Dante beyond influence

Series editors: Anna Barton, Andrew Smith

Editorial board: David Amigoni, Isobel Armstrong, Philip Holden, Jerome McGann, Joanne Wilkes, Julia M. Wright

Interventions: Rethinking the Nineteenth Century seeks to make a significant intervention into the critical narratives that dominate conventional and established understandings of nineteenth-century literature. Informed by the latest developments in criticism and theory the series provides a focus for how texts from the long nineteenth century, and more recent adaptations of them, revitalise our knowledge of and engagement with the period. It explores the radical possibilities offered by new methods, unexplored contexts and neglected authors and texts to re-map the literary-cultural landscape of the period and rigorously re-imagine its geographical and historical parameters. The series includes monographs, edited collections, and scholarly sourcebooks.

Already published

Engine of modernity: The omnibus and urban culture in nineteenth-century Paris   Masha Belenky
Spectral Dickens: The uncanny forms of novelistic characterization   Alexander Bove
The penny politics of Victorian popular fiction   Rob Breton
Worlding the South: Nineteenth-century literary culture and the southern settler colonies   Sarah Comyn and Porscha Fermanis (eds)
Pasts at play: Childhood encounters with history in British culture, 1750–1914   Rachel Bryant Davies and Barbara Gribling (eds)
The Case of the Initial Letter: Charles Dickens and the politics of the dual alphabet   Gavin Edwards
Spain in the nineteenth century: New essays on experiences of culture and society   Andrew Ginger and Geraldine Lawless (eds)
Instead of modernity: The Western canon and the incorporation of the Hispanic (c. 1850–75)   Andrew Ginger
The Victorian aquarium: Literary discussions on nature, culture, and science   Silvia Granata
Marie Duval: Maverick Victorian cartoonist   Simon Grennan, Roger Sabin and Julian Waite
Creating character: Theories of nature and nurture in Victorian sensation fiction   Helena Ifill
Margaret Harkness: Writing social engagement 1880–1921   Flore Janssen and Lisa C. Robertson (eds)
Richard Marsh, popular fiction and literary culture, 1890–1915: Re-reading the fin de siècle   Victoria Margree, Daniel Orrells and Minna Vuohelainen (eds)
Charlotte Brontë: Legacies and afterlives   Amber K. Regis and Deborah Wynne (eds)
Madrid on the move: Feeling modern and visually aware in the nineteenth century   Vanesa Rodríguez-Galindo
The Great Exhibition, 1851: A sourcebook   Jonathon Shears (ed.)
Interventions: Rethinking the nineteenth century   Andrew Smith and Anna Barton (eds)
Counterfactual Romanticism   Damian Walford Davies (ed.)
The poems of Elizabeth Siddal in context   Anne Woolley

Dante beyond influence

Rethinking reception in Victorian literary culture

Federica Coluzzi

MANCHESTER UNIVERSITY PRESS

Copyright © Federica Coluzzi 2021

The right of Federica Coluzzi to be identified as the author of this work has been asserted by them in accordance with the Copyright, Designs and Patents Act 1988.

Published by Manchester University Press
Oxford Road, Manchester M13 9PL

www.manchesteruniversitypress.co.uk

Cover Image: Text of the *Commedia* with annotations by Samuel Taylor Coleridge, 1814, held by the British Library

British Library Cataloguing-in-Publication Data

A catalogue record for this book is available from the British Library

ISBN 978 1 5261 5244 2 hardback
ISBN 978 1 5261 7891 6 paperback

First published 2021

The publisher has no responsibility for the persistence or accuracy of URLs for any external or third-party internet websites referred to in this book, and does not guarantee that any content on such websites is, or will remain, accurate or appropriate.

Typeset by
Deanta Global Publishing Services, Chennai, India

Contents

Acknowledgements	*page* vi
Introduction: What do we talk about when we talk about Dante's reception?	1
1 Reading Gladstone reading Dante: Marginal annotation as private commentary	14
2 Ephemeral Dante: Matthew Arnold's criticism in Victorian periodicals	59
3 The critic and the scholar: Christina and Maria Francesca Rossetti's Dante sisterhood	91
4 'Everyman's Dante': Philip H. Wicksteed and Victorian mass readerships	123
5 Academic networks: Dante studies in Victorian Britain	156
Conclusion: From *grande amore* to *lungo studio*: rethinking the hermeneutic turn in Dante reception history	200
Bibliography	205
Index	233

Acknowledgements

Many have contributed to the making of this book. I am indebted to Daniela Caselli and Guyda Armstrong who believed in it from the very beginning. Their incisive comments and generous encouragement made the project develop in new, exciting directions, while their example inspired me as a researcher, teacher and woman in academia.

This work could not have been carried out without the Irish Research Council Government of Ireland Postdoctoral Fellowship that enabled me to develop the book within the thriving research community at University College Cork. My deepest gratitude goes to the Department of Italian for welcoming me among its ranks. In particular, I want to thank Daragh O'Connell and David Bowe for nurturing the discussion over meetings, countless coffee runs and (occasional) pints. They demonstrated that friendship and mutual respect are the underlying conditions for the most rewarding kind of collaborative research. For this reason, I am grateful and proud to be part of the newly established Centre for Dante Studies in Ireland, of which this book is one of the many outputs to come. I am also indebted to the Leverhulme Trust for supporting the last months of the project, which gave origin to a new, larger work on *Dante's Female Transnational Public* in Ireland, Britain and Italy.

In its earlier phase, the project had been supported by the Early Career Research Fellowship at the John Rylands Library which allowed me to spend three months working within the Dante collection and benefit from the expertise and insights of Julianne Simpson and the other curators of the collection. Similarly, the Gladstone Library Fellowship enabled me to work among the shelves of his Dante collection. I also owe a substantial debt to the library staff who assisted me over multiple research visits made to the Bodleian Libraries, Manchester College, Balliol College, Oxford, Eton College, the National Archives in London and the Houghton Library at Harvard. Earlier versions of portions of the chapters have been published as journal articles in *Dante Studies*, *Strumenti Critici* and the *Palgrave Encyclopaedia of Victorian Women Writers*, with obtained permission.

I would particularly like to thank Emilia Di Rocco, Stuart Jones and Fabio Camilletti for their support at various stages in the process. My deepest gratitude goes to Anna Lanfranchi and Serena Cammoranesi for being the best friends, colleagues and zoom-office mates I could have wished for in these uncertain times.

None of this could have been even imaginable without my family. To my parents, Domenico and Donatella, goes my deepest gratitude for their unconditional love. To Gabriele, for his unflagging support since the very start of this journey, ten years ago. This would not feel the same without you. Thank you to my uncle, Giancarlo Lombardi, who first ignited the spark, and to my family who let it grow stronger every day. To Paola D'Amico, Chiara Prili and Sara Michetti: in memory of the little girls we were and in awe of the strong women we are today. For these reasons, *Dante beyond influence* is dedicated to all of them.

Introduction: What do we talk about when we talk about Dante's reception?

The publication of Paget J. Toynbee's *Dante in English Literature from Chaucer to Cary (ca. 1380–1844)* in 1909 has often been taken as the origin of Dante reception studies in Britain. Issued by Methuen & Co., the work was an unprecedented attempt at tracing the 'history and influence of Dante in English literature' over 'some 460 years' through a corpus of 'over a thousand' passages quoted either abridged or *in extenso* from the writings of more than six hundred English-speaking individuals (Toynbee, 1909: ix).

More than six decades ahead of Jauss' reader-response theory and the advent of reception aesthetics, the bulky volumes configured the phenomenon as an ever-expanding cultural and historical, imaginative and interpretive relation between the Florentine medieval poet and his transgenerational public of common Englishwomen and 'Englishmen', 'popular writers and critics of the day' (Toynbee, 1909: ix–x). This composite concept was combined with a capacious and supple notion of 'literature'. Stretching past 'books proper' (poetical, prose and dramatic works), Toynbee charted the 'the growth of interest in Dante' through a miscellaneous body of documentary sources, such as private 'letters, diaries' and personal papers (vi). 'Spreading the knowledge of Dante on this side of the channel' were also 'reviews, magazine articles' and a 'formidable array of anonymous periodical literature', of English translations and didactic works 'for English readers by foreign authors domiciled in England' (iv). Equally valuable were 'library and sale catalogues, lists of MSS., bibliographies' for the way they recorded collecting and publishing trends between ca. 1380 and 1844, the 'year of Cary's death and of the publication of the first cheap edition of his translation, by which time the name of Dante had become …

a household word with Englishmen' (iv). When, over a decade later, Toynbee recast the anthology into a more succinct chronological record – gifted to Italy as the *British Tribute to Dante* for the sexcentenary of the poet's death – he extended the *terminus ad quem* to 1921. The new timeframe captured the most recent transformations and developments of the phenomenon within the private and the public, the imaginative and the interpretative realms of experience.

Over the course of the intervening century and up to the present day, the Toynbean concern for the generic and material variety of Dante's reception has been substantially superseded by a narrower attention to the particular experience of canonical writers for whom the contact with Dante had been 'aesthetically productive' (Camilletti *et al.*, 2011: 9). The vast majority of contemporary studies demonstrate an engrossing attention to Romantic, Victorian and Modernist acts of imaginative re-creation, intersemiotic trans-codification, literary and cultural appropriation of the aspects, themes, motives and *textual loci* of Dante's works. Purposefully aimed at uncovering the permeating presence and assessing the continuing resonances of Dantean textuality in British poetry and prose, this mode of inquiry has reduced the Toynbean discourse to anxiety-led notions of literary exemplarity and canonicity.

Alison Milbank and Nick Havely have taken the investigation *beyond* the realm of productive reception to explore the many cultural and intellectual, religious and political declensions of the reception phenomenon throughout the long nineteenth century. Havely's latest study, in particular, has done essential work in re-orienting the contemporary discourse towards a markedly collective dimension epitomised in the idea of 'British public' and bound to the rediscovery of the polyphonic 'conversations' and 'expansive interaction' produced 'across more than six centuries' (Havely, 2014: xiii–xiv). No longer synonymous with a creative act performed by an exceptional individual, Dante's reception is ultimately reconfigured as a multifarious process of textual transmission and dissemination, access and consumption performed by large and socio-culturally diverse audiences.

Toynbee's comprehensive idea of 'literature' and Havely's far-reaching definition of 'public' are at the heart of *Dante beyond influence*. They constitute the ground on which this study, the first systematic inquiry into the multifarious formation of the British critical and scholarly discourse in Dante's reception history, is founded. My book, however, departs from their macro-historical perspective to focus on the inter-centenary years (1865–1921), identified as the years of the hermeneutical turn – a key historical moment in which the readers' individual and collective, private and public interest in Dante became markedly interpretive and oriented towards 'positive study of the text, the documents and the themes of [his] works' (Caesar, 1989: 37).

Dante's nineteenth-century reception: from influence to *lungo studio*

In the 'Preface' to *Prometheus Unbound*, Percy B. Shelley offers one of the earliest, most tangible signs of these broader changes in the forms and modes of readerly engagement. Directly addressing his public, the Romantic poet urged them to recognise that Dante, 'our great poet, is a masterpiece of nature which another not only *ought* to study, but *must* study' (Shelley, 1820: xii). Shelley's reiteration characterised reading as a purposeful act of extended and careful inquiry into the poet's works. The readerly relationship envisioned closely resembled the exemplary connection that bound Dante-pilgrim to the work (*'lo tuo volume'*) of his master and author, Virgil, described as *"'l lungo studio e 'l grande amore'* in *Inferno* I, 83. A semantically dense conceit that reoccurs in the *Vita Nuova*, *Convivio* and *Commedia*, Dante's notion of *'studio'* combines ideas of academic application, literary apprenticeship, zealous devotion and even deep affection in the pursuit of higher knowledge. Filled with Dantean echoes, Shelley's own *appello al lettore* posited a paradigmatic shift in the modes of engagement with the author and his oeuvre: from an erratic, idealised and highly idiosyncratic contact with the text ('ought') to a more concrete, necessarily calculated ('must') engagement shared by a wider community of readers. At the heart of his postulation was the poet's stern rejection of modes of recreational and aesthetic reading engendered by what St Clair identified as the 'boom of literary anthologies' (St Clair, 2004: 118).

A burdensome legacy of eighteenth-century publishing, these popular collections (of poetry and, less frequently, of prose) offered the British public 'an overview and general impression of foreign literature' (Saglia, 2018: 73) and evaluations of aesthetic value, cultural status or historical relevance. Although, as Saglia observed, anthologies 'contributed in crucial ways to helping British readers familiarize themselves with authors and works from other European traditions' (74), they nevertheless reduced the readerly experience to a circumscribed and episodic encounter with an abridged version of the original text. Ever-present, Dante's *Commedia* was exemplified by few, brief excerpts, generally taken from its most dramatic episodes such as the story of Paolo and Francesca in *Inferno* V and Count Ugolino in *Inferno* XXXIII. Translated into English by 'only fairly linguistically competent British intellectuals and writers' and accompanied by minimalistic commentaries, the anthologised passages lent themselves to an ephemeral consumption temporally and spatially circumscribed. They enforced a 'stop-and-start rhythm of reading' (Price, 2000: 5), which very rarely generated an interest so strong to foster a long-term engagement with the original, unabridged text.

The tide had begun to turn with the publication of two complete translations of the *Commedia* respectively by Henry Boyd (1802) and Henry Francis Cary (1814–15). Of the two, Cary's *The Vision of Dante* was the one that most successfully ensured the linguistic, intellectual and even material accessibility of the poem to the widening nineteenth-century mass public. Reproduced in its unabridged form with biographical notes and running commentaries, Cary's volumes appealed to the interest of general readers and the attention of a more specialised public of critics and periodical reviewers of the day. The biennium 1818–19 saw the convergence of various interpretive endeavours publicly pursued within the lecture halls of literary institutions and the pages of prominent periodicals. Commanding large audiences and readerships, William Hazlitt's and Samuel Coleridge's public lectures and Foscolo's articles in the *Edinburgh Review* shed a revelatory light on the poetical and linguistic, historical and ideological aspects of Dante's masterpiece. In different forms and extents, each of these interventions showcased to the British public the fruits of a more sustained readerly attention and perceptive exploration of the work as a whole.

Although lectures and articles had stimulated the public discussion, launching a wave of more interpretive responses, the critical impulse did not develop into a more coherent discourse paving an exemplary path of study. Returning to the issue in his *Defence of Poetry*, Shelley lamented his profound disappointment and frustration in the short-sightedness of recent contributions. 'Modern reader[s]', Shelley observed, were still struggling to cultivate their 'enthusiasm for Dante's apparently boundless creativity into a significant engagement with the details of his work' (Shelley, 1852: 35). The (intellectual and material) conditions for turning Dante into the object of serious, systematic and dedicated study were still far from ripe. His works, each 'a spark, a burning atom of inextinguishable thought' remained inescapably 'covered in the ashes of their birth, and pregnant with the lightning which has yet found no conductor' (35).

Unfortunately, Shelley did not live long enough to rejoice in the ground-breaking work done by the vast and varied multitude of 'conductors' – women and men of letters, literary critics and translators, scholars and lecturers – towards the establishment of a British scholarly tradition. His tragic death at sea occurred long before the beginning of what Azeglio Valgimigli hailed as 'the golden age of Dante studies in England' (Valgimigli, 1921a: 435). The intercentenary period that saw the poet and his oeuvre being 'studied with unprecedented care and completeness' attracting the attention of 'thoroughgoing scholars' and benefiting from 'learned criticism and annotation, based upon ample knowledge', 'careful attention to details', and 'rational and disciplined methods' of textual criticism (435).

Apart from being hoped for by Shelley, bibliographically recorded by Toynbee and sensationally advertised by Valgimigli in *The Tablet*, the nineteenth-century hermeneutic turn remains one of the darkest corners in Dante's reception history. Tackling this vacuum, *Dante beyond influence* is the first study to conceptualise and historicise the phenomenon across intellectual realms, agents and forms of readerly and writerly engagement. It retraces the origins of the Victorian *lungo studio* of Dante within the intimate sphere of solitary and self-regulated programmes of reading. It then charts its transition into the public arena, where critical study became an individual performative act as well as an occasion for encounter with larger interpretive communities. Ultimately, it maps the diversification of these interpretive endeavours through two modes of dissemination: that of mass popularisation and academic specialisation.

Placing itself within the theoretical framework of the new 'multi- and interdisciplinary field' (Sherif, 2017: 36) of book history, my study aligns with Coolahan's definition of reception as 'the history of how texts were read, disseminated, and consumed across media, languages, and geographical regions' (Coolahan, 2020: 1). The volume reconstructs the phenomenology of Victorian *dantismo* through a historical narrative that unpacks the Victorians' role as producers and consumers, 'receivers' and 'agents of transmission' of the critical and scholarly discourse (1). To do so, my study complements Toynbee's and Havely's broad-encompassing notions of 'literature' and 'public' with an equally capacious idea of a Victorian 'reading' of Dante. One that recognises it as a purposeful and systematic interpretive engagement able to engender textual and graphic, individual and collective writerly responses. Charted in its historical development, the act is situated within the wider socio-cultural context in which it found its manifold materialisation (private manuscript sign to public printed discourse), dissemination and popularisation. The overarching aim of this book is to demonstrate that the hermeneutic turn in Dante reception history was the product of major transformations in Victorian intellectual, social and publishing history as much as the (hidden) driving force behind major advancements in educational reform, discipline formation and women's access to literary and scholarly professions.

My investigation begins with what Acheson defines as 'materialist inquiries' (Acheson, 2019: 5) into nineteenth-century practices of Dante reading and book collecting. The volume turns to the private libraries and archives to interrogate an eclectic body of writerly traces that is 'rich enough' to overcome Robert Darnton's legendary scepticism and capture historical readers 'at work, fashioning meaning from text' (Darnton, 1990: 157). This never-before-seen corpus consists of *marginalia*, transcribed passages and reading lists found in diaries and personal copies of Dantean primary and secondary sources (Chapters 1, 2, 3), annotated course syllabi (Chapter 4), society minutes, library catalogues and accession records (Chapter 5).

Holistically interpreted, these signs of engagement provide unprecedented insights into the mechanisms of absorption, consumption and elaboration of the Dantean text. Most specifically, they reveal that many nineteenth-century readers relied on marginal annotations, lists and transcriptions as practical means for establishing their hermeneutical contact with Dantean textuality. The chapters will show that for solitary and mostly self-taught Dante readers like William Gladstone, Matthew Arnold and Christina Rossetti (Chapters 1–3) the writerly activity over and within the margins of the page or the book channelled their critical engagement into a self-referential, and hence cryptic, commentary. Graphic signs, single words or more discursive comments reveal that readers' processes of knowledge construction were often anchored to the content, form or linguistic translation of certain passages. In Wicksteed's case (Chapter 4), the annotations in the syllabi show a much later stage in his *lungo studio*: the moment where the interiorised knowledge is re-elaborated into teachable content accessible to both beginner and more experienced students. Similarly, the documentary evidence produced by Henry Clark Barlow or the Oxford Dante Society (Chapter 5) attests to the formation and refinement of (individual and collaborative) practices of philological and textual scholarship.

Materiality matters: new conditions of reading Dante

Marginalia and other writerly techniques are also central to the study of readers' uses and relations to the book as an object. The materiality or 'material form' of the book, as Ann Sherif observed, has a central part in 'inform[ing] reading and hermeneutic practice' (2017: 41) and Dante was no exception. For the Victorians' corporal proximity with and the physical materiality of the text was a crucial precondition to their *lungo studio* of Dante.

Chapter 1 discusses in detail how the nineteenth-century industrialisation of print, the changes in literacy and the mass expansion of the publishing market created new conditions of accessibility and affordability of Dantean literature in Britain. This had a salvific effect on Dante's modern reception, breaking the aestheticising crystallisation of the *Commedia* as a collectable object – a condition engendered by eighteenth-century bibliophiles who purchased medieval manuscripts and *incunabula* for their own private collections, where they kept them as inestimable relics for which any readerly or even writerly intervention would have been an irredeemable violation of the aura of their treasured possession. The Victorian revolution in print technology brought Dante within the material and intellectual reach of the mass, middle-class public. Over less than fifty years this expanded from a small enclave of Italophiles purchasing recent Italian editions, commentaries and studies on Dante imported from the Continent to a large and heterogeneous readership of men and women who carried a copy of Cary's *Vision* in their pockets.

Dante beyond influence expands the reception discourse from individual practices of annotated reading to the broader mechanisms of book production, commodification and transmission that made those readerly modes possible. Mapping the dynamic flow of books of and on Dante is key for understanding his reception as a meaningful output of what Richard Altick famously tapped as 'the great turning point in the history of English book trade's relations with the mass public' (Altick, 1957: 294). In particular, the volume aims to overcome the traditional reluctance with which reception scholars have looked at the nineteenth-century commercialisation of Dantean literature – creative, critical and even scholarly – in a kaleidoscopic variety of affordable editions and formats as a threat to their literary and cultural value. Contrary to such prejudicial contentions, my study demonstrates that it was the purposeful exploitation of 'the tempting commercial possibilities inherent in a vastly enlarged market' (Altick, 1957: 294) on the part of publishers that led to the amplification and diversification of the works of and on Dante published in Britain. The international celebration of the first Dante centenary in 1865 afforded a crucial stimulus to the production and dissemination of Dante-related material in print and periodicals.

Resonating with Kathryn Prince's work on Shakespeare's reception, *Dante beyond influence* illustrates how Victorian periodicals became key epistemological sites for the formation, maturation and popularisation of the critical discourse on Dante. Periodical literature was one of the 'most distinctive and characteristic' features of the Victorian literary history; pervasive and constantly expanding, it 'commanded an influence and prestige without parallel' as it was addressed 'on the one level, to the common reader, and at another "to the articulate classes, whose writing and conversation make opinion"' (Houghton, 1982: 3). From the *Cornhill*, *Fraser's* and *Gentleman's Magazine* to the *Athenaeum*, *Academy* and *Blackwood's*, the mid-Victorian period saw the proliferation of reviews, essays and notices on Dante-related publications, discoveries and events.

For this volume I have turned to the archives to unearth a vast, diverse body of evidence to bring forth the key aspects of Victorian Dante criticism and interpret them in relation to broader changes in forms of nineteenth-century literary criticism. Dante's reception certainly benefited from 'professionalisation of journalism' and the substantial shifts in 'the tone', 'style' and 'spirit of mid-Victorian periodical criticism' (Woolford, 1982: 109). The discourse greatly benefited from what Woolford termed 'adjectival criticism', characterised by 'over-intensity of feeling' (111) towards 'analytical criticism' (125). More securely anchored in extensive familiarity with the poet and his work, this form of criticism gave way to the expression – if not even 'the critic's self-display' – and exchange of literary, historical, biographical and (even) textual knowledge that was at once 'helpful and instructive' (115) for the public.

Each chapter highlights how periodical writings not only contributed to building the public consensus around Dante's canonicity and the linguistic, historical and literary value of his poetry but also actively stimulated the production of new publications by appealing to the generative power of reading: encouraging and supporting (at least a fraction of) this receiving public to become authors at their turn. This book delineates the proliferation of English translations, critical editions, handbooks, essay collections and biographies and the reaction of the periodical press, thus capturing at once the character of these interpretive responses and their public reception.

The overarching aim of my study is, therefore, to demonstrate that British critical and scholarly discourse emerged from the integrated actions of multiple agents that ranged from annotators and translators to publishers, printers, periodical editors and reviewers, literary critics and educators. The selection of articles and volumes featured in the volume brings to the forefront of the reception discourse the variety of means, forms and genres through which Dantean knowledge was mediated, disseminated and made relevant to the intellectual needs of the socio-culturally diverse Victorian mass public. In doing so, I shall highlight the far-reaching socio-cultural and economic impact of the hermeneutic turn as it fostered the emergence of new professional figures (Dante scholars, translators and interpreters) and research institutions, such as learned societies, university courses and library collections.

Dante beyond influence isolates the five case studies that capture the macroscopic phases through which the reception phenomenon unfolded between 1865 and 1921. It illuminates lesser-known aspects of the private intellectual life and public work of Victorian figures such as Christina Rossetti, Matthew Arnold and William E. Gladstone, thus reinvigorating the interest in these canonical figures. At the same time, it introduces a significant cohort of men and women of letters, critics and scholars whose contribution to Victorian literature and culture has hitherto passed unnoticed.

Chapter 1 focuses on William E. Gladstone, four-time British Prime Minister and a central figure in the political and cultural history of Victorian Britain. Gladstone chronicled his lifelong private study of Dante in the daily entries of his diaries, pursuing it through reading, annotating and book-collecting as well as literary tourism and encounters with Italian and European scholars in the field. Using the large corpus of marginalia and reading lists found in his personal diaries, papers, and books, the chapter historicises Gladstone's reading practices and illustrates how his personal path frequently corresponded with the one traced by the major trends of nineteenth-century scholarly practices and provide a concrete representation of the hermeneutic process through which Gladstone turned Dante's *Commedia* into an object of serious, self-disciplined study. The diaries map the development of Gladstone's reading habits and the simultaneous construction of Dantean knowledge from a chronological perspective, thus charting the growth of his interest from the primary text to secondary critical sources over a sixty-year period. The chapter showcases the progressive refinement of Gladstone's scholarly approach through the comparative close textual and material study of the marginalia recorded in three distinct copies of the *Commedia*: two nineteenth-century editions and

Cary's English translation, bringing forth the creative and critical dialogue Gladstone had established with Dante throughout his life.

Chapter 2 concentrates on another central figure in Victorian literary and cultural history: the poet and critic, Matthew Arnold. It argues that his long-neglected relationship with Dantean textuality is most representative of the initial phase of the Victorian hermeneutic turn, with the emergence of a coherent and conspicuous critical discourse in lectures, essays and reviews between 1853 and 1888. The chapter reunites for the first time the large but fragmented corpus of general references and quoted passages from the *Commedia* found in his private notebooks and published prose works. So far disregarded as unresponsive and unproductive, the chapter reinterprets these *sententiae* as meaningful hermeneutic signs revealing the inner mechanisms of Arnold's critical assimilation and manipulation of Dantean knowledge within broader interventions in literary and cultural criticism. Such macroscopic investigation, however, is complemented and enhanced with a close-reading analysis of a *uniquum* in Arnold's prose-works: 'Dante and Beatrice', an article printed in the pages of *Fraser's* in May 1863 and representing the only existing/surviving piece of unitary and extensive piece of criticism entirely devoted to Dante.

Chapter 3 argues that by the mid-1870s, the rising field of Dante studies had become one of the new territories of endeavour claimed by a growing public of women of letters, actively negotiating their critical identity and scholarly authority as professional mediators of Dantean knowledge. The chapter focuses on the paradigmatic case of Christina and Maria Francesca Rossetti for the way they negotiated with the forces of patriarchal authority represented by their male-centric 'family *dantismo*' to achieve authority as public and professional mediators of Dantean knowledge. The chapter examines their published work – Christina's periodical articles in *Churchman's Shilling Magazine and Family Treasury* (1867) and *Century Magazine* (1884) and Maria Francesca's best-selling handbook *A Shadow of Dante* – to elucidate the dynamics through which they constructed their critical expertise and scholarly knowledge, gaining cultural power and public recognition as pioneers Dante scholars on the Victorian literary market.

In exploring the mechanisms that led to the wider popularisation of Dante's works in late Victorian Britain, Chapter 4 recovers the pivotal yet long-forgotten experience of Philip H. Wicksteed. Through a comprehensive biographical reconstruction, it retraces the evolution of Wicksteed's scholarly persona: from Unitarian preacher interested in the spiritual and uplifting use of Dante's theological message in his *Six Sermons* to Dante lecturer working for the University Extension Movement; from the translator and editor of Dent's *Temple Classics* to an internationally recognised scholar with a large body of academic publications. Wicksteed achieved status and critical authority as a pioneering practitioner of what I term commercial *dantismo*: a materially affordable and academically accessible form of scholarship purposefully designed for the growing middle- and lower-class public, which fostered an unprecedented growth of the opportunities for dissemination and (creative and critical) appropriation of Dantean knowledge in British literary culture.

Chapter 5 represents the chronological and conceptual culmination of my study. By the end of the nineteenth century, Victorian *dantismo* began to be practised and understood as a form of public outreach and engagement as well as of political and cultural exchange on a national and international level. The chapter maps the dynamics of disciplinary specialisation of Dante studies from the perspective of the scholarly activities of the Oxford, London and Manchester Dante Societies established between 1876 and 1906, and the creation of Dante Collections at University College London and at the John Rylands Library. These professional institutions were responsible for catalysing the methodological turn from *dantofilia* to *dantismo*, and the institutionalisation of the teaching of Dante in academic (established and extramural) courses. Through the recovery of key archival witnesses, the chapter delivers a vivid and tangible representation of how the Victorians crafted a discipline still notable for its vibrancy and relevance today. In retracing such dynamics, the chapter pays particular attention to figures such as Henry Clark Barlow, Edward Moore, Paget Toynbee, Charles Tomlinson and Azeglio Valgimigli for the way their personal trajectories exemplified the historical and socio-cultural evolution of the Dante enthusiast into a Dante scholar: a turn that fostered the conditions for the creation of one of the most eminent scholarly traditions outside Italy.

Altogether, the reconstruction of their material readings of and interpretive responses to Dante enables this book to rethink the critical and scholarly reception of Dante as a central event in Victorian literary and cultural history. It re-evaluates it as a path-breaking phenomenon nurtured and spurred by underlying changes in the Victorian intellectual life and character in the approach to the construction of critical knowledge, and in the pursuit of literary study as a 'specialised activity with an increasingly scientific rationale and methodology' (Atherton, 2005: 61) practised by men and women professionals. It reclaims its importance as an experience conducted by and conducive to substantial advancements in Victorian educational history and university reform, print history and mass publishing.

1

Reading Gladstone reading Dante: Marginal annotation as private commentary

On the evening of 16 September 1834, the twenty-five-year-old William E. Gladstone picked up his hard-covered pocket journal to write a 'skeleton-like' account of the day spent at Fasque, his family home in Scotland (Foot, 1968–94: xix). Among the noteworthy events, the future British Prime Minister wrote: 'began Dante's Commedia, read Canto 1' (GD [*The Gladstone Diaries*] 18/09/34). As he jotted down the entry in his minute handwriting, little did he know that he was inaugurating a sixty-year-long companionship with the Florentine poet and his *Commedia*, which represented 'not merely a pleasure, an endeavour, a lesson' but 'the most rigorous of disciplines for the heart, the mind and the whole person' (Mazzoni, 1996: 314).

Thanks to Gladstone's almost compulsive activity as diarist and annotator, the chronological, topographical and critical memory of this *lungo studio* of Dante has been variously preserved in his intimate diaries, personal papers and marginalia (glosses, annotations and marks) covering the pages of the books of his Dante Collection at the St Deniol's – now Gladstone's – Library. While biographers and historians have asserted the strategic importance of these manuscript sources for the reconstruction and monumentalisation of Gladstone's private and public persona, Dante reception scholars have shown uneven interest. Although Chadwick (1979), Isba (2006) and Havely (2014) variously discussed the Gladstone–Dante relationship, they did not address the specificity of Gladstone's experience as a historical reader and its representativity of broader changes in the dynamics of nineteenth-century reception. Tackling this vacuum, the chapter illustrates how Gladstone's readerly, annotating and collecting practices reflected the modern transformation of Dante into 'a criticized thing': an object of serious commentary and scholarly consumption (Gilson, 2018: 8).

The lack of consideration for Gladstone's interpretive endeavours stands out as a countertrend given the substantial 'resurgence of interest' for the 'editorial, rhetorical, historical, and theoretical study' (Parker, 1993: 8) of medieval, Renaissance and modern Dante commentaries that has spread over the last thirty years. Beyond the strictly philological dimension, the renewed appreciation encompassed (and still encompasses) the way these commentaries 'illustrate the evolutions of notions of "literariness" and literature, genre and style, intertextuality and influence, literary histories, traditions and canons, authorship and readerships, paratexts and textual materiality' (Nasti *et al.*, 2013: 11). Interpreted from a reader-response perspective, they also function as a strategic tool for mapping the transhistorical, transcultural and transnational interpretative history of Dante's oeuvre.

Despite the bespoken concern for both local and foreign readerships, the investigation has moved thus far within clearly defined national, chronological and genre boundaries. It has privileged full-length commentaries and erudite glosses in Latin and vernacular, appearing in manuscript and print form, and generally authored by commentators active in Italy between the fourteenth and early nineteenth centuries. This is particularly evident in the Dartmouth Dante Project (DDP), the ground-breaking online database launched in 2015 which collates the fully searchable text of seventy-seven commentaries to the *Commedia* (1320s–2015). Within the DDP canon, the exemplars of British *dantismo* are drastically narrowed to four works, all published towards the end of the century and representative of a discrete type of commentaries: Oelsner's and Wicksteed's notes to the Temple Dante (1899–1901), Ruskin's incidental *Comments* (1903), Frederick Tozer's stand-alone English commentary (1901), and John S. Carroll's expositions in three volumes (1904–11). The Checklist of Commentators compiled by Robert Hollander as 'aid to the systematic computerization' of the DDP (Hollander, 1983: 181) is slightly more inclusive as it acknowledges also the *Notes* by J. W. Thomas (1859–66), A. J. Butler (1880–92), Plumptre (1886–87) as well as Vernon's *Readings* (1889–1909). Neither one of them accounted for the core of the century, conveying the representation of the Romantic and Victorian ages as periods of hermeneutical stasis. Yet, this picture is far from the truth: the aesthetic and literary hyperactivity in poetry, prose and visual arts for which the long nineteenth century owes its fame was combined with an equally spirited critical industry practised and vehiculated through unconventional forms of commentary.

The traditional notion of commentary as a full-length edited and published work by which Hollander *et al.* abide bypasses altogether the disparate range of generic possibilities covered by the term (Botterill, 2005). This strict codification decimates the British tradition by excluding the most practised form of commentary: that of marginal annotation. More than anecdotal materials, the marginalia are the first means of configuration of the British critical discourse on Dante and his works: an interpretive endeavour first originated in the private realm of the individual readerly experience, which progressively grew into a public and collective effort. Common among notable British readers like John Flaxman, Samuel Coleridge, the Shelleys as well as Matthew Arnold, George Eliot, William Gladstone and John Ruskin among others, marginalia record the emergence and sophistication of their hermeneutic interest towards Dantean textuality. The heterogeneity of the annotation marks reflects the broad diversity of approaches autonomously designed to penetrate the meaning of the *Commedia* in the absence of an English exegetical tradition of reference providing linguistic, interpretive and material support.

Commenting Dante in nineteenth-century Italy and Britain

In Italy, the early 1800s marked a turning point in the critical and editorial fortune of Dante's exegetical tradition. Thanks to technological advancements in the printing industry, Italian publishers were able to bring new editions of both ancient and modern commentaries to widening readership – from those of l'Ottimo (Pisa, Capurro 1827–29), Pietro Alighieri (Firenze, Piatti 1845), Benvenuto da Imola (Imola, Galeati 1855–67), Francesco da Buti (Pisa, Nistri 1858–62), Jacopo della Lana (Milano, Civelli 1865), the Anonimo Fiorentino (Bologna, Romagnoli 1866–74) and Lodovico Dolce (Venezia, Occhi, 1812) to Gaetano Volpi's edition of the *Accademia della Crusca* (Padova, Comino, 1727),

Baldassarre Lombardi (Roma, Stamperia De Romanis, 1815–17) and Pompeo Venturi (Firenze, Formigli, 1830). Parallel to this came the publication of brand-new commentaries by Giosafatte Biagioli (Silvestri, Milano 1820–21), Brunone Bianchi (Firenze, Le Monnier, 1844, which had nine re-issues between 1849 and 1863 for a total of 22,750 copies sold), Pietro Fraticelli (Firenze, Formigli, 1837), Niccolò Tommaseo (Venezia, Gondoliere, 1843), along with schoolbook editions like Raffaele Andreoli's (Firenze, Barbera, 1870). Although Lord George Vernon and his son William, dantophilists and members of the Anglo-Florentine community, funded these editions (Bombagioli, Jacopo and Pietro Alighieri, falso Boccaccio and J. P. Lacaita's five-volume edition of Benvenuto da Imola), British *dantismo* was still far from producing its own original contribution to the exegetical tradition.

While Italian Dante studies were leaning towards the material and intellectual popularisation of tradition and criticism, in Britain the development of the scholarly was halted by *bibliomania*: a phenomenon described as 'a distortion of properly literary and readerly values, a perverse lust after physical properties' of the books as 'made objects' (Ferris, 2004). Minutely diagnosed by Thomas Dibdin in 1809, this pathological obsession for hunting and collecting rare books spread between 1775 and 1825 among 'wealthy, well-educated and well-born amateur bibliographers with investment capital and a sharp eye for a bargain, as well as nouveaux riches anxious to consolidate their social status' (Connell, 2000: 25). As a peculiar declination of the phenomenon, *Dantemania* was a legacy of 'the cultural programme and conventions of the Grand Tour' (Havely, 2014: 136) and of the genteel, 'conservative desire for the preservation of Europe's literary heritage in the form of great libraries' (Connell, 2000: 32). According to Havely's reconstruction, the 'avid and competitive' hoarding of Dante manuscripts and incunabula had begun early in the seventeenth century with Henry Wotton (1568–1639), Kenelm (1603–65) and George Digby (1612–77) and Bishop John Moore (1646–1714). These were followed by Anthony Storer (1746–99), whose collection 'comprise[d] a virtual publishing history of the poem [*Commedia*] in the sixteenth century', and Thomas Coke (1747–1814), 'owner of the largest number of Dante manuscripts that are still to be found in a British private collection', namely Holkham. This type of ownership severely limited their material circulation and fruition among an emerging British public, while also reinforcing the aura of literary elitism and obscurity that was still burdening the poet's popular reputation (Havely, 2014: 106).

In Britain, the popularisation and transformation of Dante into an object of criticism and scholarship depended on the rhizomatic growth of the publishing industry and 'the demographic extension of print culture in the nineteenth-century' (Connell, 2000: 29) fostering the 'expansion of reading across all strata of society, whether categorised by income, by occupation, by educational attainment, by geographical location, by age, or by gender' (St Clair, 2004: 11). The overcoming of the intellectual stasis caused by bibliomaniac *dantofilia* was made possible by the 'mechanized revolution' of the book industry (Raven, 2014: 143) that redefined the material conditions of accessibility and affordability of Dantean literature in Britain. In particular, the implementation of cost-reducing technologies of 'printing, papermaking, bookbinding and transportation' (146) gave a strong impetus to the production and import of multiple and competitively priced editions of Dante's works (in original and translation). Issued in longer print runs, these cheaper editions were presented in embellished cloth bindings and 'slighter', more portable formats that replaced the more expensive and 'often cumbersome multi-volumes' treasured by collectors (151).

Throughout the century, the cheapening of literature was repeatedly critiqued by those who feared the perils of 'a distinct deterioration in the taste and industry of the general reader' and a weakening of 'the love of, and perhaps the capacity for study, research and scholarship' (Raven, 2014: 151). In Dante's case, however: the critical and scholarly discourse began to form the moment the *Commedia* was made 'accessible to the nation', 'shewn to, and handled by the multitude' (D'Israeli, 1795: 216) in a multifarious variety of editions and translations 'competing' for the reviewers' attention and sales on the British book market (Havely, 2014: 137–8).

The phase of broad commercialisation began with an increase in the number of 'annotated and plain-text copies' (Havely, 2014: 137) of the poem printed in London, supplementing the import of titles, such as Pompeo Venturi's (Lucca, 1732) and Antonio Zatta's

(Venezia, 1757–58, one of the 'most "desirable"' exemplars for British collectors) editions (Havely, 2014: 120). In 1808–9 alone, there were two new releases. The first work was authored by Romualdo Zotti, an expatriate printer and teacher of Italian in a girls' school, and consisted of a three-volume annotated edition of the *Commedia*, printed in 12mo and 'competitively priced' at £1. 11s. 6d. (Havely, 2014: 138). Compared to Zotti's bulky format and didactic commentary, G. B. Boschini's edition was slimmer in format and more concise in content: printed in two volumes in 16mo, and presenting a short, prefatory 'Vita di Dante' and the plain text of the *Commedia* with condensed *argomenti* introducing each *canto*. These editions initiated a trend that continued throughout the following two decades with Petroni's (three volumes in 16mo, Shulze and Dean, 1819) and Pickering's plain text edition in the *Miniature Classics* (two volumes in 32mo, 1822–23), the first in which 'no foreigner's name appears'. In 1826, John Murray published Gabriele Rossetti's highly controversial *Commento Analitico alla Commedia*. The monumental work in six volumes was followed by the first 'single-volume edition' in 610 pages by Pietro Cicchetti (Chiswick Press, 1827 in 12mo). In 1842–43, the Italian printer Pietro Rolandi completed the project begun by Pickering in 1825 and gave to the presses Ugo Foscolo's four-volume octavo edition of the poem 'containing the Italian text along with various illustrative matter' (Toynbee, 1905: 17). After Foscolo's, English editions of the *Commedia* lost appeal as stand-alone works and were used to complement the flourishing number of English translations with the facing, Italian text.

It was the publication of Henry Francis Cary's *Vision* that marked a turning point in Dante reception history. The book engendered a revolutionary process in the forms and modes of reading the *Commedia* throughout the entire century. The first innovation was that introduction of the Italian facing text in his two-part translation of *Inferno* (1805–6) 'then for the first time printed in England' (Toynbee, 1912: 226) so that readers 'moderately skilled in the Italian tongue' (326) could experience and appreciate the *cantica* in the original and mediated form. The success of his complete translation (1814–19) disproved all past, prejudicial contentions about the poetic, linguistic and material inaccessibility of the *Commedia*. Increasingly adopted by many as 'replacement of the

Divine Comedy' (Braida, 2004: 28), Cary's translation launched the process of commodification of Dante's poem into a classic bestseller, an object of wide production and consumption among the English-speaking public.

The first edition published in 1814 consisted of three volumes in 12mo, printed at the translator's expenses and sold for 'the modest price of twelve shillings, in boards' (Toynbee, 1912: 326). Disliked by Cary, the 'diminutive' format proved itself particularly practical for readers who could keep the first fully annotated English translation of Dante's masterpiece in their pockets. After initial struggles, the translation was (re-)discovered by the general public in 1818 thanks to Samuel Coleridge's overt praise in his public lectures as well as the positive reviews by general and specialised readers, like Ugo Foscolo in the *Edinburgh Review*. These interventions engendered a subitaneous mass demand for the work, leading to the sale of 'nearly a thousand copies' granting Cary 'more than £200 as profits' and the prospect of a revised and expanded edition, which was published in July 1819 in 'the more marketable format' (Toynbee, 1912: 326) of three handsome octavos sold at 36d. Exploiting the propulsive power of industrial publishing, *The Vision* underwent multitudinous reincarnations in high-end and cheap editions, with and without the facing text and the critical apparatus, proliferating both nationally and transnationally. The third edition came out in 1831, while the fourth – the last to be revised by Cary before his death – was published in 1844 in 'a single volume 12mo, at 10/6 to compete with a pirated American edition, 8vo in double columns, at 6/-, which was sold out within a fortnight' (Toynbee, 1912: 327). The translation 'had the rare distinction of being edited like an ancient classic: twice at least in America, three times at least in England' (Beatty, 1914: 576). As such, it soon became a pillar of high-end and popular book series: from Bell's *Bohn's Standard Library* (1876), *Routledge Popular Library* and Warne's *Chandos Classics* (1877) to Methuen's *Little Library* (1892–1902), Newnes' *Thin Paper Classics* (1903) and Dent's *Everyman's Library* (1908). Throughout this time, the translation was also printed in luxury editions where the text was complemented with the designs of John Flaxman and Gustave Doré, thus exerting a lasting influence on the literary and visual imagination of the poem. The commercial success of *The Vision* stimulated the emergence of a new and vibrant sub-segment of the British book trade devoted to the production and import of critical, scholarly and literary works of and on Dante. By 1914 the *Commedia* alone had had twenty-four complete English translations along with an array of partial interventions on single canticles and fragments. At the same time, in the eyes of generations of men and women of letters, it was glaring proof that Dante could be made the object of specialised and remunerative professional labour in Britain as much as in Italy.

In redefining the conditions for affordable ownership and proactive use of Dante's works among a large and socio-culturally varied public of English-speaking readers, the industrialisation of book publishing was crucial to the formation and professionalisation of Dante studies throughout the nineteenth century. By the 1830s, new habits and more stimulating modes of acquisition and interaction with books had exceeded the 'dysfunctional compulsion of bibliomaniacal collectors' (Connell, 2000: 38). For many, the restoration of the physical, sensuous proximity with the object vehiculated a more intimate interpretative relationship, which materialised as marginalia in its pages, flyleaves and endpapers.

Before Gladstone: nineteenth-century readers of Dante

Reconstructing the history of modern marginalia, H. J. Jackson noted that 'in their everyday life, readers of the Romantic period were accustomed to work with the books they had as schoolbooks and then in their jobs and avocations' (Jackson, 2005: 60). Since the mid-eighteenth century, educational writers like Isaac Watts (1741) and Thomas Sheridan (1775) had promoted the practice of marginal annotation as a virtuous habit for cultivating the analytical and critical faculties of the mind. Among basic methodologies, they promoted 'traditional techniques of assimilation (glosses, heads, cross-references) and enrichment (correction, supplement, commentary) that had been carried over from manuscript to print culture' along with markedly personal interventions on the intrinsic qualities of the text (Jackson, 2005: 300). Specifically,

> readers should mark passages that contained matter 'new or unknown' to them, for a second reading; they should detect the writer's faults make note of them in the margin, and 'endeavour to

do better' (NB); they could find it convenient to create a rough-and-ready index, if the book did not come with one; and they might make 'remark' about the faults and beauties observed along the way.

(Jackson, 2005: 61)

Once the phase of analytical dissection was completed, readers were invited to reflect upon 'what real improvements' they had made in 'reading that author' (61) and how their acquired knowledge could have been 'put to use intellectually, professionally and socially' (305). As the century progressed, the readers' degree of self-conscious scrutiny and theorisation increased, and annotation practices came to be gradually adopted as a coping mechanism for preserving the profitable qualities of intensive reading within the new, extensive conditions of mass publishing.

Along with Gladstone, many nineteenth-century readers embarked on Dante's journey with a pencil in their hand, a notebook on their side, and a vast range of external aids at their disposal (such as multiple editions, translations, commentaries and vocabularies) for linguistic and critical reference. Indeed, the traces of common reading have long faded but those of poets, novelists, critics and artists have survived thanks to librarians, archivists and scholars. Despite the broad variety and relatively easy accessibility of such material evidence, however, Dante reception studies have remained tied to a metaphorical notion of reading productively intended as the 'reactivation' – through intertextual rewriting, appropriation and absorption – of Dantean 'linguistic and narrative structures, characters and stories' in poetry, fiction, art and criticism (Camilletti et al., 2011: 12). Much remains to be said about reading as a cognitive process and the peculiar epistemological practices through which readers interacted with textuality to construct their own knowledge and understanding through two distinct annotating practices: commonplacing and marginalia.

Nineteenth-century readers and the art of commonplacing Dante

John Flaxman, Samuel Coleridge, Matthew Arnold and George Eliot were among those who relied on the practice of commonplacing to record their readerly experiences. To different extents, their notebooks, journals and personal papers acted as portable repositories of extracted knowledge – passages, transcribed for intellectual reflection, moral uplifting and creative inspiration. These objects activated a complex epistemological process that engendered the almost simultaneous 'reception' and 'conception' of new visual, critical and literary ideas reworked and 'assembled' into new textual 'patterns' (Darnton, 2000: 82). In Dante's case, the use of commonplace books and papers ranges from the recording of episodic encounters with the *Commedia* to lengthier and more diversified endeavours carried out over recurring programmes of extensive reading of the poet's oeuvre.[1]

John Flaxman, painter and illustrator, recurred to commonplacing in the period between the preparatory and revision phases of his *Compositions*: the series of line drawings of the *Commedia* commissioned by Thomas Hope in 1792 and completed in 1793. First kept by the commissioner, they were later published in Rome in 1802 and England in 1803. In his case, the passages were transcribed on four sets of blank sheets later bound in volume held at the British Library and containing numerous notes. These included a *canto*-by-*canto* outline of the poem, which he likely kept as an aid to the navigation of the overall narrative along with two lists of passages in English from *Inferno* and one in Italian for *Purgatorio* and *Paradiso*. Altogether, the papers detail the artist's process of comprehension and appropriation of the text: from the initial, intensive reading of Zatta's Italian edition, signalled also by a significant body of marginal annotations described and discussed by Charlotte Miller in her study (2003), to the subsequent extensive re-readings at later stages in the revision process, where he also resorted to Henry Boyd's English translations. Commonplaced lists and passages illustrate the deconstruction of each canto into a single, paradigmatic quote serving as the 'textual basis' for the designs, while the plate number on the upper-left corner signals its re-organisation into a pre-visual text divided into 109 plates: thirty-eight plates for *Inferno* and *Purgatorio* and thirty-three for *Paradiso*.

Perhaps the 'best-known scribbler in books in the English-speaking world' (Jackson, 2012: 272), Coleridge talked about his notebooks as 'his "full confidantes", "day books", "memorandum-books", "fly-catchers" and "commonplace books"' (Hess, 2012:

473). These reunited a 'multiform, diverse collection of textual extracts, fragmented ideas, sketches, reading notes and the occasional recipe' recorded over the course of thirty years (Hess, 2012: 473). Reflecting the broadly romantic approach, Coleridge conceived them as 'sites not just of reception but of conception, of producing new ideas to accompany the old' (Hess, 2012: 475).

The corpus of transcribed and annotated passages from Dante date back to two distinct historical moments in the history of his Dante reading, likely characterised by different material conditions of access to the texts. As Jackson noted, in fact, Coleridge's practice of commonplacing was often bound to a condition of limited, circumscribed access to a book, generally borrowed from friends and acquaintances, while the marginal annotations were made (in pencil and, more rarely, ink) once 'the book was staying on his own shelves' (Jackson, 2012: 282): a prized possession, the object of later re-readings.

The chronology of Samuel Taylor Coleridge's reading and study of Dante has been amply reconstructed by Pite (1994) and Braida (2004) in their respective studies. The point of origin is 1796, the year in which Coleridge read Henry Boyd's translation of *Inferno*. This first contact remained largely superficial, leaving a delayed trace in a notebook entry from 1803 which reproduced Dante's admonishment to the door. The interest was revived during his prolonged sojourn in Malta, which began in May 1804. From his correspondence with know that before his departure, Coleridge requested 'Dante and a Dictionary', and William Wordsworth provided him with a copy of Venturi's commented edition of the *Divina Commedia* edited by G. B. Placidi in three volumes. During this time the reading in original Italian became more intensive as well as more extensive, encompassing the rest of his prose and lyrical production. In 1807–8 his notebooks show that Coleridge had begun developing the ideas at the heart of his epoch-making lectures in 1818–19, identifying Dante as the 'dawn of modern' European 'Literature' (Coleridge, 1957–89: 3203). At this time, Coleridge recorded that he had 'read Dante's prose intermixed with Poetry, il convito, Vita nuova, & c. & and all the works of the old Italians prior to, contemporary with, or the immediate successors of Dante' (Coleridge, 1957–89: 3203). By the time of his first encounter with Henry Francis Cary in the autumn of 1817, Coleridge could 'recite whole passages of the version of Dante, and though he had not the original with him, repeated passages of that also, and commented on the translation' (Cary, 1847: 18–19).

Coleridge's developing familiarity with Dantean textuality is testified by the commonplaced passages extrapolated from the *De Vulgari Eloquentia*, Dante's linguistic treatise largely unknown to British readers, as well as several *rime* and *canzoni* copied integrally and abridged form. After a decade-long hiatus (1808–18), traces of Dante reading reappeared among the pages of his notebooks in preparation for his lectures. In addition to these, there is an undated and small body of marginal annotations written in ink and pencil in the third volume of his personal copy of Cary's *Vision*, undated.

At this point, the notebooks' pages became spaces of critical and creative elaboration of reading matter. From this, we can infer that in 1807–8 Coleridge did not own a copy of Dante's *Opere minori* and the transcriptions were 'separable entries' of the elements that struck his attention. The conceptual proximity between the lengthy excerpt from *De Vulgari Eloquentia* 2, iv and the lines from *Voi che 'ntendendo il terzo ciel movete* (Alighieri, 1995: 53–5, II) can be seen in juxtaposition as theorisation and application of the ideas about the broadening of the 'subject-matter suited to the poetic volgare illustre' as able to 'express poetically the intricacies of scholastic reasoning' and philosophical knowledge (Coleridge, 1957–89: 1304). The second extract from *Convivio* IV, i, 1–2 on 'amore' 'belta' and 'amista' is transcribed as an example of the 'force as well as the elegance of the Italian, which painfully exemplifies the great poverty of our Language in philosophical Language' (Coleridge, 1957–89: 3203). Particularly noteworthy is the selection of *Rime* composed during Dante's youth and around the time of the *Vita Nuova*, ranging from 'Un di si venne a me Malinconia' (25, LXII) to 'Di donne io vidi una gentile schiera' (22, LXIX). The *canzone* 'Tre donne intorno al cuor mi son venute' (47, CIV) is prefaced by a short annotation in which Coleridge argued that 'fra le rime di Dante is a wild & interesting Images, intended as an Enigma, and to me an Enigma it remains, spite of all my efforts. Yet it deserves transcription, and translation' (Coleridge, 1957–89: 1304). A shorter, abridged section (91–100) from the same is transcribed shortly after, signalling a continued interest in the text. The poems also include three by Cino da Pistoia, 'Questa Donna, ch'andar mi fa pensoso', 'Nelle man vostre, o dolce donna mia' and 'Perchè nel tempo rio' – the former described as 'sweet and pathetic' (Coleridge, 1957–89: 3012) – and one by Fazio degli Uberti, 'Io miro i crespi e gli biondi capelli'. Coburn's edition of the *Notebooks* list these under Dante: at this point, we don't know whether Coleridge copied it from a spurious edition or was, in fact, erasing attribution. In any case, Coleridge certainly demonstrated a pioneering knowledge of and interest in the works of Italian poets of the Duecento and Trecento, who came to be more widely known to the British public only in 1861 with the publication of Dante Gabriel Rossetti's volume of translations, *The Early Italian Poets from Ciullo D'Alcamo to Dante Alighieri (1100–1200–1300)*. The contact with Dante's lyrical production informed aspects of Coleridge's own poetry, although intertextual echoes are sparse and hardly traceable.

The Dantean notes from 1818–19 are mostly what Hess defined as 'thoughts in the early stages of development, complete with an undetermined horizon of possible revisions and interpretations' (Hess, 2012: 475). These include a series of synthetic discussions on Dante's historical context; the importance of scholastic philosophy in understanding the genius of Dante; the poet's place within the Italian and European literary tradition; as well as a more discursive exposition on the subject. The latter is, to all effects, a draft of Coleridge's 1819 lecture on Dante. The manuscript evidence offers an insight into the private, reflective elaboration of public, critical discourse. With a skeleton-like structure, the draft alternates full paragraphs, signs and abbreviations; bullet point lists of topics to be covered; reminders for inserting passages; page numbers for the original and translated texts; and a potential comparison with Milton (Coleridge, 1957–89: 4498–500). The 1818 and 1819 public lectures marked a turning point in the history of Dante's British reception sparking a critical discourse on the poet and his oeuvre. Far from being isolated interventions, they were part of a blooming tradition of Dante teaching that flourished throughout the entire century as we will see in the following chapter.

George Eliot established a stronger, more programmatic correlation between readerly and writerly practice. Kept separate from her (daily and travel) journals, the commonplace books were mediating objects and 'sites of the epistemological process' in which she stored the (literary and historical, religious and scientific) knowledge harvested through the studies and research activity underpinning her compositional process (Hess, 2012: 475). Eliot transcribed the majority of her Dantean excerpts during the two most prolific decades of her career as a novelist. The years between 1862 and the late 1870s, during which she wrote and published *Romola* (1863), *Felix Holt* (1866), *Middlemarch* (1871–72), *Daniel Deronda* (1876) and *Impressions of Theophrastus Such* (1879). In this period Eliot repeatedly immersed herself in the reading of Lombardi's edition of the *Commedia* and Fraticelli's *Vita Nuova* and *De Vulgari Eloquentia*, occasionally complemented by Boccaccio's *Trattatello*, Ozanam's *Dante et la Philosophie Catholique au Treizième siècle* and Balbo's *Life and Times of Dante*, among others. Each return to (the whole or specific *cantiche* of) the *Commedia* was directed to the surgical extraction of lines, terzine and wholesome passages stored under the occasional headings of 'Dantesque phrases'. Dispersed among five main notebooks, the corpus encompasses thirty-seven passages from *Inferno*, fifty-four from *Purgatorio* and thirty-one from *Paradiso* along with a sonnet, 'Negli occhi porta la mia donna Amore' from the *Vita Nuova*.[2]

On various occasions Eliot inscribed the textual extracts within lengthier pieces of self-directed commentary, revealing the continuous 'reflection on the process of writing', 'of textual creation' and 'on the reasons for and the implications of a certain choice' that underlined the writerly appropriation of the Dantean material into her fiction (Boldrini, 2001: 28). The result was a protean 'literary relation' at once plainly (and verbatim) exhibited in chapter epigraphs and direct speeches, and subtly woven in the 'specific literary structures, themes, stylistic and linguistic choices' of her novels (12–13). Eliot reworked and diffracted the commonplace entries to feed into the imagery, scenery and atmosphere of the moral landscape of her novels. They substantiate the historical context as well as the physical, intellectual and spiritual description of the characters while influencing the narrator's judgement of their actions. More acutely than Flaxman and more extensively than Arnold, George Eliot was the reader of Dante who seized the prodigious capacity of commonplacing as a readerly mode that in redefining the material and intellectual consumption of the *Commedia* also vehiculated its continuous textual and literary regeneration.

Scribbling in the margins: Romantic practices of Dantean annotation

While many Romantic and Victorian readers relied on a mediating object to stimulate the epistemological and creative process, others like Walter Landor, John Keats, Percy Shelley, William Gladstone, John Ruskin and Francis Palgrave established immediate contact with the text through the means of marginal annotation. They anchored their writerly responses onto the physical surface of their personal copies of Dante's works: books that they generally owned in Venturi's five-volume Italian edition and Cary's English translation.

At a glance, these marginalia appear graphically homogeneous, encoded within a system of marking where each sign describes a distinct degree of engagement with the text. Here, symbols such as asterisks, checks and crosses, exclamation and question marks record the reader's extemporaneous reactions of notice and doubt, approbation or dis-approbation of particular loci. Differently, horizontal underlining (of single words and full verses and even entire groups of terzine), brackets and vertical bars (single or double, on one or both margins for emphasis) signal a more substantial 'desire' to 'single out a part of the work to be mentally registered and guarantee further attention on later reading' (Jackson, 2005: 182). These graphic markings are generally complemented with more textual (linguistic and interpretive) aids such as interlinear glosses and marginal comments, summaries and extra-textual references to secondary sources. End-papers are usually devoted to indexed lists of headings and summaries of passages, along with an occasional general note surveying and evaluating the book in its entirety.

Behind such ostensible uniformity, however, lies a broad diversity of 'conscious motive[s]' underpinning each distinct writerly practice. Like Arnold and Eliot, Romantic poets isolated the *materia poetica* more functional 'to the thematic and structural needs of their own poetry' and more instrumental to their critical discourses on literary authority, canonicity and tradition (Braida, 2004: 176).

In the winter of 1817, John Keats began reading the *Commedia* upon the advice of his friend, Benjamin Bailey, who suggested it for 'the serious purpose of providing a background to his own prospective epic of Hyperion' (Gittings, 1956: 14). The recommendation

– 'You said I must study Dante' – turned into a three-year-long endeavour pursued over three different editions of the poem.[3] According to John Saly's reconstruction, these were a two-volume 1805 edition of Cary's translation of *Inferno* received from Bailey; an 1814 edition in three 32mo volumes of *The Vision* that he carried and read on his 1818 tour of Scotland; and an unidentified Italian edition read in the summer of 1819 as he was learning the language (Keats, 1958: 212). Of these, the miniature set is the one that reached us, and which bears a substantial corpus of reading marks in Keats's handwriting. Interestingly, however, only *Inferno* is densely annotated while the other two are seemingly untouched. For Gittings, the discrepancy denoted the poet's lack of interest in the *cantiche*, a position recently disproved by Saly's analysis of letters and intertextual references in *The Fall of Hyperion* proving Keats's acquaintance with, at least, 'cantos XXX to XXXI of the *Purgatorio*', 'canto I of the *Paradiso* and probably also the beginning of Canto II' read in Italian as part of his language practice (Saly, 1965: 75).

Closely observed, Keats's markings in his copy of *Inferno* show a somewhat erratic readerly interest localised around three discrete groups of *cantos* rather than encompassing the *cantica* in its entirety.[4] Within the fourteen annotated cantos (*Inf*. I, IX to XV and XXII to XXVII), the stroke of the poet's pen appears to be particularly insistent in highlighting 'narrative sections', 'extended similes', those employed for the description of the Infernal landscape, and the 'references to classical figures' (Braida, 2004: 133–4). Gittings first, followed Pite, Saly and Braida recognised in these annotations the formative ground where Keats began moulding the literary and textual relation that bound his own poetry to Dante's. Weaved through direct references, allusions and echoes, the intertextual dialogue initially born out of the specific need for a model of a modern epic for *Hyperion* soon exerted its shaping influence over a sizable portion of the works composed in that same period.[5]

Among the annotating readers of the Romantic period, Percy B. Shelley was the one who reached 'the complete saturation of his mind with the poetry of the great Florentine' over the course of two decades of continuous study (Kuhns, 1904: 212). The transcriptions from *Inferno* II and V found in his notebooks fix the earliest encounter with Dantean textuality to 1814, while in 1815 he completed his first translation of the sonnet 'Guido, i' vorrei …' (Webb,

1976: 279–81). The dexterous movement from the *Commedia* to the *Rime* attests that Shelley already owned the five-volume Italian text of Dante's *Opere col Comento del M. R. P. Pompeo Venturi* (Venice, 1793). Though the year of his acquisition of Cary's 1805 *Inferno* remains unknown, the correspondence with Ollier, his publisher, demonstrates that he had requested and received the English-text edition of *Purgatorio* and *Paradiso* in 1817. Notably, Shelley did not share the enthusiasm of his contemporaries for *The Vision*, 'praising the fidelity of the version' but remaining critical toward the translator's decision to render the poem in blank verse instead of *terza rima*: a choice that he considered an 'injustice' to the author (Medwin, 1913: 244). Medwin's testimony supports the contention that Shelley used the translation as an external reading aid, while he employed Venturi's edition, printed in a portable small octavo (4.5 by 7 inches), and equipped with *argomenti* and *annotazioni*, as his reference text. Such preference also explains the reading chronologies advanced by Pite, Webb and Braida that fix the date of the first reading cycle to 1816–17 in light of the 'early intertextual reference' to *Purgatorio* II in Alastor, and the multiple allusions to the poem in *The Revolt of Islam* (Braida, 2004: 101). The re-reading commenced on 11 April 1819, a week after he and Mary arrived in Milan: 'by the 19th he had finished the Purgatorio and three days later he embarked on the Paradiso' (Webb, 1976: 283).[6] In Pisa, the couple read the *Vita Nuova* together over the span of two weeks, from 30 January to 12 February 1821. That same year, Shelley approached the *Convivio*, while working on *Epipsychdion*, translating the first *canzone* and transcribing two passages from it in his notebook along with a brief comment.

The large corpus of external and internal evidence indicates that Shelley's readerly experience was the product of a unique combination of solitary and communal, intensive and extensive modes of reading. In Milan, in particular, the act acquired an aura of transcendentalism as Shelley took on the habit of visiting the Duomo and sitting in 'one solitary spot among those aisles, behind the altar, where the light of day is dim and yellow, under the storied window [...] to read Dante' (Shelley, 1964). In the summer of 1820, such intimate endeavour became a collaborative enterprise shared with Mary. With and to her, Shelley would read aloud two *cantos* a day and, later on, chapters of the *Vita Nuova* 'after dinner'. Initially undertaken to alleviate the sorrows of the loss of their son William, the reading of Dante soon became part of their commitment 'to a shared existence of reading, writing and a radical philosophy that would challenge the values of the society in which they lived' (Mercer, 2019: 1). Although there is no evidence suggesting whether they were inscribed during individual or collaborative occasions – both Percy and Mary were heavy annotators – the thick layer of marginalia in Venturi's edition attests to Shelley's reliance on both intensive and extensive modes of reading. The three surviving volumes contain a miscellaneous mass of signs, which range from the dense network of annotations covering the first twenty-two *cantos* of *Inferno* (I), numbered indexes of the *canzoni* of *Convivio* and vertical highlights for poetry and prose sections in the *Vita Nuova* (vol. IV) to lines along selected passages in *De Vulgari Eloquentia* and verses from the *Rime* (vol. V). As such, the marginalia substantiate with graphic evidence what the intertextual analysis of his published work has already revealed.

The uncommon comprehensiveness and far-sightedness of Shelley's readerly activity overcame the Romantic obsession with *Inferno* to pioneer the (re-)discovery of the beauty and significance of Dante's entire oeuvre. In this respect, the loss of the two volumes of *Purgatorio* and *Paradiso* deprives us of observing the inner mechanisms that elevated these *cantiche* to favourite sources for his own writing as discussed by Pite and Braida. Nevertheless, the markings in *Inferno* illustrate the reader's movements around the text as well as between the text and the commentary paratext constituted by Venturi's *argomenti* and *annotazioni* placed respectively at the opening and at end of each *canto*. Although he relied on the latter to clarify the meaning of the more obscure passages – generally marked with an 'X' – Shelley did not always accept Venturi's authority, as in the case of *Inferno* IX, 63. As Robert Hartley noticed, the 'No' inscribed on the side of this line refers to the note on page 88 (Hartley, 1990: 26), where the commentator questions the importance of this *appello al lettore* (60–3, underlined) in which Dante-poet warns his reader that 'this is a central moment in the story, where the literal event configures an important moral event, which requires a greater interpretive effort on his part' (Chiavacci, 2005: 283n). Here, Shelley disagreed with Venturi who contended that the poem contained '*infiniti altri passi molto più degni di osservazione* (a multitude of passages worthier of comments)'. It is possible that Shelley had perceived the significance of the passage in relation to the parallel *appello* in *Purgatorio* VIII, 19–21, which similarly invited the reader to distinguish truth ('*vero*') from the 'allegorical veil' ('*velo*') (Chiavacci, 2005: 236n, II). At the same time, this opinion might have been formed on the basis of the two-volume *Comment of Dante* written by his friend, John Taafe. This was the first English commentary (published in Britain in 1822), regarded by the poet 'a most excellent work, & one without which the history & spirit of Dante as relates to him will never be understood by the English students of that astonishing poet' (Shelley, 1964: 304, II).

Throughout the copy, the annotations signal minute attention to the linguistic detail (in *Inferno* V and VI, where individual words are singled out), to mottoes, to the similes underlying the descriptions of the infernal scenery (the '*sabbione infuocato*' and the *foresta dei suicidi*) of the punishments and of characters (Beatrice, Pier delle Vigne, Tyresias). As the journey through the underworld progresses, the markings become scarcer and more fragmentary until the last mark: a line pencilled over the *argomento* of *Inferno* XXII. The signs of the intensive consumption of *Inferno* demonstrate the degree of seriousness and critical acuity with which Shelley pursued his reading of Dante. This was practised not on the basis of personal taste – he was more inclined towards *Purgatorio* and *Paradiso* and 'Dante as a celebrator of nature, of love, and of ideal beauty' (Webb, 1976: 317) – but as the fulfilment of the intellectual imperative according to which 'one great poet is a masterpiece of nature which another not only ought to study, but must study' (Shelley, 1820: xii).

In spite of Shelley's own conviction that 'the reading of Dante was unfavourable to writing, from its superiority to all possible compositions' (Medwin, 1913: 160), this fuelled a writerly impulse channelled through translation, poetic composition and literary criticism. In 1816 Shelley translated the sonnet exchange between Dante and Guido Calvanti and the adaptation of three lines from the *Vita Nuova*. In 1820, he turned to the first *canzone* of the *Convivio*, 'Voi che 'ntendendo', and the scene of Matilda gathering flowers in Earthly paradise from *Purgatorio* XXVIII, 1–51.[7]

Shelley's maturation as a reader of Dante had a two-fold effect on his poetry and criticism. It enhanced the modes and forms appropriation of Dantean textuality from 'flashes in metaphor and figure, or even single words and expressions' into a 'kinship' in the themes and structures, style and ideological substratum of *Prometheus Unbound* (1820), *Epipsychidion* (1821) and *The Triumph of Life* (1822).[8] At the same time, it stirred the formation of a ground-breaking critical discourse conveyed in his 'A Defence of Poetry', written between February and March 1821. A 'major document in the history of aesthetics' and of British *dantismo*, the 'Defence' eloquently discussed the nature of Dante's oeuvre, of his place and function within the canon, and on the necessity of an English-speaking tradition of Dante studies. The 'Defence' was the first critical essay to make evident the unity of vision between the *Commedia* and the *Vita Nuova*, emblematised by the 'apotheosis of Beatrice in Paradise, and the gradations of his [Dante's] own love and her loveliness' (Shelley, 1821: 29). Similarly, it proposed a pioneering reassessment of Dante as a lyric poet who 'understood the secret things of love' (28) in his *Rime*, *libello* and *Paradiso* as much as the 'epic poet' of *Inferno* (31). More effectively than Coleridge's lectures, the 'Defence' discussed Dante's poetic excellency from a comparative perspective, asserting his centrality within the Italian tradition: foremost to Petrarch, Boccaccio, Ariosto and Tasso, and one of the three true epic poets, along with Homer and Milton. Finally, and most pragmatically, the 'Defence' voiced the frustration of the growing public of English 'modern reader[s]', who were struggling to turn their 'enthusiasm for Dante's apparently boundless creativity into a significant engagement with the details of his work' (Caesar, 1989: 468). In the absence of accessible scholarship and popular interpretive tools, Dante's 'very words', each 'a spark, a burning of inextinguishable thought', were left 'covered in the ashes of their birth, and pregnant with a lightning which has yet found no conductor' (Shelley, 1821: 65).

Forty more years passed before Shelley's call found an answer, channelled into a collective effort that led to the rise of a British tradition of Dante studies from the private endeavours of few solitary yet scholarly-committed readers like William Gladstone: individual readers who had overcome the Romantic poetic fascination and turned Dante into an object of Victorian positivist study.

Retracing Gladstone's early reading of Dante between diaries and papers

Straddling the Romantic and the Victorian ages and their respective readerly practices, Gladstone's experience as a reader of Dante bears notable traits of continuity as well as striking elements of originality. Similar to these were the periodic campaigns of solitary and communal, intensive and extensive reading of Dante's works, often carried out in correspondence of his sojourns in Italy.[9] Unparalleled was the intellectual drive underlying the readerly commitment, which had very little to do with the creative-oriented attitude of poets and artists. In Gladstone, the reading of Dante manifested as a sheer, self-interested desire of *canoscenza* (*Inf.* XXVI: 120) and for the rectification of the flaws and 'superficialities of the male education he had received at Eton and Oxford' (Windscheffel, 2003).

Undertaken as part of his lifelong and self-disciplined knowledge-accruing project, his Dante studies were pursued through the regular compilation of diary entries, the dense annotation of marginalia, the creation of a rich and diverse book collection, the contact with eminent scholars frequented individually or in the context of the activities of the Oxford and the London Dante societies. Gladstone minutely recorded his Dantean education in the *Diaries* kept from 1825 to 1896, the year of his death. Annotated as part of his 'terse note(s) of the day's activities' only rarely accompanied 'with an occasional gloss or comment' (167), the entries detailed the precise chronology, topography and bibliographical diversification of Gladstone's reading and book-collecting activities; his 'visits to and comments on major libraries'; his 'meetings with librarians and other bibliophiles' (Windscheffel, 2003: 14).

Between 16 September 1834 and 12 February 1893, Gladstone undertook twelve distinct bouts at 'in-depth study' or 'casual reading' of the primary texts (*Commedia*, *Vita Nuova*, *Monarchia* and *De Vulgari Eloquentia*) read in various editions and translations, as well as a corpus of secondary criticism. Initially picked up during his stays at the family house Fasque or in London, later in life he 'avoided tackling Dante or books about him at all during the parliamentary session' (Isba, 2006: 20). Rather, he made it into a ritualistic activity of sojourns in Italy: the country to which he escaped as a sort of 'voluntary exile during periods out of political life, and which provided the opportunity for reflection and respite' (45). To his friend and biographer, John Morley, Gladstone confessed the self-imposed decision to 'never look at Dante unless I can have a great continuous draught of him', explaining that the Florentine was 'too big, he seizes and masters you' (Morley, 1903, II: 497).

According to Windscheffel, in the summer of 1834, the reading 'regime' at Fasque was somewhat 'punishing' as it included the extension of the 'habitual reading period to cover the whole day, aiming to read and write for at least nine hours, sometimes working for eleven or more' (Windscheffel, 2003). Commenced on 6 September, the first reading of the *Commedia* unfolded slowly over a three-year period that saw Gladstone dividing the effort into three intensive bouts of study each separated by hiatus. The programme included an average of two *cantos* a day 'excluding Sundays, when his reading was more specifically devotional' (Isba, 2006: 49). The *Diaries* show that *Inferno* was finished on 4 October 1834 with the last three *cantos* accompanied with a (partial) re-reading of his friend Arthur Hallam's critique of Gabriele Rossetti's *Disquisizioni sullo Spirito Antipapale*: a work already read in 1832 in the aftermath of his friend's death and which represented Gladstone's initiation to Dante (see Chadwick, 1979). *Purgatorio* spanned from 6 November to 4 December 1835, while the passage into *Paradiso* was delayed until 26 February, and completed on 24 March. Notably, here the diary entries become slightly more detailed and let on the reader's emotional engagement with 'the dear Paradiso' uttered in entranced comments describing the *cantos* as '*veramente deliziosi*' (*Paradiso* III and IV) or 'delightful' (*Paradiso* XVII and part of XXVIII).

On 11 November 1836, Gladstone had 'recommenced with great anticipations of delight, the Divina Commedia' to which four days later he added Rossetti's *Spirito* (GD 11/11/36). The parallel reading continued until 8 December, when he 'finished Purgatorio, & drew an abstract of the cycles of punishment in that & the Inferno', while Rossetti's work was concluded on Christmas Day. On New Year's Eve, Gladstone's triangulated reading went full circle with the return to Hallam's Rossetti. Interestingly, the second re-reading of *Paradiso* was delayed once again: began on 23 March 1837 but also quickly abandoned after the first few *canti*, a behavioural pattern that Gladstone repeated over two consecutive years, in June 1838 and 1839.

Halfway between the first and second re-reading, Gladstone tried his hand at 'translat[ing] a little Dante' (GD 9/11/38): three passages from the *Commedia* in English *terza rima*. More than an outburst of creativity, the creative endeavour was an applied test of the 'poetical faculty' developed 'between twenty and thirty, due perhaps to having read Dante with real devotion and absorption' (Gladstone, 1930: 34). Gladstone's first translated passage in 1835 was 'the mediation on the Lord's Prayer recited by the penitents on the cornice of the Proud (*Purgatorio* XI, 1–21)'; then, 'the first part of Piccarda's speech expounding the willing submission of the souls in Paradise to the will of God (*Paradiso* III, 70–87)', undertaken at the beginning of 1836, and finally 'Ugolino's account of his betrayal and death (*Inferno* XXXIII, 1–78)' composed in 1837 (Davie, 1994: 387). The order of production is synchronic to various stages of the reading programmes carried out at the time. Although Gladstone did not motivate his choice of grand passages, they are nevertheless symptomatic of the originality of his readerly interests. The imprisoned Ugolino is a declared *trait-d'union* with Gladstone's eighteenth- and nineteenth-century translators. Along with the Paolo and Francesca episode of *Inferno* V, the story of Ugolino was the breach that modern readers opened into the *Commedia*. From Jonathan Richardson (1719), Thomas Gray (1737), Thomas Warton (1781) and William Hayley (1782) to the pictures of Sir Joshua Reynolds (1773), Henry Fuseli (1806) and William Blake (1827), *Inferno* XXXIII had already undergone manifold literary and pictorial transformations. His voice and image 'haunt[ed] the Romantic imagination' not just as a gothic tale of 'paternal despair and horrors of death' but as 'an exemplary case of political oppression' (Tinker-Villani, 1989: 294).[10]

While the choice was typical of the taste of 'an age which so much admired and reviled in the pathetic' (Yates, 1951: 97), the other passages testifies to Gladstone's youthful spirit of enterprise. The Lord's Prayer in *Purgatorio* XI, 1–21 represented a 'formidable challenge to the translator' for the level of sophistication of both language and themes, spanning 'the divine love for creation, and the response of creation in adoration; humanity's dependence on divine grace' and 'life as a pilgrimage' (Davie, 1994: 390). Here, Gladstone successfully reproduced the semi-liturgical nature of the passage with its alternation in each *terzina* between the Latin of the Pater Noster and the vernacular, 'first paraphrasing and then expanding it or reflecting on it' (392). Throughout, the reader-turned-translator demonstrated interpretive insightfulness for distinguishing and valorising 'the underlying principles of Dante's poetry and recreating them in his own version, while preserving his independence from the letter of Dante's text' (394). Comparatively less successful is the rendering of the 'subtlety and complexity' of Piccarda's discourse in *Paradiso* III verses, limited by the lack of 'variations' for the keyword '*volere*' (398).[11] Kept among his private papers for almost thirty years, in 1861 the passages were included in a volume co-edited with Lord Lyttleton and printed for private publication by Bernard Quiltch.

More than in the translations as finished products, Gladstone's readerly engagement emerges from preparatory flyleaves and a second set of related papers held at the British Library.[12] Despite the clear ink calligraphy, the marginalia, crossings and additions in pencil let one in on the linguistic and interpretive struggles that Gladstone was facing as he tackled the passages from the *Commedia* – the experience that brought out the conviction that translating Dante was neither a 'slight matter' of lyrical inspiration nor 'an after-dinner relaxation' or 'the plaything of the butterflies of literature' (Gladstone, 1884: 1). Rather, it required 'the greatest mental effort to reach his level' on the part of the individual who needed to let 'his intellectual being be in great part absorbed in that of his original'; willing to 'imbue and saturate himself with the spirit of Dante' (3) first as a reader and only subsequently as a translator – a sanctioning judgement to which Gladstone gave public and resonant expression in his polemic review of Lord Russell's translations of *Inferno* V (see Davie, 1994).

Like many of his contemporaries, for Gladstone the translational endeavour was an instinctual response to the *Commedia* that he soon superseded by a more reflective interaction with the text. The second set of *Papers*, in fact, show Gladstone establishing a more private, hermeneutical dialogue with Dante. Midway between the inwardly contemplative and outwardly instructional (veined by strong rhetorical addresses, 'Let us say' or 'No man') the notes offer an unparalleled insight into Gladstone's theory of reading the *Commedia*. In order to reach the 'true poetical appreciation' of the poem, Gladstone argues, the reader should be subservient to the text: he/she 'cannot truly understand what the poem is writing about unless he receives his ideas as a servant receives the commandment of his superior' (*Gladstone Papers*, 44731: 134f). Notably, Gladstone's appreciation and understanding are primarily oriented to the theology of the 'supreme' *Paradiso* and the readerly experience is conceived as an immersive spiritual experience where the reader's mind progressively coalesces into the Poet's, who guides him:

> Let no man read the *Commedia* Paradiso first written then crossed out] as a work of art. Let him first brace his understanding for its highest effort, and hush his tumultuous thoughts, his roving impulses, into a heavenly stillness. Let him become as little conscious as may be of his external organs of sight and hearing; the inward receptive energies, into which those organs will have enough and more than enough to fill them. Let him associate himself with the mind of his Poet. Let Dante be to him what Beatrice was to Dante.
> (*Gladstone Papers*, 44731: 134f)

From this perspective, the value of the *Commedia* transcends the simply literary or artistic dimension and gains a greater theological power: a contention that anticipates those uttered by Philip H. Wicksteed, who adopted Dante's poem as a moral, ethical and philosophical exemplum in his cycle of *Six Sermons*, which will be discussed in Chapter 4.

Gladstone's critical turn: 1840s–1860s

After this period of creative experimentation, the 1840s recorded three new bouts of study – first, in July–August 1841 when the reading (initially shared with his wife, Catherine) stopped at *Purgatorio* XVIII. In February–March 1844 Gladstone 'read and wrote about Dante', having been commissioned by *The English Review* to review Lord John Russell's translation in the *Literary Souvenir*. Finally, in August–October 1846 Gladstone completed his first full re-reading of the *Commedia* at the end of which he sentenced: 'I had really read and digested that astonishing work' (GD 11/11/46).

Following two episodic returns to *Paradiso* in 1853 (Good Friday and 1 June, respectively), on Christmas Day 1855, Gladstone devoured the *Vita Nuova*, in one sitting. In October 1859, the reference to 'Dante's Poems' in October 1859 might suggest a certain acquaintance with the *Rime*. After that, in 1861 the reader's attention moved onto the Latin works, with the completion of the *De Vulgari Eloquentia* between 2–5 January, and the *Monarchia* on 5 January. The reading sequence, from which the *Convivio* was inexplicably left out, corresponds to the order in which the works appeared in Alessandro Torri's *Della Prose E Poesie Liriche di Dante Allighieri: Prima edizione illustrata con note di diversi*, published in Livorno between 1843 and 1850. Valid on the textual and philological level, the edition conveyed a derogatory vision of the place of these works within the canon of Dante's oeuvre, presenting them as 'secondary (or even inferior) to the *Commedia*, reason for which it is worth publishing them ... only as aid to the "preparatory introduction to the study" and the commentary of the poem' (Vatteroni, 2017: 448).

Possibly influenced by this judgement, in the winter of 1866 Gladstone returned to the *Commedia* during his three-month stay in Rome. At this point, however, the deeply intimate and solitary reading of Dante was turned into a communal experience shared with his wife Catherine and his daughters, Agnes, twenty-four, and Mary, nearly nineteen. According to Mary's diaries, the lessons took 'place after breakfast and to have lasted about an hour' and reached the end of *Purgatorio* before their return to England. Apart from manifesting the reader's intimate desire to share his reading with his wife and daughters, the institution of these 'morning lessons' is an event of greater historical significance for it exemplified the way in which many Victorian women readers came into contact with Dante and gained access to the realm of high culture as part of a patriarchal heritage, which they eventually transcended by writing and publishing their own pieces of criticism as I will illustrate in Chapter 3.

The last two decades of the nineteenth century marked a critical turn in Gladstone's Dante studies. After a number of unfinished re-readings in September 1874, June 1876 and a more sustained effort in October 1878 – signalled by 'Read Dante, good progress' 'Read much Dante' – the last re-reading of the *Commedia* ('Finished my

Dante') was concluded on 9 September 1886. From that point onwards, Gladstone only read and acquired 'books of commentary on Dante, his life and work' (Isba, 2006: 60).

Although Gladstone had already begun integrating into his programmes the reading of Rossetti's *Spirito Antipapale* and Hallam's critique, Dean Church's 'Dante: An Essay' and E. H. A. Scherer's *Etudes Critiques* (October 1879), December 1887 witnessed a more marked turn towards scholarship with the reading of Giovanni Scartazzini's *Dante Alighieri: seine Zeit, sein Leben, und seine Werke*. Published in 1869, the book monopolised Gladstone's attention to the point that it was exceptionally read even on Sundays, thus making 'the study of Dante ... intensely sabbatical' (GD 22/01/88). Scartazzini's work set forth a solid scholarly methodology for the study of Dante's time, thought and poetry, to which Gladstone responded promptly as demonstrated by the thick layer of reading notes and marks covering the pages of the book, and the echoes found in his own original piece of criticism published on 14 June 1892 in *The Nineteenth Century*. The admiration for the Swiss scholar was such that Gladstone also acquired a copy of his 'vast and erudite' commented edition of the *Commedia*. Published by Brockhaus (Leipzig) between 1874 and 1882, the work had the ambitious objective of providing '*non solo un commento, man nello stesso tempo un repertorio esegetico-critico della* Divina Commedia (not just a commentary, but at the same time an exegetical and critical repertoire of the *Divine Comedy*)' (Lindon, 2013: 443). The result was monumental in both size (first volume 'only 444 pages long, whereas *Purgatorio* ran 817') and scope, for 'it popularized at once so many things and so many glosses, through wide examination of the ancient commentators and a sudden transference of German erudition and speculation' (444).

Gladstone combined the study of Scartazzini with a selection of recently published Italian scholarship, ranging from Giovanni Cornoldi's *La divina commedia di Dante Alighieri: col Commento* (1888, read 16–18 December), to Pietro Fraticelli's edition of the *Vita Nuova* (1873–87, read 11 January) and Giosué Carducci's *L'opera di Dante: Discorso* (1888, read 29 January). While Cornoldi's and Fraticelli's critical editions provided an up-to-date philological reconstruction and interpretation of Dante's works, the essay of the poet and teacher advanced a witty critique of 'the underdevelopment of Italian scholarship on Dante', and an attack 'towards the dantomani and ... the works of the dantofili' (Tognarelli, 2012: 514). Along with them, Gladstone also read Margaret Oliphant's *The Makers of Florence* (1888, read 28 December), which reconstructed the history of the city through the lives of Dante, Giotto and Savonarola. In March, Gladstone turned to the most authoritative source of biographical knowledge, reading Giovanni Boccaccio's *Vita di Dante* in a day. Finally, on 24 January 1893, the last critical work to be recorded was Frank Sewall's study on *Dante and Swedenborg*.

It is possible that the awakening of Gladstone's critical interest had been fostered by the intensification of his interactions with a growing network of *dantofili* and *dantisti* in Italy and abroad. During these years, the *Diaries* record noted repeated visits to Ignatius Von Dollinger, German theologian and Dante enthusiast, Edward H. Plumptre, Dean of Wells and author of an article 'Two studies in Dante' for the *Contemporary Review* (which Gladstone read and annotated) and a translation of the *Commedia* (received as a gift in April 1883), and finally Prof. Pasuale Villari, with whom Gladstone visited the Vatican Libraries in Rome and the Laurentiana in Florence.

On 14 February 1885 Gladstone was nominated Honorary Member of the Oxford Dante Society together with two other eminent Victorians, Walter Pater and John Ruskin. As I will discuss in Chapter 5, this was the first learned society founded with the aim of producing and disseminating a philological, historical and textual knowledge of Dante within and beyond Britain. Gladstone's election, supported by Edward Moore and Paget Toynbee, President and Honorary Secretary of the Society, was an act of public recognition and legitimisation of Gladstone's serious interest in Dante as a reader, interpreter and collector. Although the Society minutes do not record his active intervention during the plenary debates, his participation placed him at the very centre of the flourishing of the British scholarly debate on Dante as it was unfolding within the earliest community of British *dantisti*. The interaction with this enclosed group of private Dante enthusiasts-turned-public scholars engaged in philological recovery and traditional exegeses, commentary and translation gave the final impetus to Gladstone's burgeoning scholarly consciousness.[13]

Gladstone as a modern collector of Dante

With utmost conciseness and efficacy, the *Diaries* provide the chronological, topographical, bibliographical and social coordinates necessary to chart the developmental shifts of Gladstone's readerly experience over the span of sixty years. Along with the explicitly Dantean information, the entries also record ulterior activities, equally instrumental to the material realisation of such *lungo studio*: the purchase, use and systematisation of the books into his own personal and private Dante collection.

One of the reasons that made his sojourns in Italy most conducive for his Dante studies were the recurrent visits to various bookshops and bookstalls (as well as printers and binders' shops) in Milan and Turin, Florence, Rome and Naples, where he browsed catalogues and conversed with booksellers and other clients. The acquisition in loco was supplemented by an international network of book-buyers employed by Gladstone as well as a crowd of publishers, admiring authors (often seeking reviews) and the general public who would send him their books as gifts.

Such voracious, and at times compulsive, appetite for book-buying subsided with the actual consumption of the work, and its ultimate 'transition' into his library collection: a space in which the books remained highly movable objects that Gladstone – as well as his family and closest friends – picked up at various points. Initially housed in a sui-generis gentleman's library denominated the 'Temple of Peace' at Hawarden Castle, the 35,000 volumes were later transferred to St Deniol's, the 'public', residential library that Gladstone built in 1899. In both libraries, Dante was granted a prominent position as one of the centres of organisation of the collection: a status shared with a canon of great individuals such as Homer, Shakespeare, Johnson, Scott and Burns.

Perfectly preserved to this day, the Dante collection is situated on the Upper Floor of St Deniol's – now Gladstone's – Library, and occupies two whole, floor-to-ceiling bookshelves on the left-hand corner. A *uniquum* for completeness and the pristine conditions of the individual books, the collection is crucial for seizing the depth of Gladstone's individual readerly endeavours as well as its broader historical significance for British *dantismo*. Taken as a whole, the collection provides a synoptic representation of the state of the field in both Britain and continental Europe throughout the nineteenth century. Individually examined, the books and, specifically, those containing marginalia offer the unparalleled opportunity to assess the reader's receptivity of both primary texts and secondary sources. The eighty-two titles encompass works from the three great nineteenth-century traditions of Dante studies: the Italian, the Anglo-American and the German, with a smaller number of examples in French and even Greek. Italian *studi danteschi* accounts for fifty-three works among editions, biographical, critical and philological studies published between 1821 and 1890. Along with Boccaccio's *Vita*, Torri, Scartazzini, Cornoldi and Carducci, Gladstone owned the Minerva edition of Baldassarre Lombardi's *Opere di Dante*. Comparatively smaller, German scholarship is exemplified by Karl Witte's Italian edition (1864) and German translation (1865) of the *Commedia*, along with those by Hettinger (1880) and Braun (1883), and general criticism by Wegele (1865).

British *dantismo* is represented by a selection of forty-four titles, published between 1802 and 1896. The first, macroscopic group encompasses English translations in various formats, sizes and editions. For the *Commedia*, Gladstone owned not only the first edition of Henry Boyd's translation (1802) and the new and corrected edition of Cary's *Vision* (1844), but also John A. Carlyle's literal prose translation of *Inferno* (1849), Frederick Pollock's in blank *terzine* (1854), John Thomas' *Inferno* and *Purgatorio* (1859–62), Ernest Ellaby's *Inferno* (1874), a new edition of Ichabod Wright's translation with Flaxman's designs (1883), James Minchin's *terza rima* (1885) and Butler's prose translation of *Purgatory* and *Paradise* (1885). American translations included Thomas Parsons' translation of *Inferno*.

As for the minor works, Gladstone owned Charles Lyell's pioneering English rendition of the *Canzoniere* (1840), Dean Church's *De Monarchia*, to Perini's commented translation of the *Vita Nuova* (1893). Among them, particularly valuable is a private press numbered copy of the Ashendene edition of the *Vita Nuova di Dante Alighieri Fiorentino* (1895): this second book to be printed by the Ashendene Press, and of which Gladstone owned n° 46 out of 50.

The translational and critical efforts of the Rossetti family are also well represented in the collection. From Gabriele's *Osservazioni Sul Comento Analitico Della Divina Commedia* (1832) and the heavily annotated *Sullo Spirito Antipapale* (1832) to a rare edition of William Michael's *Comedy of Dante Alighieri ... pt 1: The Hell* (1865) gifted by the author with dedication, Maria Francesca's handbook *A Shadow of Dante* (1871), read on 14 February 1872 and Dante Gabriel's *Dante and his Circle* (1874) containing his ground-breaking translation of the *Vita Nuova*.

In terms of British scholarship, Gladstone owned foundational works such as the first volume of Taaffe's *Commentary* to Edward Moore's *Time references in the Divina Commedia* (1887); *Dante and his Early Biographers* (1890) and *Studies in Dante* (1896) as well as John A. Symond's *Introduction to the Study of Dante* (1872). Interestingly, the collection also included works by women *dantiste*: from the aforementioned Maria Francesca Rossetti and Margaret Oliphant's *Dante* (1877) to Arabella Shore's *Dante for Beginners* (1886) and Eleanor F. Jourdain's *Three Papers on Dante's Divina Commedia* (1895). Additionally, we find Catherine Potter's best-seller translation of *Cantos from the Divina Commedia of Dante* (1896), Phoebe Anna Traquair's beautifully designed *Dante: Illustration and Notes* (1890) as well as Mary Hensman's *Dante Map* (1892) and Norley Chester's (pseudonym of Emily Underdown) creative reworkings of Dantean episodes in her *Dante Vignettes* (1895).

Gladstone as annotator: marginalia and the challenge of private *dantismo*

A conspicuous number of the books in the collection contain marginalia of various forms and extents. While light and neutral annotations and notice lines are mostly found in books received as gifts from authors and publishers – signs of acknowledgements rather than genuine interest – a smaller group of books are covered by a thick layer of reading marks, signs and notes that extend over the text and its extremities, with indexes and annotations penned on flyleaves, front and endpapers. Altogether, this body of marginalia illuminates the manifold ways in which Gladstone sought to establish a hermeneutic and epistemological relationship with Dante by employing an articulate system of annotation (partially) deciphered by Windscheffel. Compiled in February 1836, the 'annotation key' listed and explained the following marks:

Notice ... |
/
Special notice ... NB
/
n. [note] with approbation ... +.
/
Disapprobation ... X, =.
Special do. [ditto] ... XX, XXX.
/
A doubt ... ?
/
A reservation or qualification ... ma.
/
Disbelief or surprise ... ! (Windscheffel, 2001:141)

The key, however, 'is not complete' as it 'does not define a mark he frequently used which resembles a "v" but which is likely a tick of approbation' (141). Other known annotation marks include obvious elaborations, such as a double line beside text, as well as more obscure marks found throughout. Along with these non-verbal annotations, the 'glossing of individual words and occasionally lines ... reflects Gladstone's interest in the art of translation' (Havely, 2014: 182).

Of the many annotated books extant in his collection, progressive refinement of Gladstone's scholarly approach is most tangibly recorded in three distinct editions of the *Commedia*: the 1822 Minerva edition of *La Divina Commedia col Comento del Baldassare Lombardi*, the 1827 pocket-size *Divina Commedia* curated by Lorenzo Pezzana, and the 1844 edition of Cary's English translation. Probably acquired personally during his Italian travels and book-hunts in London, the exemplars are all fine editions preserved in mint condition, bearing Gladstone's bookplate as a sign of ownership. While Lombardi's and Cary's volumes are housed in Hawarden, the Comino edition was gifted by Gladstone's son, John, to the Eton College Library and presented in a red morocco slipcase with an embossed inscription in gold letters, reading 'Mr GLADSTONE'S POCKET DANTE'.

Gladstone's copy of Lombardi's edition was a limited reprint of 1,500 copies from la Tipografia della Minerva presented in royal thick octavo, with exceedingly wide margins, in five volumes luxuriously bound in white calf with red inserts, marbled borders and gilded titles, enriched by engraved illustrations and a portrait of Dante. Lombardi presents a commented text of the three cantiche (I, II, III), a *Rimario della Commedia* (IV), and Giovanni Boccaccio's *Trattatello in Laude di Dante* (V) along with other critical writings. Originally in three volumes, Lombardi's was the first edition of the *Commedia* to be printed in Rome by the Stamperia De Romanis in 1791–92. In 1802 Tommaso Pироли printed a non-authorised version of Lombardi's edition which was complemented with Flaxman's designs. Soon after its publication, the Lombardina became a reference text for the nineteenth-century Dante scholars such as Ugo Foscolo, Karl Witte and Giovanni Scartazzini – a reason that might have encouraged Gladstone to acquire it for his collection.

Materially and substantially dissimilar is Lorenzo Pezzana's 1827 single-volume edition of the *Commedia* printed in Venice by Gaspari and based on Giovanni Antonio Volpi's Comino edition published in 1727. Printed in a portable size (32mo), the edition only consists of 'a plain text *Commedia*' with no commentary apparatus but Leonardo's Bruni's *Vita di Dante*. Such minimalism differed significantly from Volpi's original edition in three octavo volumes. Introduced by Aretino's *Le vite di Dante e del Petrarca*, the first volume presented text of the *Commedia* 'per la prima volta con i versi numerati' (I), the second *Rimario* (II), and third 'three alphabetical indexes, one devoted to linguistic matters, one of characters and toponyms, and the last to the exegesis of periphrasis and antonomasia' (Colombo, 2011: 338; my translation). The inclusion of the latter volume marked a watershed in the modern history of Dante's reception in Italy. The indexes were designed to 'the advantage of those beginners who do not master Latin, ignore difficult terminology and cannot afford to buy additional books' (Colombo, 2011: 322; my translation).

Finally, Gladstone's copy of the one-volume 1844 edition of *The Vision* is another fine exemplar in small octavo bound in brown full calf, raised bands to spine with decorative gilt panels and marbled endpapers. Published by William Smith, this was a new, corrected edition – the third impression following those published in 1814 and 1819 – of Cary's translation which included along with the translated text with commentary, an essay on 'The Life of Dante', a 'Chronological View of His Age' and additional notes and index.

Despite their material heterogeneity, these editions contain a similar corpus of marginal annotations and reading signs written not only in English, but also in Latin, Greek, Italian, while flyleaves and endpapers are filled with similar indexes of passages and lists of topics. The two editions and the translation are part of a larger and unitary system of study, within which each text fulfilled distinct yet complementary functions in Gladstone's private routine of Dante study. In particular, the continuities between the annotations found in each book suggest an integrated, if not even, simultaneous, use of the three books: each fulfilling a different practical use and didactic functions directly related to their distinctive material and substantial features. It is possible that Gladstone used the Comino edition as a book of hours: carried in his pockets along with his current diary, opened occasionally when he sought to read 'a little Dante for quiet'. Similarly to Cary's octavo edition, the pocket Dante was a small travelling object brought along not only in his journeys abroad, but likely employed as 'a coping mechanism such that after a difficult day in parliament, he would write in his diary that he read a little Dante for quiet', immersing himself in the 'pure text' without the visual and critical obstruction of the commentary (Isba, 2006: 4). Conversely, the five-volume Minerva edition was likely used in more sedentary conditions, at home: first in the family library at Fasque, and then at Hawarden in his 'Temple of Peace'.

Dating between mid-1782 and early 1788 and based on the *vulgata Nidobeatina*, Lombardi's edition did not envision students as its target public. Rather, it was addressed to a more selected audience of cultivated readers, who had the means for not only purchasing, but handling – both materially and intellectually – the quarto volumes enriched with frequent latinisms and references to theology and philosophy. Each *canto* was expounded in the 'complex of its different motifs, literal, allegorical, historical, conceptual and, even in some instances, rhetorical and stylistic' (Roda, 2017). Lombardi is highly indebted to the Cominiana on the ecdotic level as he adopts it as a reference text. On the critical level, Lombardi transcribed from the indexes explanations on toponyms and on the characters' biographies, and on the methodological level, he borrowed the greatest lesson: that the *Vocabolario della Crusca* is the access-door to the interpretation of the *Commedia*. The corpus of reading signs illuminates Gladstone's responsiveness as a *lector studiosus* of Lombardi's edition, keen to go perfection his intelligence of the text, acquire new knowledge and face the challenges posed by Lombardi's text and its paratext.

The annotating behaviour runs throughout the three *cantiche* and shows the peculiarity of Gladstone's interventions on Lombardi's edition. Here, the marginal annotations are light, and spatially limited to a specific part of the page located between the text and paratext. On the text, the sparse annotations, pencilled on the side of a single verse or lengthier passage, are the only traces of a more discursive, yet intermittent interaction with Dante. More frequent are the interpositions of punctuation marks such as commas and full stops, parenthesis and inverted commas. This kind of intervention could signal Gladstone's attempt at unpacking the line to either facilitate his understanding of its content (accompanied, sometimes, by an overwritten translation of a keyword) as well as isolating a notable aspect or passage to highlight, as in the case of ll. 31–3 in *Purgatorio* XIV. In this case, however, the parenthesised passage is also marked by a notice line that establishes a direct correspondence between the poetical text and the corresponding note of commentary in which Lombardi expounds the literal and allegorical meaning of the passage The high frequency with which Gladstone marks this connection unveils the specific function fulfilled by this edition: that of acting as a reference-text, an instrument for building and securing his core knowledge of the *Commedia*. Such annotating practice is strikingly different from that adopted for the Comino.

The relative limitedness of the marginalia on the text page, with a general intensification around the space of the commentary rather than the text, suggests that Gladstone saw this edition as a designated space for silent learning and absorption of knowledge from the paratext, rather than problematic engagement with the text. Strictly related to this choice is the displacement of his notes found in the material extremes of each volume, front and end flyleaves. With rare exceptions, the index lists of passages, topics, and characters appear hectic and cryptic: features that could suggest that they were compiled simultaneously with the reading to enhance the assimilation of selected contents of the text. Similarly, the non-dialogic nature of the index lists is emblematic of the level of self-referential nature of those annotations as part of Gladstone's strategy of private self-learning and construction of Dantean knowledge. In only a few cases, the lists are more easily intelligible and revealing of the reader's specific interests in certain aspects of the *Commedia*.

The lists found in the front flyleaf of volume I (*Inferno*) and second rear flyleaf of volume IV (*Rimario*) show Gladstone's interests in mapping the geography of the poem, references to Italian and European cities (Florence, Pisa, Genoa, Bruges, Lille, Paris) and countries (England, Germany, France) as well as rivers. Gladstone's selective attention is also directed to poetical features as he compiles a substantial list of similes from *Inferno*. Noteworthy are the lists relating to the Church, Popes and doctrinal aspects of the text, an interest that speaks of Gladstone's tendency to the religious and spiritual appropriation of the *Commedia* (see Havely, 2014). This was a critical disposition, which in the case of Lombardi's commentary eventually made him its ideal reader able to grasp Dante's extensive 'references to philosophy and theology'.

Finally, the front flyleaf in the *Paradiso* volume presents an inscription devised as Gladstone's own creative re-composition or summa of the *Commedia*, through the juxtaposition of four lines selected from the *cantiche*, and describing Dante's journey through the three realms of the afterlife:

> Giu per lo mondo sanza fine amaro (Inf.)
> E per lo monte, del cui bel cacume (Purg.)
> (XVII. 112) Gli occhi della mia Donna mi levaro
> (XXI. 59) La dolce sinfonia di Paradiso. (Parad.)

The choice of passages and their reconfiguration into an alternative collection could indicate the conclusion of Gladstone's reading process: a mark of his achievement of a greater degree of understanding and familiarity with Dante's *Commedia*.

The marginalia in Cary's translation refer to a later moment in the development of Gladstonian scholarship when the reader sought to engage in a dynamic critical dialogue with the Dantean text in both original and translation. Here the annotations do not just amend mistakes or misprintings and suggest alternative translations of certain loci, but vehiculate a direct critique of the authority of the translator as a commentator by questioning the validity of the paratextual corpus of notes.

While Gladstone recognised Cary's ground-breaking accomplishments as a linguistic mediator, the inquisitiveness of the marginalia reveals a certain scepticism towards Cary's authority as a 'cultural mediator'. Raising the reader's suspicions was the fact that the running commentary was ostensibly overcoming the traditional exegetical function to exert a more intrusive, domesticating influence over the original text. Gladstone's scepticism, in fact, was directed towards what Crisafulli describes as Cary's 'complex strategy of authorial control' (Crisafulli, 2003: 273).[14] Reflecting the domesticating approach used at a linguistic level, the translator designed the paratext as aimed to 'consolidate the impression' of the *Commedia* 'as a text already present in the English tradition', 'associated with an established English genre' like the Gothic (Braida, 2004: 45–6; 53). Another possible point of friction was the eminently literary and aesthetic nature of the translator's approach to the *Commedia*: a perspective in contrast with Gladstone's own spiritual appropriation of the text. As Pite observed, in Cary 'Dante's Catholicism and the religious significance of the allegory is toned down' as Cary insisted on interpreting *The Vision* according to 'the eighteenth-century meaning of the word, as of fiction or dream rather than "religious experience"' (Pite, 1994: 14–16). Despite these tensions, however, for Gladstone, the reading and re-reading of Cary's text and paratext remained crucial for securing the greater understanding, familiarity and memory of the poem in its entirety.

The 1827 Comino edition represents the point of convergence of Gladstone's hermeneutic endeavours and of the knowledge harvested from Lombardi's edition and Cary's translation. The distinctive material features of the book played a central part in both reinforcing his physical connection to the text as a reader, while also keeping his critical engagement active. The portable format enabled Gladstone to carry it in his pockets, to consult and annotate it at all times and occasions, from journeys abroad during long parliamentary recesses or in between daily activities. Proof of this is the rather trembling calligraphy in which the marginalia are written, perhaps caused by the movements of the carriages he was travelling in.

With the exception of Bruni's 'Vita di Dante' as an introductory essay, the page layout of Pezzana's edition presents a short paragraph of *argomento*, with the text of each *canto* centred on the page and the lines sufficiently distanced in between, thus leaving sufficient space for Gladstone's construction of his own running commentary made of (historical, literary, stylistic, philosophical) annotations, inscribed in the external and lower margins of the page as well as interlinear glosses of micro-elements (Jackson, 2001: 28) Similarly, the four blank flyleaves on the front and the back of the book also provided a relatively wide space to use not just for his usual, compact index lists, but for more meticulously schematic surveys of the poem as a whole. Generally clear and well-ordered, notes and signs appear only in a few instances superimposed, suggesting a potential re-reading and re-interpretations of the passage over time.

Throughout, the marginalia show formal and conceptual continuities with those seen in his copies of Lombardi's and Cary's editions, along with additional kinds of manuscript interventions on and around the text. Yet, the pocket Dante marks the maturation of Gladstone's readerly experience, with 'a progressive distancing from the text' to articulate a parallel critical discourse (Jackson, 2001: 42). The formal and conceptual improvement of Gladstone's system of annotation mirrors the central turn of his critical understanding and proto-scholarly approach towards the hermeneutic study of Dantean textuality. This maturation, however, becomes most tangible when examining Gladstone's enriched use of underlines and side-lines, interlinear glosses as well as the range of editorial interventions made on the text and paratext of Pezzana's edition.

On several occasions Gladstone amends misprints, comments on the quality and validity of the introducing *argomenti* through either extensive notes or reading signs (+, *), and pinpoints with marginal notes the names of characters mentioned in specific sections of the *canto* as a functional aid for future re-readings. The most intrusive intervention is represented by the dissection of the *canto* into smaller narrative and thematic units, to each of which the reader associates a headline usually referring to the name of the character portrayed. The structural deconstruction of the *canto* could be interpreted as an expression of the reader's attempt at manipulating the text into 'a unique personalised possession', reflecting his own comprehension needs (Grafton, 1997: 147).

Within the 'pocket Dante', underlines and side-lines are polysemantic. They single out individual lines or longer sections of the *canti* that altogether form a system of mottos and moral 'canons for living', ranging from Beatrice's words in *Inferno* II, 87–90; the close of Ulysses' monologue from *Inferno* XXVI, 118–20; the passage in *Purgatorio* VI, 91–3; and the *proemio* in *Paradiso* I, 1–9. At the same time, they signal greater critical awareness and sensibility towards the formal features of Dante's poetry, varying from the choice of metaphors and imagery to linguistic and rhythmic elements like the use of internal rhymes, anaphora and assonances. Furthermore, throughout the copy the side-lines are used as signs of approbation, reinforced by a corollary of marks ('NB' and '+'), and two types of marginal annotation that Gladstone devised as he attempted to penetrate into the depths of the poem.

The first is a network of minimalistic signs through which the reader made evident both the thematic, literal and stylistic elements of continuity within the poem on both a micro- and a macro-structural level, as well as the references to a range of external sources, including the Bible, Latin and Greek text. In this regard, the apparently inconsistent use of both Arabic and Roman numerals to punctuate references to specific textual loci could signal that the detection was not immediate but realised over the course of multiple re-readings of the poem. The second is a series of short marginal annotations that occur limitedly in *Inferno*, become increasingly present in *Purgatorio* and predominant in *Paradiso*. Gladstone's personal (and eminently private) discourse on the *Commedia* in which the knowledge harvested from Lombardi's and Cary's commentaries – openly acknowledged on multiple occasions – is re-elaborated into his own original output. What emerges from the synergistic reading of these marginalia is the reader's particular interests in Dante's anthropological, natural and astronomical theories, in the poetic and theological descriptions of God and in time references investigated by Edward Moore's in his 1887 study. Similarly, they reveal Gladstone's interest in the *appelli al lettore* in *Purgatorio* IX and XXVI. The spatial and conceptual unification of the marginalia is reached in the back endpaper of the 'pocket Dante'. Along with the numeric column list of page references, in fact, the endpaper presents a miniaturised table of contents of the *Commedia*, providing a simple coupling of sin and *contrappasso* to a more extensive description of key themes and characters, thus unveiling Gladstone's strategies for systematising and absorbing the knowledge acquired through intensive reading.

Reading Gladstone reading Dante 53

The marginalia inscribed in the three editions of the *Commedia* are the traces of Gladstone's personal archaeology of reading and stand out as monuments of his life-long readerly experience grasped in its far-reaching methodological, interpretive and scholarly development.

The end of private scholarship: Gladstone's (attempt at) public *dantismo*

Towards the end of his life, Gladstone embarked on a final scholarly enterprise titled 'Did Dante Study at Oxford?'. Likely drafted during his last sojourn in Italy, it was first published in June 1892 in *The Nineteenth Century* and then delivered as a lecture to the London Dante Society in 1908, after which it was re-published in the society's third volume of lectures. The piece was the public sublimation of Gladstone's *lungo studio* of Dante.

Standing at a median position halfway between 'the scores of commentators' and the 'crowds of readers' (Gladstone, 1892: 1041), Gladstone's intent was not to break new ground in Dante scholarship, but rather to cement an interpretive path opened up by more authoritative figures such as Giacomo Laicata, Andrea Scartazzini, Dean Plumptre and Cesare Balbo. The article sought to 'present in connected form' the body of 'direct' and 'corroborative evidence' scholars have produced in their individual studies, enhanced by his own original survey of 'the internal evidence as a whole' (1040–1). Gladstone's contribution to the ongoing discussion was a critical compilation of the multitudinous textual traces found in the *Commedia*, Giovanni Boccaccio's *Vita* – read in Fraticelli's edition (1861) – and in a manuscript in the Vatican Library containing testimony from Giovanni of Serravalle, Bishop and Prince of Fermo.

The opening statement confirms the ideological coherence and overall purposefulness of Gladstone's proto-*dantismo*, always oriented from the very beginning towards the *Commedia* as the sole object of his reading activities: 'no fresh light' can be thrown on the matter 'except that that comes from the text', which Gladstone as the 'firm ground of positive and primary source', a judgement applied also to Boccaccio's *Vita* (Gladstone, 1892: 1040). Demonstrating great methodological dexterity as well as an in-depth understanding of the compositional process and the overall narrative of the *Commedia*, Gladstone dissects the poem to trace 'the limit of his [Dante's] travelling experience' through Italy, France and Britain (1040). With order and clarity of exposition, he pinned down all 'local allusions' to Britain as a geographical and historical reality – 'from Purg. VIII, 130 and Par. XIX, 121–3 to Inf. XXIX and Purg. IX, 89' – to prove Dante's 'academical travel' and residence in Oxford, interfacing them with supporting secondary criticism (1040).

The distinctive characteristic of Gladstone's contribution lies in the high degree of textual accuracy of his cartographic reconstruction made possible by the annotating and indexing work done on Lombardi's and the Comino copies of the *Commedia*. For this reason, it is through the reconstruction of the intimate readerly experience (and the materials traces produced) that the public intervention unravels in its broader significance. Far from being 'a jeu d'esprit towards the end of his life', Gladstone worked on the article to apply the knowledge built and the analytical approach developed through decades of self-motivated and self-taught study (Ramm, 1992: 10). Breaking away from the private dimension, Gladstone chose a highly circulated monthly magazine like *The Nineteenth Century* and (later) the community of amateur and professional scholars gathered in the London Dante Society to test the validity of his work into the public arena, and ultimately leave his mark on the fast-developing tradition in Britain of Dante studies: a strain of scholarship that he saw happily extending before him thanks to individual and collective, private and public scholarly endeavours. Despite its methodological and interpretive limitations, the piece earned itself a space in Paget Toynbee's *British Tribute to Dante* where it was canonised the Gladstonian work as a pillar of the nineteenth-century scholarly reception of the poet's life and oeuvre.

Gladstone readerly engagement with Dante encompassed the entire nineteenth century, moving across and in parallel to major changes in the history of British Dante studies. The traces of reading left in diary entries, personal papers and a macroscopic corpus of marginalia, his *lungo studio* of the poet and his oeuvre constitute an unmatched historical record for Gladstone's self-creation as a serious critical and scholarly reader of the *Commedia*. While undoubtedly important for his individual biography, his approach to the reading, collecting and annotating Dantean textuality holds greater socio-cultural significance for the way it illustrates the transformation of Dante into an accessible object of daily, dynamic consumption within the private sphere. Similarly, his translational and critical interventions also demonstrate how the act of reading and re-reading engendered a drive for public expression: the impetus that sparked the wider critical conversation in periodicals and learned societies, and from which British *dantismo* drew its very origins.

Notes

1 For a history of commonplace books from the early modern to the Romantic period, see E. Havens, *Commonplace Books: A History of Manuscripts and Printed Books from Antiquity to the Twentieth Century* (New Haven: Yale University Press, 2001); A. Moss, *Printed Commonplace Books and the Structuring of Renaissance Thought* (Oxford: Oxford University Press, 1996); L. Dacome, 'Noting the Mind: Commonplace Books and the Pursuit of the Self in Eighteenth-Century Britain', *Journal of the History of Ideas*, 65 (2005), pp. 603–25.
2 For a discussion of Eliot's relationship to Italy and intertextual use of Dante in her novels, see A. Thompson, 'George Eliot, Dante and Moral Choice in *Felix Holt, the Radical*', *The Modern Language Review*, 86:3 (1991), pp. 553–66; *George Eliot and Italy: Literary, Cultural and Political Influences from Dante to the Risorgimento* (Basingstoke and New York: Palgrave Macmillan, 1998); 'George Eliot's Borrowings From Dante: A List Of Sources', *George Eliot George Henry Lewes Studies*, 44/45 (2003), pp. 26–74; R. Cortese, *George Eliot and Dante* (PhD dissertation, University of Winsconsin-Madison, 1981). For her practice of annotations and annotated books see W. Baker, *The George Eliot and George Henry Lewes Library. An Annotated Catalogue of their Books at Dr. Williams's Library, London* (New York and London: Garland, 1977).
3 *Inferno*, trans. by Henry Francis Cary, 2 vols., 1805–6 (KC, I, 254); *The Vision; or, Hell, Purgatory, and Paradise*, trans. by H. F. Cary, 3 vols., 1814. Vol. II inscribed 'J-K' and vol. III 'F. B – n'; contains marginalia (at Yale's Beinecke Library); another 3-vol. ed. (based on Severn drawing).
4 Keats's annotating behaviour has been widely explored over the last decades by B. Lau, 'Editing Keats's Marginalia', *Text* 7 (1994), pp.

337–48; 'Keats and the Practice of Romantic Marginalia', *Romanticism*, 2:1 (1996), pp. 40–53; *Keats's Paradise Lost* (Gainesville: University Press of Florida, 1998). On Keats as reader and book-owner, see S. J. Wolfson, *Reading John Keats* (Cambridge: Cambridge University Press, 2015); F. N. Owings, *The Keats Library: A Descriptive Catalogue* (Keats-Shelley Memorial Association: University of California, 1978); B. Lau, 'Analyzing Keats's Library by Genre', *Keats-Shelley Journal*, 65 (2016), pp. 126–51. See also: 'Keats Family Books in the Harvard Keats Collection' (list compiled by Leslie A. Morris), available from http://hcl.harvard.edu/libraries/houghton/collections/modern/keats.cfm.

5 Along with Saly, Pite and Braida, the influence of Dante on Keats's poetry has been explored by P. Vassallo, 'Keats's "Dying into Life": The Fall of Hyperion and Dante's Purgatorio', in *Challenge of Keats: Bicentenary Essays, 1795–1995*, ed. by A. C. Christensen (Amsterdam: Rodopi, 2000), pp. 206–17; P. Levine, 'Keats against Dante: The Sonnet on Paolo and Francesca', *Keats-Shelley Journal*, 51 (2002), pp. 76–93; D. Pollack-Pelzner, 'Revisionary Company: Keats, Homer, and Dante in the Chapman Sonnet', *Keats-Shelley Journal*, 56 (2007), pp. 39–49.

6 Mary's journals document her progress with the poem. She started reading '7 Canto's of Dante [*sic*]' from *Inferno* in Este in September 1818 and she continued till 20 January, when she noted: 'Finish the Inferno of Dante' (Shelley, 1987: 9). She must then have proceeded with *Purgatorio*, which was finished on 20 August 1819, and continued with *Paradiso* in August and September, with some shared readings. On Mary Shelley's reading of Dante see A. Braida, 'Mary Shelley in Italy: Reading Dante and the Creation of an Anglo-Italian Identity', *L'analisi linguistica e letteraria, Vita e Pensiero*, 17:3 (2020), pp. 107–18.

7 On Shelley as translator see also J. Raben, 'Milton's Influence on Shelley's Translation of Dante's "Matilda Gathering Flowers"', *The Review of English Studies*, 14:54 (1963), pp. 142–56; V. Ravinthiran, 'Dante and Shelley's Terza Rima', *Essays in Criticism*, 61:2 (2011), pp. 155–72; A. O'Connell, 'Dante's Linguistic Detail in Shelley's Triumph of Life', *CLCWeb: Comparative Literature and Culture*, 13.4 http://docs.lib.purdue.edu/clcweb/vol13/iss4/13 [accessed 3 December 2020].

8 On Dante's influence on Shelley's poetry see S. Ellis, *Dante and English Poetry: Shelley to T. S. Eliot* (Cambridge: Cambridge University Press, 1983); A. Weinberg, *Shelley's Italian Experience* (London: Macmillan, 1991); 'Shelley and the Italian Tradition', in *The Oxford Handbook of Percy Bysshe Shelley*, ed. by M. O'Neill and A. Howe (Oxford: Oxford University Press, 2012), pp. 444–59.

9 Peter J. Jagger noted that 'Aristotle, Augustine, Dante and Bishop Butler all had made their contribution to the formation of Gladstone,

the churchman, statesman and lifelong student' (Jagger, 2007: 251). A more unitary representation was provided by David Bebbington (1993, 2004) who pointed out that along with Homer's poems, Dante's works were made the objects of a 'detailed and sustained' study to which 'he repeatedly returned [...] for intellectual stimulus and spiritual nourishment' throughout his entire life (Bebbington, 1993: 139; 128).

10 The Romantic obsession for Ugolino has been widely discussed: along with Pite and Braida, Yates reported that 'Toynbee reckoned that there were twenty-seven translations of the Ugolino passage into English, the last which he had noted being 1899', F. A. Yeates, 'Transformations of Dante's Ugolino', *Journal of the Warburg and Courtauld Institutes*, 14:1 (1951), pp. 92–117.

11 Despite its shortcomings, *Paradiso* III is a noteworthy case of commonplacing: Gladstone's extrapolated the solemn remission to God's own will conveyed in the emblematic 'in sua volontade / è nostra pace' (l. 85) and adopted an engagement promise to Catherine and a 'passage ... for canons of our living' (Davie, 1994: 385).

12 To my knowledge, those more extensively relating to Dante are the following: London, British Library Add. MS 44503, f. 6; BL Add MS 44689, ff. 209–11; BL Add MS 44726, f. 24, MS 44731, f, 139 v.; BL Add MS 44792, ff. 63–5.

13 On many occasions, Gladstone's private correspondence with British and Italian *dantisti* was brought to the public eye *via* local and national newspapers. Between January 1883 and 1884, the *Pall Mall Gazette*, the *Daily Gazette For Middlesbrough*, the *London Standard* and the *Manchester Courier* published *verbatim* the letter addressed to Professor Giuliani in which he famously described the 'reading of Dante' as 'not only a pleasure, an effort, a lesson', but a 'strong discipline of the heart, the intellect, the man' (*Manchester Courier*, 1884: 8). According to the *Edinburgh Evening News*, 'the original text of Mr Gladstone's letter [was] published by the *Opinione* of Rome' after being given to 'F. Mariotti, one of the deputies to the Italian Parliament, with a declaration that the letter, placed in a small frame, should be deposited in Dante's house [...] to serve as a stimulus and encouragement to Italians' (*Edinburgh Evening News*, 1884: 4). In 1895, the *Manchester Courier* recorded Gladstone's exchange with J. B. McGovern, *dantista* and first advocate of a Dante Society in Manchester, to complement his 'highly ingenious and satisfactory' solution of the difficult lines in Inferno VII, 1' (*Manchester Courier*, 1895: 6). In 1896, the *Edinburgh Evening News* printed Gladstone's letter addressed to Hermann Oelsner praising his essay on *The Influence of Dante on Modern Thought* ('I am agreeably surprised at the amount of information you have brought

together') and the way in which 'the study of Dante should decidedly have gained ground in England during a period in which Italian studies generally have so miserably fallen off' (*Edinburgh Evening News*, 1896: 4).

14 Tinker-Villani, Crisafulli and Braida provided the most detailed analysis of Cary's strategies of translation. For further reference, see also G. F. Cunningham, *The Divine Comedy in English: A Critical Bibliography 1782–1900*, 2 vols (Edinburgh and London: Oliver and Boyd, 1963–65); R. W. King, *The Translator of Dante* (London: Secker, 1925).

2

Ephemeral Dante: Matthew Arnold's criticism in Victorian periodicals

In one of his harshest comments, T. S. Eliot found that Matthew Arnold lacked 'the power of connected reasoning at any length: his flights are either short flights or circular flights. Nothing in his prose work, therefore, will stand very close analysis' (Eliot, 1932: 346). What Eliot intended as a derogatory remark offers itself as the ground for a series of more productive research questions on an aspect of Arnold's private life and public works that has remained largely unexplored. What kind of 'flight' was Arnold's hermeneutic interest for Dante? Was it short, circular or all encompassing? And how does it stand the challenge of close (textual) analysis?

The answers to these questions are conditional to re-evaluating the condition of material fragmentation that characterises his critical discourse on Dante. More substantially than Gladstone's, the traces of Arnold's hermeneutic engagement with Dante are scattered between the public *text* of published essays, periodical articles and lectures, and the 'spatial field of the paratext' and, specifically, of his 'intimate epitext' (Genette, 1997: 5) mainly consisting of his notebooks. Once reunified, the *text* and the *epitext* reveal a multifaceted hermeneutic endeavour simultaneously carried out in the public sphere of literary criticism where Dante is employed as a literary and stylistic paradigm, and the private domestic sphere of self-learning, where it was part of a self-imposed habit of continuous reading and self-directed study.

Much like Coleridge and Gladstone, Arnold's history of Dante reading can be mapped from his notebooks where the margins functioned as the material spaces in which the hermeneutic act was first performed. Altogether, they help situate the readerly encounter within a specific chronological and topographical coordinate. Differently from them, however, the outward use of the private knowledge was not circumscribed to an isolated intervention. Rather, it was diffracted among lectures, essays and periodical articles unified by an underlying theorisation on the nature of poetry and the function of literary criticism. Articulating the discussion over three related movements, the chapter reassesses Arnold's *dantismo* as an element of mediation between fragmented and unitary forms of critical reception in a momentous phase in the history of Dante in Britain, prior to the emergence of a scholarly tradition of study.

Arnold's private *dantismo* between reading lists and annotations

Writing the 'Preface' to her abridged edition of the *Notebooks*, Eleanor Sandhurst recalled that her father was in his thirties when he acquired 'the habit of always having with him a long narrow book' in which he transcribed passages read 'in the British Museum, at the Athenaeum, in continental hotels, on railway trains, at home, and even in America' (Arnold, 1902: ix), and drawn from 'six great literatures and from newspapers, pamphlets, periodicals' (Arnold, 1952: xi). Kept until the day of his death in the spring of 1888, Arnold filled the pages of (at least) forty-one notebooks with notes that have so far been met with scant interest or even outright dissatisfaction. In the review of the more comprehensive 1952 edition of the *Notebooks*, Lionel Trilling complained that they defied common expectations since they 'contained no original observations, no personal memoranda, or germinal notions, or early drafts' of works showing Arnold's mind at work (Trilling, 1952: 496). Disappointingly, they presented instead 'a collection of quotations from his reading' that Arnold had copied in 'to bind them upon his mind, we might say, like phylacteries on the brow' (496).

Complicating the reading and raising eyebrows was the fact that entries did not follow any commonplacing organisational criteria. Rather, they were 'written in and out, wherever a convenient space offers itself: filling the gaps among more practical annotations on his travels, appointments and financial transactions' (Arnold, 1902:

vii–viii). With the exception of a few years in which 'the pages were left blank', Arnold filled the front and back-leaves of the diaries with a 'continued list of all the reading, hoped to accomplish during the year', updated on a monthly basis (xii). Minimalistic, the lists recorded the place, time and purpose of his reading along with either the title of the book or the name of the author, but no specification of editions and translations used. On some occasions, Arnold used headers highlighted in capital letters for instructions and status updates: 'to read', 'at the end of book', 'compose and read'. Complete readings were crossed off with a line. A concrete and continuous stimulus for intellectual self-reflection and self-improvement, the lists were part of a 'larger system of note-taking and record-keeping' (Jackson, 2001: 96) that Arnold grounded on the belief that 'a man's life of each day depends for its solidity and value on whether he reads during that day, and, far more still, on what he reads during it' (Arnold, 1902: xii).

Despite the vagueness of some entries, the overall high degree of orderliness of the lists offers a reliable account of the historical, geographical and bibliographical development of Arnold's private *dantismo*. Between 1857 and 1883 his reading went through several different stages that mimicked Gladstone's changes, marking a gradual passage from the exclusive use of primary sources to the integration of secondary literature, supporting his study of Dantean textuality. The reading of the first fifteen *cantos* of *Inferno* was accomplished by December 1857; in January 1858, he completed the first *cantica* and promptly moved on to *Purgatorio* and *Paradiso*. Among the many 'books for the summer' of 1860, Arnold noted again the two remaining *cantiche*, adding an Italian dictionary, an Italian grammar and Cary's Dante: a combination that could signal a more systematic commitment in learning the language of the *Commedia*. Although Arnold's personal copy of *The Vision* has not been recovered, it is possible that he resorted to the 'new corrected edition' published in 1850 by Henry G. Bohn in London, complemented by the poet's biography and chronological overview of his age. For his Italian *Commedia*, it is difficult to establish which of the many contemporary editions Arnold used. The only paratextual information inferable from the lists are memoranda from 1858 with which he reminded himself to 'bind Dante': a note that could either suggest that he had an acquired three-volume edition that he wanted to unify into a single volume, or that he intended to customise his edition with the standard binding used in his personal library as many Victorian book collectors did at that time.

In September 1861 at Fox How, Arnold finished *Purgatorio* and began *Paradiso*, which proved to be the most problematic and time-consuming of all. Dragging the reading over the following two years, in March 1863 Arnold interrupted or at least alternated the *cantica* with the *Vita Nuova* as an aid for redrafting a lecture into the article for *Fraser's Magazine*. Compared to the reading of *Inferno* and *Purgatorio*, the completion of *Paradiso* haunted the Victorian critic for more than a decade, between 1864–68 and 1876–77, when he finally crossed it off the list. Among the many factors that could have obstructed his reading, the theological and philosophical elevation of the language was likely the hardest to overcome. To escape the conundrum, Arnold began resorting to an interesting set of secondary studies.

Like Gladstone, this opened a new phase in Arnold's *dantismo*. Although most of his evocative uses and responses to Dante are ascribable to the years between 1857 and 1863, the last two decades 1864–83 saw the sophistication of his critical understanding of the *Commedia*. As in Gladstone's case, the passage from the exclusive use of primary sources opened a new phase of his *dantismo*. In fact, although most of Arnold's evocative uses and responses to Dante are ascribable to the earliest period (1857–63), the second phase (1864–83) is equally valuable because of the way in which the use of new sources granted Arnold a range of scholarly notions to enhance his critical understanding of the *Commedia*.

Arnold's choice fell on two French Romantic writers: Abbé Félicité Robert de Lamennais (1782–1854) and Frédéric Ozanam (1813–53). The former was a Catholic priest, philosopher and intellectual of the French Restoration who devoted his final years to the composition of a French prose translation of the *Commedia*. The latter was a Dante scholar, Catholic thinker and critic who had lectured on the *Commedia* at the Sorbonne between 1841 and 1853. First penned in the list for the year 1864, the block of entries noted: 'Ozanam's Franciscan Poetry*; Ozanam's Germany; Ozanam's Dante; Dante's Paradiso; […] Novels – Review & magazine articles & c– Lamennais on Dante' (Arnold, 1952: 576). The bibliographical references provided by the 1952 edition of the *Notebooks* help identify three items of the list: Ozanam's *Dante et la philosophie catholique au treizième siècle* (1845, appeared in English in 1897) and *Les Poétes franciscains en Italie au treizième siècle* (1852), reported as 'editions Arnold could have used at the time an entry was made', and Lamennais' *La Divine Comédie de Dante Alighieri*, the first tome of the six-volume collection of *Oeuvres posthumes* (1855–59) and 'known to be owned by Arnold himself' (Arnold, 1952: 637).

The sub-category under which the book is listed could also suggest a reference to a detailed article that appeared in the *Westminster Review*. After introducing the rather unknown Abbé Lamennais to the English-speaking public, the reviewer commended the translation, and 'the long and brilliant dissertation on the life, doctrine and works of Dante, which is prefixed to it', praising it as 'the best introduction to the study of the *Divina Commedia* that has yet appeared' (*Westminster Review*, 1866: 371–2). The emphasis on Lamennais' work as a seminal scholarly achievement unparalleled in Britain supported Arnold's comparative critique voiced in the lecture on *The Literary Influence of Academies* and later included in his *Essays in Criticism: First Series*. In the absence of a British authoritative scholarly work to guide 'the large class of readers who are students and admirers of that immortal poem' (*Westminster Review*, 1866: 371–2), Lamennais' work was a concrete reminder of the damaging effects of the cultural, political and academic isolation of England from the Continent.

Differently from Lamennais, Ozanam was a trained Dante scholar with a solid national and international reputation. In 1838, competing for the title of Doctor of Letters, he had presented his first scholarly essay on Dante, and six years later he was appointed Professor at the University of Paris Sorbonne. There, he designed a course on the *Commedia* that he taught for almost a decade. His doctoral thesis was published in 1845 with the title *Dante et la philosophie catholique au treizième siècle* and represented 'a major breakthrough in French Dante studies', soon translated into Italian, English and German (Caesar, 1989: 515). Ozanam's work shed light on the inner poetic potentialities of the Catholic philosophical language used by Dante throughout the whole poem and, most extensively, in *Paradiso*.

In 1873 Arnold jotted down two passages from the fourth chapter of *Dante et la philosophie* dealing with the same subject: the nature of the souls corresponding to the threefold partition of the afterlife in Dante's *Divina Commedia*. As Arnold had previously glossed, these were not Ozanam's original contentions but quotes from two of Dante's early commentators: one in medieval Latin from Benvenuto da Imola, and the other by Jacopo Della Lana in vernacular Italian. A *unicum* in the notebooks, those annotations provide tangible proof that Ozanam granted Arnold access to a broader range of exegetical sources and to a defined hermeneutical approach to the *Commedia*. Read intermittently between 1864 and 1876–77, in 1880 the entry 'Ozanam, Dante vol. 1' inaugurated a four-year-long integral re-reading of the *Commedia*, carried out in two distinct moments: first continuously in 1880–81, and then divided into two distinct moments, beginning in 1882 (*Inferno* 1 to *Purgatorio* 16) and coming to a definite conclusion in 1883 (*Purgatorio* 16 to the end of *Paradiso*).

As much as the reading lists are instrumental for historicising Arnold's reading habits between 1858 and 1883, the annotated passages scattered throughout his notebooks unveil the inner mechanisms of absorption of Dantean textuality. Once pieced together, the annotations *from* and *on* Dante reinforced the figure of Arnold as an unconventional Victorian *dantista*: susceptible to the minute beauty and the grand style of certain turns of phrase, usually found in lesser-known *loci* of the poem. Here lies the originality of Arnold's readerly experience, where the annotations form a reconfigured version of Dante's poem in which crucial moments such as Virgil's first speech in Canto I (*Inf.* I: 118–20) illustrating to Dante the condition of the souls in *Purgatorio* and Beatrice's 'lovely words to Virgil' (*Inf.* II: 70, 91–3) are juxtaposed with overlooked instances such as another metaphorical description of Dante's journey (*Inf.* XVI: 61–3). This can also be seen where Virgil's exhortation to Dante to fight against spiritual laziness and be ready to undertake the hardest of paths (*Inf.* XXIV: 46–8) is combined with a line from *Purgatorio* XIV (93) in which Dante reiterates the importance of intellectual (*vero*) and moral (*trastullo*) virtues in a man's life.

Throughout, the reoccurrence of specific entries exemplifies Arnold's 'theory of re-reading' (O'Gorman, 2012: 245) first formulated in *The Study of Poetry* (1880). Francis O'Gorman described it as a 'critical procedure' that 'primarily figures a return to texts as a renewed source of pleasure, a reminder of "what is really excellent, and of the strength and joy to be drawn from it"' (2012: 245). More than just an instrument to 'counter forgetfulness', Arnold's practice of re-reading was a hermeneutic instrument through which one could experience poetry from a twofold perspective (245). Arnold conceived 'all those returns, those "once agains"' as an intellectual practice through which the critic was able to fulfil his professional task, that of evaluating literature, and concurrently fully relish the pleasure of re-discovering true poetical excellence (245). Thus, the reappearance of certain passages is evidence of the continuous renewal of his critical and aesthetic experience of Dante's textuality: thus, *Inferno* XXVI (46–8) was annotated four times between 1858 and 1868, while *Purgatorio* XVI (93) was quoted in 1859 and 1862. Selecting the contents of her father's notebooks for publication, Eleanor Sandhurst became aware of the constant repetition of 'certain favourite quotations' and maintained that they hold crucial bearing within Arnold's critical framework because 'they furnish living illustrations of many of the principles again and again insisted upon in his prose writings' (Arnold, 1902: v). A comment that reiterates the existence of necessary connection and correspondence between the inward and the outward dimension of Arnold's readings: between what was privately recorded in the pocket diaries and what was publicly used in his lectures, articles and essays.

The fragmented discourse

Robert M. Zweig posited that 'throughout his career Arnold looked to Dante in light of some of the major questions he was concerned with and mentioned him constantly in *rankings* of great poets' while 'lines from the *Commedia* were used as touchstones and as examples of noble sentiments or thoughts' (Zweig, 1984: 156). Excluding passing mentions and general redundancies, the list of references can be narrowed down to a selection of exemplary cases, whose publication history and compositional background provide valuable information about the development of Arnold's critical discourse on Dante, and its public legitimisation.

Between the late 1850s and 1860s the name of Dante echoes in lectures, essays and an article, in which the critical discourse expanded to different lengths. While 'a lecture of March 1859 entitled "Dante, the Troubadours and the Early Drama," is mentioned in Arnold's notebooks but has not been published' (Zweig, 1984: 156), Dante's poetry is then amply discussed in a triptych of lectures given at Oxford in the winter of 1860–61, then published with the title *On Translating Homer*. The second documented instance is 'Dante and Beatrice' (May 1863), redrafted from a lecture given in March 1862 entitled 'On the Modern Element in Dante' for which no manuscript evidence was left, apart from a brief mention in a letter to his mother. Subsequently, *On the Study of Celtic Literature* had Arnold returning to some features of Dantean style previously expounded in the Homeric lectures; initially appearing in the *Cornhill Magazine* (1866), it was published in 1867. Finally, yet unrelated to his lecturing activity, was Arnold's extensive use of Dantean textuality in 'The Study of Poetry': an introductory essay written for T. H. Ward's anthology on *The English Poets* (1880), which was then reprinted in the *Second Series* in the late 1880s. Furthermore, a number of slighter interventions can be found in which Dante's name stands out with particular strength: the 1864 Oxford lecture on 'Pagan and Medieval Religious Sentiment' printed in the *First Series*, and three later monographic studies on *Milton* (1868), *Wordsworth* (1880) and *Byron* (1881) collected in the *Second Series*. Finally, Arnold quoted a passage from Ulysses' monologue in *Inferno* XXVI in the conclusion of an address entitled 'Ecce, Convertimur ad Gentes' delivered to the Ipswich Working Men's College, published in the *Fortnightly Review* in February 1879, and ultimately included in the collection of *Irish Essays and Others* in 1882. In it, Arnold reprised 'the words Dante has given to Ulysses (*Inf.* XXVI, 118–20): "*Consider whereunto ye are born! Ye were not / made to live like brutes, but to follow virtue and knowledge*"' (Arnold, 1882: 39; original emphasis).

This body of evidence places Arnold within an emerging British tradition of public lecturing on Dante, which originated with the Romantics at the beginning of the nineteenth century and continued developing manifold academic and popular expression over the whole Victorian period. Aware of their transitory nature of the medium, most of Arnold's lectures found a second life in print, either as periodical articles or essays in volumes.

Romantic legacies: Dante public lectures from Hazlitt to Carlyle

The first time the name of Dante Alighieri resonated among the rows of a British lecture room, the walls that surrounded it were not those of the university. Rather, they were those of one of the many literary institutions that flourished in London, Edinburgh and the provinces at the beginning of the century. Along with their scientific counterparts, these institutions organised 'slates of lectures by "recognized authorities in their fields" that held "high educational standards" while remaining "popular in approach"' (Zimmerman, 2019: 1). The lectures were 'open to anyone who could pay the entrance price'; they attracted young and older crowds of middle- and upper-class men and women eager to 'acquire an informal literary education' and social visibility through these popular events (1–2).[1] The socio-cultural diversity of the audience commanded wide-ranging curricula within which poetry – tackling issues of aesthetic criticism, literary history and canonicity – gained a central space, along with philosophy, history and music.

Despite its growing popularity, in Britain Romantic literary lecturing did not get the same recognition that it had in Germany where 'state-supported universities fostered lectures as a regular and largely academic form of inquiry and public scholarship' (Klancher, 2013: 5). Particularly debated was the 'utility' and 'appropriateness' of the medium for the study of poetry. Zimmerman's reconstruction of the dispute between *Blackwood's Edinburgh Magazine* and James Jennings conveys a paradigmatic opposition between private and public, individual and collective, amateur/self-organised study and authoritatively guided/administered reading of poetry. Jennings sustained a notion of study as a sociable and collaborative moment of 'collision of minds' (Jennings, 1823: 43–4) and of lectures as crucial means for bringing large audiences in a mediated proximity to great works and authors otherwise unachievable. Negating the validity of these practices, for *Blackwood's* the study of 'the works of great poets' belonged to 'the privacy of the mind' and should be carried out 'in undisturbed solitude' rather than 'in the midst of the contagious emotions of a thronged assembly, listening with excited feeling to a mixture of reasoning and passion' (*Blackwood's*, 1819: 165–7).

Seen from a Dantean perspective, the *Blackwood's* approach reflected the solitary, silent and self-designed modes of reading practised by Gladstone and the contemporary Romantic annotators. Jennings' defence of the literary lectures intercepted the impetus that many lone readers felt for sharing their critical understanding of the poet and his *Commedia*. The Romantic literary lectures had a central role in raising the interest and shaping the British critical discourse on Dante as poetic, linguistic and stylistic *exemplum*: as the first national poet, founding father of the modern literary traditions in Italy and Europe.

Moving past the eighteenth-century translational endeavours – generally circumscribed to *Inferno* V and XXXIII – the lectures advanced aesthetic, historical, political, ideological and philosophical readings of the *Commedia*. Reading passages in original aloud and commenting on them in English, the lecturers stirred the very 'contagious emotions of a thronged assembly' (Zimmerman, 2019: 28) to kickstart the circulation of the poem and, particularly, of its ground-breaking English translation authored by Cary. The support given by prominent organisations like the Philosophical Society, the Surrey Institution and the Marylebone Literary and Scientific Institution to programmes that featured Dante and the *Commedia* had far-reaching effects on its legitimation as a taught subject.

As oral performances, the lectures introduced to the critical reading of Dante large, but socially homogeneous audiences of 'self-taught and self-improving' men and women from the upper classes and 'the newly wealthy commercial class', who were admitted to these 'exclusive, high-society events' as paying subscribers (Hessel, 2016: 509). Once fixed into printed form, they reached the public at large (at first national, and then even transatlantic) through lecture notes circulated by hand and letter, then through the reports, reviews and excerpts featured in journals and newspapers in the following days and, ultimately, as edited (often annotated and improved) volumes published in the following years. Significantly, these very publications gave the first impetus to prolific trends in the nineteenth-century periodical writing and book publishing, characterised by the increase of Dante-related articles and reviews, primers, thematic studies and biographies for the expanding readership.

The British tradition of Dante-lecturing was highly derivative of the work of German philosophers and theoreticians of Romanticism, such as the Schlegel brothers, August and Friedrich, and Friedrich Schelling. Particularly influential were August W. Schlegel's seminal *Lectures on Dramatic Literature*, translated into English in 1815 by John Black, editor of the politically radical *Morning Chronicle* and glowingly reviewed by William Hazlitt in the *Edinburgh Review*. Bringing Dante 'out of [the] enclosed academic world into the public sphere' of 'the widest circles of educated and literate society', Schlegel's Berlin lectures offered a detailed 'systematisation of the critical discourse about the poet – history, subjectivity, the text, the audience – into a new description predicated on the principle of unity' (Caesar, 1989: 51). Arguing that the *Commedia* expressed the spirit of the age and the linkage to the Medieval Christian past, Schlegel's lectures demonstrated the feasibility of a markedly biographical and historiographical approach. One through which the critic could reconstruct the poet's intellectual development, with an outlook for understanding how 'the events of his age' and ideas about science, religion and poetry influenced the poetic genius (Caesar, 1989: 51). This interpretive perspective, however, did not exclude the possibility of a purely 'sentimentalist approach' (52): the lectures also demonstrated that the *Commedia* could also be read on the basis of shared human feelings rather than erudition, bridging literature, philosophy, theology and science.

On the evening of 18 February, the critic William Hazlitt inaugurated his course of eight *Lectures on the English Poets* at the Surrey Institution in London. The introductory lecture, 'On Poetry in General', was concluded with 'some remarks on four of the principal works of poetry in the world at different periods of history – Homer, the Bible Dante and ... Ossian' (Hazlitt, 1930–34: 34). Here, Hazlitt explained Dante's role as 'the father of modern poetry' (34): the node of conjunction between ancient and modern worlds, and author of 'the first lasting monument of modern genius', the *Commedia* (34). Repeated in March 1819 at the Crown and Anchor Tavern on the Strand, the lecture was grounded on two Dante-articles that Hazlitt had published in the *Edinburgh Review*: the review of Schlegel's *Lectures* and Sismonde de Sismondi's *De la literature du midi de l'Europe*, a recently translated volume based on a series of lectures delivered in Geneva in 1811. In the latter, Hazlitt had derived the historiographical material and the idea of Dante's place within the tradition of Italian Medieval literature

(69), while the former allowed him to place the Florentine within a broader European perspective.

Schlegel's *dantismo* also shaped Samuel Taylor Coleridge's epoch-making lectures on Dante, delivered on 27 February 1818 at the London Philosophical Society, and on 11 March 1819 at the Crown and Anchor Tavern. Commonly taken to mark a paradigmatic shift in Dante reception history along with Foscolo's articles in the *Edinburgh Review* (1818) and Cary's blank-verse translation of the *Commedia*, the lectures presented the British public with a new interpretative practice based on the combination of historicist and aesthetic criticism.

The manuscript remains of the 1818 lecture evidence how Coleridge devised a highly structured didactic approach in which the appreciation of the socio-historical context of the poet's intellectual (religious and philosophical) formation was the precondition for the understanding of Dante's poetic genius and the 'satisfactory perusal of the *Divina Commedia*' (Coleridge, 1884: 292). The teaching objective was to instruct ('prepare') the public to recognise and appreciate 'Dante's chief excellences as a poet' (292) on the basis of aesthetic categories that Coleridge identified as style, use of images, profoundness of vision, picturesqueness, topographic reality and mastery of the pathetic. To elucidate each of these categories, the lecturer used a selection of passages from *Inferno*, first quoted (better, 'recited') in Italian, then reproduced in Cary's ground-breaking translation. Although Coleridge's acts of close reading were less detailed than those in his lectures on Shakespeare (1811–19), the critical use of the *exempla* stimulated a proactive hermeneutic engagement on the part of the learners, dialogically invited to 'consider', 'observe', 'note and dwell' on (292) these aspects of Dantean textuality. Similarly, the juxtaposition of the Italian and the English text invited them to reflect on the unmediated beauty of Dante's verses, and concurrently reassess the aesthetic and practical value of Cary's translation in making the poem linguistically accessible to foreign audiences.

The combination of historicist and aesthetic approach along with extensive use of close reading was also characteristic of Ugo Foscolo's own lecture 'On the life, the poem and the age of Dante' delivered on 15 May 1823. Lesser known than his 1818 articles in the *Edinburgh Review*, the lecture was the fourth of a series of twelve *Lectures on Italian Literature* organised by his aristocratic friends, Lord and Lady Dacre, to help him repay his debts. Foscolo welcomed this offer of assistance with mixed feelings and a certain reticence to take on the commercial office of *public* rather than *academic* lecturer, exposing himself 'con la vergogna sul viso e col cuore afflittissimo, a dare lezione in pubblico, non in un'università che sarebbe un onore, bensì in una specie di teatro' (Foscolo, 1917: 241). The course took place in Willis's Rooms in St James Street, London at the presence of a 'numerous and elegant assembly' (145) of 140 subscribers (many friends and acquaintances of Foscolo), who paid the exorbitant price of £5 5s for a problematic and, at times, frustrating learning experience compromised by the cryptic use of Italian as the only language of delivery.

Later in the century Thomas Carlyle, the Scottish historian and essayist, placed Dante at the centre of two of the four courses of lectures delivered throughout his career. The *Lectures on the History of Literature or the Successive Periods of European Culture* were given between April and June 1838, on twelve successive Mondays and Fridays at three o'clock at 17 Edward Street, Portman Square, London. Challenging the insularity of the Victorian mind, the fifth lecture (14 May 1838) centred on Medieval Italian culture and Dante's *Commedia*. Surveying Dante's early biography and the composition history of the poem, Carlyle's initially fixed the traits of the moral character of the poet as a sublime example of 'depth', 'nobleness' and earnestness 'of heart', and 'grandeur of soul' (Carlyle, 1892: 86–7). He then used these very features as aesthetic criteria instrumental for the study of selected episodes from the poem from the *Commedia*: from the 'scene of the monster Geryon', the 'description of the city of Dis' and the 'dawn of morning' (Carlyle, 1841: 147) on the shore of Purgatory to the dialogic encounters with Francesca, Brunetto Latini, Farinata, Cato and the joyous vision of Beatrice. More limitedly than Coleridge, Carlyle's aesthetic criticism of these key moments rested on the incorporation (rather than close reading) of specific verses, quoted only in translation. The most distinctive feature of the lecture, however, was the attempt at widening the audience's horizons beyond the *Inferno*: 'the favourite of the three' which 'has harmonised well with the taste of the last thirty of forty years' (Carlyle, 1841: 147), to (re)discover the luminous beauty of *Purgatorio* and *Paradiso*, and learn to appreciate the moral, spiritual and literary unity of the poem as a whole. In the course on 'Hero, Hero-worship and the Heroic in History' delivered in May 1840, Carlyle expressed an even sterner critique towards 'the general Byronism of taste' that was hindering the perfect balance of 'Dante's world of souls', in which 'the three kingdoms, *Inferno*, *Purgatorio*, *Paradiso* look-out on one another like compartments of a great edifice' (147).

Canonised as a paradigmatic expression of nineteenth-century Dante criticism, these lectures have been largely undervalued as early pedagogical endeavours, on the account of the limited scholarliness of the knowledge they produced and on which they were also grounded. With the exception of Foscolo, whose work expressed a 'philological sense, a knowledge of the editorial history of the text superior to any in England (and most in Italy)' (Caesar, 1989: 450), they were the product of 'peripheral', 'occasional' and largely self-taught knowledge of Dante's works, which rarely extended beyond the *Commedia*, and was generally confined to the letter of the text. The result of their endeavours was a form of aesthetic criticism guided by poetics of taste that saw the lecturers expounding passages of the poem and aspects of Dante's life, language, style and imagery to support their own particular reflections on poetry and poetical genius, literary imagination and tradition, religious morality, political idealism.

Nationalism was the driving force behind the pedagogical activities of many Italian exiles, disseminating the aesthetic and critical appreciation for Italian literature and language across the British Isles as a cultural mission and professional endeavour. While a few like Antonio Panizzi (1825–29), Carlo Pepoli (1838) and Evasio Radice (1839) taught within academic institutions – Panizzi and Pepoli at the University of London and Radice at Trinity College Dublin – the majority carried out their Dante-lecturing at the Willis's Rooms and Marylebone Literary and Scientific Institution, the Manchester Royal Institution and the Tipperary Mechanic's Institute (central Ireland).

Felice Coen Albites and Alessandro Galleano Rivera were among those who lectured at the Willis's Rooms, one of London's principal concert rooms established in 1765 and known for its weekly subscription balls, musical events, vocal concerts and readings.

Differently from Hazlitt's, Coleridge's and Carlyle's lectures, the material memory of these critical interventions survived not in personal notebooks and published volumes but in a scattered array of newspaper reports and periodical advertisements. According to the women's magazine *La Belle Assemblée*, Professor Albites delivered a successful six-part public course on Dante in 1838, designed 'to give a sort of introduction to the reading of his principal poem, by presenting to you the essence and its form on a reduced scale' (*La Belle Assemblée*, 1838: 50). The first lesson sketched Dante's life and earlier works (*Convivio*, *De vulgari Eloquentia* and *Monarchia*) and concluded with an 'outline' of the *Divine Comedy*. Most interestingly, the magazine reported the 'very agreeable change' the Professor made for his more analytical lectures. Despite being 'thoroughly acquainted with the English language', Albites adopted French as the vehicular language for his commentary, with occasional quotes in 'the Italian original' (*La Belle Assemblée*, 50). Although praised by the reviewer for the way it 'conveyed more forcibly and without interruption to the minds of his auditory, the force, fire and beauty of his own conception of the renowned and beautiful original' (*La Belle Assemblée*, 51), the shift was made possible by the sophisticated nature of his close circle of auditors: cultivated upper-class men and women with a fluent command of the modern languages.

Advertised in *The Times*, Galleano Rivera's lectures at the Willis's Rooms took place on consecutive Saturday afternoons in June 1852 with 'a plan quite novel and exceedingly effective' where the *Commedia* was 'read, translated and recited' in the original Italian: 'copies of Dante's Canto could be purchased at the doors' (*Times*, 1852: 1). It is possible that the public lectures were organised following the success of Galleano Rivera 'Italo-English afternoons' in May 1852: smaller events taking place at his residence with limited admission priced at 5s for the 'numbered seats', 2s 6d for the 'reserved' and 1s for the 'unreserved' spots (*The Times*, 1852: 2). While the first lecture covered 'the political and literary life of Dante', the second offered a 'sketch of Beatrice and his Holiness Pope Boniface the Eighth' (*The Times*, 1852: 2).

Later in the decade, the Marylebone Literary and Scientific Institution hosted two lectures on 'The Age of Dante' by the Principal of Owens College, A. J. Scott, which 'exhibited' the poet 'in his relations to language and literature, to woman and love, to the State and, lastly, to religious thought' (*Daily News*, 1857: 2). In the winter of 1860, Italian dramatist Giovanni Battista Nicolini delivered on consecutive Wednesdays 'a course of ten lectures in the Italian language on the "Inferno" of Dante' at the presence of a small 'but attentive' audience 'consisting of ladies chiefly' (*Daily News*, 1860: 2). The lecturing activities continued well outside the capital. In the industrial north, Luigi Mariotti taught a nine-lecture course on Dante for the price of £2. 2s. at the Manchester Royal Institution (*Manchester Courier*, 1846), followed by the Principal of Owens College A. J. Scott in 1854 (*Manchester Times*, 1854). In Ireland, the *Tipperary Free Press* reported that in November 1849, Mr Wright had presented to the public of the Tipperary Mechanic's Institute the first 'instructive and entertaining' lecture on the 'biography of Dante and the analysis of his great work' (*Tipperary Free Press*, 1849: 2).

More than their content, the historical significance of the lectures dwells in the distinctive nature of the *medium* and the socio-cultural and pedagogical context in which Dante and the *Commedia* were turned into taught subjects between the 1810s and 1840s. These early forms of Dante teaching, in fact, took place within the new, public learning environments of cross-disciplinary (scientific, technological, philosophical, literary and national) institutions, which flourished in London and wider Britain at the beginning of the nineteenth century. Ideologically and structurally distinct from other knowledge organisations such as universities and academies, these institutions became dynamic producers and mediators of public knowledge through the promotion of courses of lectures in sciences, fine arts and humanities delivered by a salaried group of critics, intellectuals and more rarely, academic scholars.

The critical uses of Dante in Arnold's lectures and essays

The 1860s marked a shift in the nature of the pedagogic endeavours as well as in the spaces that housed them, fostering the conditions for the institutionalisation of Dante courses within traditional universities and centres for extramural teaching. Although excluded from Kuhn's and Cooksey's canons, Arnold's lectures carry the early nineteenth-century public lecturing tradition, transferring them into the realm of academic teaching. His hermeneutical approach aligns with the Romantic predecessors by promoting the familiarisation with Dante's poetry through the analysis of representative passages of the *Commedia*. Similarly, it reasserts Dante's inclusion within the European and British literary canon, adopting a comparative and synchronic approach 'illustrate well-formulated theories' (Zweig, 1984: 140) on the history of literature and the connection between works of the present and past. Like his Romantic and early Victorian predecessors, Arnold's critical discourses 'in making Dante a familiar, they also laid the groundwork for his real historical recovery by stimulating serious study' (Cooksey, 1984: 381).

Arnold's lectures took place within the academic dimension of the University of Oxford, where they introduced the teaching and the study of Dante to a specialised audience of university students, significantly different from the one attending Coleridge's and Carlyle's public lectures. On 5 May 1857, in fact, Arnold was appointed to the Professorship of Poetry at the University of Oxford. The post required him to give at least three lectures a year on a variety of topics without interfering with his job as a Royal school inspector. Arnold inaugurated his position with a lecture series 'On the Modern Element in Literature', which sought 'to redefine the notion of *moderness*, expanding it from a merely temporal category to an aesthetic and even moral dimension' (Kirsch, 2008: 40) while also laying the groundwork for his future discourse on literary criticism, theory of poetry and the idea of tradition. The original plan was only partially accomplished as Arnold felt that his 'knowledge was insufficient for treating in a solid way many portions of the subject chosen' (Arnold, 1960–77: 18, I): an act of retraction and self-criticism that would second Eliot's dismissive contention that Arnold was not a man of vast or exact scholarship. Yet, Dante was one subject on which Arnold felt confident enough to deliver an entire academic lecture on the poet's modernity for a demanding public of Oxford students. Taking place at two o'clock on Saturday 29 March, the Dante-lecture was publicly advertised in the *Evening Mail* (24 March) and in the 'University Intelligence' section of *The Morning Post* (27 March), two London-based daily newspapers.

At the origins of Arnold's critical use of Dante in both lectures and essays stand the theoretical principles set out in his 'On the Modern Element in Literature', the inaugural lecture delivered on 14 November 1857. To be rightfully called modern, Arnold argued, every age should strive to comprehend its 'copious and complex' present and past that lies sublimated in 'the poetical literature' of every given age (Arnold, 1960–77: 22) In order to access 'the spectacle of the vast multitude of facts awaiting and inviting comprehension', modern readers were to rely exclusively on 'the illuminating and revealing' power of the 'poetical intellect' (20–1). A critical function that will enable them to understand 'the immense development of knowledge and power of production' of their present age while 'contemplating the refinement of feeling and intensity of thought manifested in the works of the older schools' (21). It is through the establishment of this necessary link between men and the literatures of the past and the present that Arnold creates the conditions for the critical use of Dante.

In continuity with the Romantic critical discourse, Arnold recognises in Dante an 'exemplary figure' and in the 'evocation' of his name the very 'textual moment at which the authority of the past is brought to bear on the reader's response to the text' (Hampton, 1990: 3). With his works abiding by the same 'conditions of excellence' of Greek and Latin classics, Dante was a pillar of the literary canon along with Homer, Sophocles, Virgil, Shakespeare, Milton and Goethe. Like them, Dante served an exemplary pedagogical function of acting as 'the best model of instruction for the individual writer', inspiring with his literary greatness and spiritual nobility and leading him to achieve a fuller understanding of what poetic excellency is (Arnold, 1960: 12). Apart from providing intellectual stimulus, the reading of Dante lifts the creative genius from their immanent condition of poetic and aesthetic confusion Arnold explains that

> the multitude of voices counselling different things are bewildering, the number of existing works capable of attracting a young writer's attention and of becoming his models, immense: what he wants is a hand to guide him through the confusion, a voice to prescribe to him the aim which he should keep in view, and to explain to him that the value of the literary works.
>
> (1960: 8)

Such redeeming force is also beneficial for the critic, educating the poetic intellect to recognise and evaluate literary excellence. From this perspective, the evocation of Dante appears as a complex attempt at establishing a permanent model of literary exemplarity, able to inspire future generations of poetic and critical minds. This is a discourse theorised in *The Study of Poetry*, where Dante's works are extensively employed.

> Indeed there can be no more useful help for discovering what poetry belongs to the class of the truly excellent, and can therefore do us most good, than to have always in one's mind lines and expressions of the great masters, and to apply them as touchstones to other poetry [...] when we have lodged them well in our minds, an infallible touchstone for detecting the presence or absence of high poetic quality, and also the degree of this quality, in all other poetry, which we may place beside them. Short passages, even single lines, will serve our turn quite sufficiently.
>
> (Arnold, 1880: 21)

The use of examples guides the subject through a process of critical maturation, learning to rely on the literature of 'the great masters' for more than aesthetic satisfaction or intellectual pleasure: as standards for the evaluation and detection 'of the presence or absence of high poetic quality' (Arnold, 1880: 17). Thus, the profound knowledge and understanding of the model revive the critical receptiveness of the mind, enabling it to grasp the true, literary excellence that uplifts the (poetic and critical) spirit of men.

In the following paragraph, the theory is ultimately applied to 'short passages, even single lines' from Homer's *Iliad*, Dante's *Divine Comedy*, Shakespeare's *Henry IV* and Milton's *Paradise Lost*, which are presented as the most representative cases of what he would later call 'high poetical quality' (Arnold, 1880: 21). The reproduction of the passages in their original language and the selection of particular episodes demonstrates Arnold's deep familiarity with the *Commedia* through which he was able to identify the textual moments in which the exemplary quality of Dante's verse is best conveyed. This is concentrated in a triptych of quotes, two from *Inferno* (XXXIII: 49–50 and II: 91–3) and one from *Paradiso* (III: 85). The immediacy of Dante's Italian verse is strategically mediated by introductory comments that are laconic and yet emphatic, given the range of hyperbolic adjectives used, working as essential instruments of interpretation.

> Take that incomparable line and a half of Dante, Ugolino's tremendous words
>
>> 'Io no piangeva; sì dentro impietrai. Piangevan elli ...'
>
> take the lovely words of Beatrice to Virgil
>
>> 'Io son fatta da Dio, sua mercè, tale,
>> Che la vostra miseria non mi tange,
>> Nè fiamma d'esto incendio non m'assale ...'
>
> take the simple, but perfect, single line
>
>> 'In la sua volontade è nostra pace.' (33)

The juxtaposition of those three non-sequential passages from the *Commedia* gives origin to a peculiar Dantean *tableau* with no thematic continuity or formal consistency, since they differ in verse length, respectively a half-, whole and the closing line of a *terzina*. The dramatic climax set by Ugolino's tremendous speech in *Inferno* XXXIII (with the word '*impietrai*' in the final position to sublimate the image of the father transformed into rock) seems counterbalanced by the echoes of Beatrice's heartening voice in *Inferno* II as she speaks to Virgil about her heavenly condition: a description that contributes to 'isolate and detach the character of Beatrice within an immutable composure, and in a world far away' (Chiavacci, 2005: 63). In the third passage, this imagery is reiterated and reinforced in the ascetical solemnity of Piccarda's line that seals the tragic story of her life by revealing that men can find their peace only in God's will.

Despite the limited popularity of this latter episode, the preceding commentary establishes a direct and functional connection with the very first instance of the use of Dante's exemplarity, thus reinforcing the initial contention of the substantial coherence and continuity of Arnold's discourse on Dante. In fact, in defining the verse from *Paradiso* III 'simple but perfect' (Arnold, 1960–77: 100, i), Arnold made an open reference to his own definition of *grand style*, a concept formulated in the lectures *On Translating Homer*

Ephemeral Dante 79

given in the winter 1860–61 and of which the 'high poetic style' presented in *The Study of Poetry* was a more substantial evolution (100). Here, the *grand style* was a poetic feature manifested 'when a noble nature, poetically gifted, treats with simplicity or with severity a serious subject' (146). In Homer's case, what made his style 'as *grandiose*, as Phidias, or Dante, or Michelangelo' was the 'rapidity, plainness, directedness, and nobility' of his poetry (100). To exemplify the concept, Arnold extracted passages from Homer's *Iliad*, Virgil's *Aeneid*, Milton's *Paradise Lost* and Dante's *Divine Comedy*.

> Lascio lo fele, et vo pei dolci pomi Proniessi a me per lo verace Duca;
> Ma fino al centro pria convien ch' io tomi, that is in the grand style.
>
> (137)

Although he does not provide any explanation of the passage nor reason for his choice, the identification of such a liminal, non-dramatic passage of the *Commedia* for his evocative use of Dante is a significant gesture proving the seriousness of his hermeneutical endeavour towards Dante's textuality.

A meaningful exception to this rule is represented in *On the Study of Celtic Literature*, four lectures delivered between 1865 and 1866. On this occasion Arnold recalled once again Dante's example, and acknowledged him along with Pindar, Virgil and Milton as one of 'the eminent masters of style, the poets who best give the idea of what the peculiar power which lies in style is' producing 'masterpieces of poetical simplicity' (Arnold, 1960–77: 361, iii). This time, the notion of *grand style* is developed with a more discursive approach fostering the idea that 'great works, such as the *Agamemnon* or the *Divine Comedy*' are shaped by 'the true art, the *architektoniké*' (345). An Aristotelian concept derived from Goethe, this was 'the power of execution which creates forms' and transcends 'the profoundness of single thought', 'the richness of imagery' and 'the abundance of illustration' (348). From this perspective, Dante's *Commedia* could be held as 'true art' because it possessed 'the magisterial qualities of depth, comprehensiveness, grandeur, seriousness, and organisation which Arnold demanded' (Gottfried, 1963: 67). For Arnold, Dante's poetical excellence was found in the very 'completeness of his architectonics' coupled with 'the clear and precise use of language' freed of any 'clutter, bombast, decoration', and the ability to perform 'that fusion of symbol, object and idea at the greatest intensity of imaginative power which marks the greatest poetry' (Gottfried, 1963: 67). As such, *The Study of Celtic Literature* (1867) displays the progressive intensification of Arnold's hermeneutical endeavour, and the articulation of his critical discourse on Dante.

Once put in dialogue with one another, the fragments configure a new *textus*, thus proving the substantial continuity and consistency of Arnold's use of Dante, given the complementary nature of the information they individually convey, and the compositional background and publication history they share.

'Dante and Beatrice': critical *dantismo* in Victorian periodicals

The substantial continuity of Arnold's *dantismo* pertains to the similar compositional and pre-publication processes underlying his four Dantean key-texts: initially designed as lectures for the restricted Oxford audience, they reached a far larger and socially heterogeneous public when published in prominent periodicals such as *Cornhill's* and *Fraser's* magazines. A selection of these articles was subsequently collected into bound volumes, once again 'extracted' from the ephemeral original 'context' (Brake, 1994: 67) of (re)production and granted more permanent status in book form. These redrafting processes generally involved the repurposing of the text with regard to the subject, the length and the tone of the intervention to accommodate the specific requirements of the periodical. Laurel Brake has argued that the passage from the oral to the written mode 'often involved the careful suppression of topical allusions in order to enhance the illusion of timelessness of the new "art" text' (60), hence flattening that captivating allure of originality that would have kept alive the interest of the readers through time. This dynamic is particularly evident in 'Dante and Beatrice' in *Fraser's* where 'the sense of the engaging conversational presence of the author is exceptionally vivid' (Collini, 1994: 10), characterised by irreverent irony, dictatorial accents and continuous topical references.

In the absence of original draft papers, the compositional and publication history of Arnold's only Dante-piece emerges from a series of letters dated between 1863 and 1864. On 4 February 1863, the critic wrote to his mother:

> I hope before I come to Fox How (if I come there) this summer, to have printed six articles – one on Spinoza in the *Times*, one on Dante and one on the Emperor Marcus Aurelius in *Fraser*, one on a French Eton and one on Academies (like the French Institute) in *Macmillan*, and one on Eugenie de Guerin in the *Cornhill*. Perhaps I may add to these one on Joubert, an exquisite French critic, a friend of Chateaubriand.
>
> (Arnold, 1978: 212)

On 5 March, Arnold mentioned that he had to 'get ready an old lecture, which I am going to give to Froude for *Fraser*' (214). The lecture in question was the one he had delivered at two o'clock on 29 March 1862 at the Taylorian Institution, titled 'The Modern Element in Dante' and part of his first cycle as Professor of Poetry. This time, however, the change of *medium* likely involved a particularly drastic and invasive intervention onto the focus and the substance of the work. What had been originally conceived (and performed) as a comprehensive academic discussion on the modernity of Dante's poetry was repurposed into an article 'only about one-fourth the length of his usual lecture' (Super, 1960–77, III: 7), centred on Theodore Martin's recent translation of the *Vita Nuova*.

Although the reworking was functional to earning him a living as a reviewer (*Fraser's* paid £3.78 for the article) Arnold worried that the change of focus had hindered the broader cultural value of his intervention. In the summer of 1864 he confided to Alexander Macmillan, editor and friend, that he was toying with the idea of 'including one [essay] on Dante and Beatrice which appeared in *Fraser's* in May or April 1863' (Arnold, 1958: 67) in the first volume of his *Essays in Criticism* published in 1865. As the 'doubt' persisted, however, the article was ultimately excluded. The 'piecemeal collection' opened with the seminal *The Function of Criticism at The Present Time* and consisted of pieces that were structurally and substantially necessary for 'interpret[ing] the rest' and 'conduce to the general object' of promoting a 'principle of culture, rather than a programme for or a synthesis of poetry' (Arnold, 1979: 12). Removed from the prose work canon, 'Dante and Beatrice' faded from view until Richard H. Super's integral edition which recovered the article and placed it at the opening of the volume of *Lectures and Essays*. This act of retrieval put the Dantean intervention on the spectrum of scholars such as Steve Ellis, Alison Milbank and Julia Straub who referenced it in passing in their discussion on the Victorian afterlife of Dante's *Vita Nuova*.

Despite Arnold's doubts, the transition from the universality of the lecture form to the contingent nature of the periodical article did not hinder the significance of his first and only extensive piece of Dante criticism. The intervention diverged from the trodden paths of puff reviewing to carry out a polemic denunciation of Martin's ideological use of the paratext. Urging the public to pursue more interpretative perspectives, 'Dante and Beatrice' resounded as a dissenting voice among the lively but monotonous chorus of commentaries on the *libello* crowding the pages of weeklies, monthlies and quarterlies since the discovery of the Bargello portrait in July 1840. Painted in the Maddalena Chapel of the Palazzo del Podestà around the 1290s allegedly by Giotto, it showed Dante 'holding a flower in his hand and a book under his arm, plausibly Virgil or Statius's works or even the newly published *Vita Nova*' (Camilletti, 2019: 59). The unveiling of this new youthful image of the Florentine poet – unearthed 'a real vision of Dante's person, such as he had been seen upwards of five hundred years ago, ... in the lover's day of early manhood' (Barlow, 1857: 853).

In Britain, the first to report the news had been the poet and *dantofilo* Walter Savage Landor from the pages of the *Examiner* in August 1840, followed in January by an anonymous article in the *Gentleman's Magazine*.[2] Following a short notice in 1847, the lengthier articles penned in 1857 and 1860 by Henry Clark Barlow for the *Athenaeum* proudly clarified the crucial role that the English painter and antiquarian Seymour Kirkup had had not only in convincing the Italian authorities to undertake the restoration work, but also in obtaining the facsimile of the head by bribing a jailer to lock him up for the night in the prison.[3] Initially shared among his intimate circle of *dantofili* and *dantisti* that included Gabriele Rossetti, Charles Lyell, Henry Clark Barlow and Lord Vernon, the portrait was then given to the Arundel Society which commissioned its reproduction by Vincent Brooks in 1859. The resulting chromolithograph presented the portrait 'inscribed on the mount with details of its discovery, the tracing made by Kirkup in 1841 (and its ownership by Dante scholar Lord Vernon), with production details of the "facsimile"' (Ward, 2016: 36). Rapidly becoming 'one of the Society's enduringly popular prints' (70), the work commodified the portrait into a collectable relic for bibliophiles and art connoisseurs among whom 'sold steadily until 1897' (101) and was iconised as a title-page portrait reproduced in editions and translations.

The popularisation of the Bargello portrait catalysed a whirlwind of translational and critical endeavours all concentrated on the new image of the young Dante, 'the lover of Beatrice' charged with 'sensibility, gentleness and love' (Camilletti, 2019: 59). Arthur Hallam, Gabriele Rossetti and Thomas B. Macaulay were among those who put the *Vita Nuova* and the figure of Beatrice under the light of historical, aesthetic and religious scrutiny. The critical debate resolved at the end of the century when Edward Moore, a pioneering Dante scholar, offered a scholarly interpretation of Beatrice – 'the symbolic, the real, and the ideal' – in his first series of *Studies in Dante* (Moore, 1896).

The greatest effort, however, was made towards the translation of the very text that the young Dante could be seen carrying under his arm. The poems of the *Vita Nuova* had been translated by Charles Lyell in his (mildly) successful *Canzoniere of Dante Alighieri* (London: John Murray) which went through at least five editions 1835 and 1845. The first complete translation of the *libello* came in 1846 from the pen of the expatriate Anglo-Indian Joseph Garrow with the title of *The Early Life of Dante Alighieri* (Florence: Le Monnier). The 1860s saw the transatlantic publication of three ground-breaking translations by the American scholar Charles E. Norton (Boston: Houghton Mifflin, 1859), the Pre-Raphaelite poet-painter Dante Gabriel Rossetti (London: Smith, Elder & Co., 1861) and Theodore Martin (London: Parker, Son and Bourn, 1862).[4] These new translations enjoyed unprecedented critical and commercial success.

Published in 1862 by Parker, Son & Bourn, a small London-based press, Martin's translation was first printed in crown octavo and sold for 7s 6d, cheaper than Rossetti's 12s volume. From 1864 onwards, the book was re-issued by Blackwood and Sons, with ensuing editions in 1871, 1893 and 1904. Advertisements were placed in the *Examiner*'s 'Books of the Week' (21 December 1861), *National Review* (January 1862) and *Literary Gazette* (15 February

1862) while reviews appeared in the *London Review* (25 January 1862), *Athenaeum* (February 8, 1862), *The Critic* (5 April 1862), *Westminster Review*, *Fraser's Magazine* (May 1862), *Saturday Review* (25 October 1862) and its side-publication, *Reader* (14 February 1863).

From single-column notices to fourteen-page-long essays, reviewers warmly welcomed the work for the way it rendered 'an interesting fragment of Dante's autobiography' (*Westminster Review*, 1862: 588) in a 'highly-finished and poetical' (*The Critic*, 1862: 338–40) but also 'modern and straightforward' language that filled the reader with the same 'pleasure of being able to read Dante in the original' (*London Review*, 1863: 93). The commendations extended to the 'highly serviceable' paratextual apparatus that complemented the volume, opened with an introductory study and closed by line-by-line notes of commentary. While *The Critic* reproduced Martin's words verbatim to describe 'the nature and object of Dante's work, the circumstances under which it was composed and the effect these had on the poet' (*The Critic*, 1862: 339), the *Saturday Review* praised it as most 'valuable' hermeneutic support available through which the translator

> assists the reader in disentangling from the very poetic and mystic style of the *Vita Nuova*. He grapples vigorously with all the peculiarities and uncertainties in the record which might tend to shake the reader's faith in its biographical character. He discusses shrewdly, but with singular decision, all those enigmatic questions over which habitual admirers are prone to muse with reverent bewilderment.
> (*Saturday Review*, 1862: 517–18)

Exceeding the realm of stylistic evaluation, the reviewer asserted Martin's authority as a linguistic *and* critical mediator of the *Vita Nuova*: a trustworthy and reassuring guide for those readers who still doubted the biographical and historical authenticity of the events recounted. Ironically, however, the most emphatic endorsement of Martin as an interpreter of the *libello* came from *Fraser's*: the same periodical that exactly a year later hosted Matthew Arnold's disparaging critique. After proclaiming absolute confidence in the 'existence of a personal Beatrice as an existing object of love' (rather than 'a merely allegorical personage, or fictitious creature of the imagination'), the reviewer dictated that *Vita Nuova* must be taken to be a genuine record of facts and feelings, undertaken as one means of consolation for the early loss of the lady to whose memory it is, in fact, dedicated. It is thus the most remarkable true love story that was ever committed to paper.

(*Fraser's*, 1862: 582)

The assertive tone of the reviewer is noteworthy for it showcases the rhetorical measures through which periodical criticism shaped the public discourse, influencing the reception of authors and works among the rapidly expanding readership of the press. In Martin's case, the reviews in *Fraser's*, as much as the *Saturday Review*, *The Critic* and *The Reader* acted as a powerful sounding board for the translator's views, pushing sales while setting the *Vita Nuova* down a narrowly historical path of interpretation from which it struggled to diverge. The first to tone down the enthusiasm was Barlow from the pages of the *Athenaeum*, appraising the work from a more grounded scholarly perspective. More concisely and gently than Arnold, Barlow's refutation mapped the genealogy of such interpretive behaviour, tracing it back to Giovanni Boccaccio and his *Trattatello in Laude di Dante*. While in Britain the work had been canonised as the reference biography of the poet's life, Italian scholars had long debated the historical veracity of the reconstruction, so tainted by the overly dramatic representation of the poet 'all full of love and sigh and burning tears' (Barlow, 1857: 188). Building on Leonardo Bruni's pronouncement, Barlow warned the English public about the distorting effect that Boccaccio's 'tale-telling talent' had specifically had on the reception of the *libello*, launching it 'down the stream of time as something very different from what Dante intended' (188). In bowing to Boccaccio's authority, Martin had become one of his many modern 'disciples' who 'stopped short at the mere superficial sense, without caring to penetrate this semi-transparent pellicle, and so to arrive at a deeper, truer, more solid and abiding meaning beyond' (188).

The review was the first warning bell rang against the romanticising oversimplifications that had been hampering generations of readers from recognising the greater poetic and ideological complexity of the *libello*. Furthermore, Barlow's call to the suspension of all interpretations marks a distinction between the Dantean criticism practised by the *folta schiera* of general reviewers and the type of historically and philologically grounded discourse he was delineating in the *Athenaeum*. Although Barlow's pioneering role as the forefather of the first generation of British *dantisti* will be discussed in Chapter 5, his cautionary approach was an act of sensible scholarship born in rejection of amateur absolutism and in the awareness that the Dantean textual and historical scholarship study of the *libello* had only recently begun to form.

Matthew Arnold's essay-like article in *Fraser's* is the bridge between the amateur past and the scholarly future of the history of the reception of the *Vita Nuova*. Published in May 1863, Arnold wrote the article without the pressures of the marketplace sales (already sustained by the first round of reviews) and with a far-sighted understanding of the impact that Martin's interpretation had on the British reception of the *libello* and of Dante as a young poet.

For its rhetorical and structural features, the article was a dynamic exercise in Platonic dialectics, determined to foster the 'recognition and removal of error' by breaking away from the 'perceptual set' of commonplace knowledge advanced by Martin (Berlin, 1983: 34). For the tone and the interpretive approach, it epitomised the rise of 'a new self-consciousness on the part of the critics, a belief in the profession of "the critic" as opposed to the amateur performances of the earlier generation, and a wide-spread conviction of the importance of literary criticism in literary culture' (Shattock, 2002: 387). Thus, the article opened with the confutation of two diametrically opposed but equally radicalised modes of Dante-reading hitherto practised in periodicals reviewing, (early) lecturing and studies. Here, Arnold draws a distinction between two categories of critics, placed at each end of the interpretive spectrum. Those

> who allegorize the *Divine Comedy*, who exaggerate, or, rather, who mistake the super sensual element [reducing] to nothing the sensible and human element and those other critics who exaggerate, or, rather, who mistake the human and real element [seeing] in such a passion as that of Dante for Beatrice, an affection belonging to the sphere of actual domestic life, fitted to sustain the wear and tear of our ordinary daily existence.
>
> (Arnold, 1863: 664)

Where the former demonstrated an utter obliviousness (or disregard) of the universal laws under which the poetic genius informs his creation, the latter undermined the poetic element with an excess of topicality and domesticity. While the name of Gabriele Rossetti as the originator of the allegorical method is left unspoken, the initiator of the approach is unhesitantly recognised in the 'accomplished recent translator of Dante, Mr. Theodore Martin', who was spreading the behaviour from the *Commedia* to the (re-)discovered *Vita Nuova* (Arnold, 1863: 664). A self-fashioned critic who was laying claim upon the profession on the basis of the unwieldy, fifty-page introduction appended to the volume, Martin was panned for failing to provide a 'disinterested' interpretation of the *libello*, entirely devoid of partisan preconceptions. This was because the criticism he was feeding to a public hungered for intellectual guidance was distorted by the lenses of a modern hypotext. Explicitly mentioned, this was William Wordsworth's *She Was a Phantom of Delight*, a lyrical ballad celebrating the meeting of, the love for and the marriage to his wife, Mary Hutchinson. Throughout the entire introduction, Martin could be seen 'ever quoting these lines in connection with Dante's Beatrice; ever assimilating to this picture Beatrice as Dante conceived her; ever attributing to Dante's passion a character identical with that of Wordsworth' (Arnold, 1863: 665).

Ideologically divergent from Arnold's productive comparatism, this reiterated association was an act of forced modernisation that sought to make a thirteenth-century work satisfy the literary taste, the moral criteria and the biographical obsessions of the mid-Victorian public. A widespread 'anxiety', as Milbank described it, 'for establishing an historical link' with the events narrated in the *Commedia* and the *Vita Nuova* that originated from the emphasis on 'the Incarnation and the human nature of Christ and recreation of the life of Christ in a novelistic manner' of Victorian theological immanentism (Milbank, 1998: 103). Far from absolving a traditionally explicative function, Arnold deemed Martin's introduction manipulative because it gave Dante's love for Beatrice the 'flesh-and-blood character' of Wordsworth's very own passion (Arnold, 1863: 666). A transference that degraded the poetic feeling to a 'substantial human affection, inhabiting the domain of real life, at the same time that is poetical and beautiful' (666). Martin's obstinate pursuit of this interpretive path let his introduction drift into the realm of the purely imaginative where the story was 'developed and amplified' to the point that the *libello* is turned into as 'a sentimental, but strictly virtuous, novel!' (665). A transformation so to make Arnold exclaim 'what a task has Mr. Martin to perform! how much is he obliged to imagine! how much to shut his eyes to, or to disbelieve! ... Mr. Martin seeks ... and when he cannot find him, he invents him' (665). What lies behind the irony is a vehement contestation of Martin's bypassing of the interval evidence found in the *libello* as a manipulatory act that precluded readers to fully appreciate the text for the richness of its authentic biographical content. Events 'recorded', 'told' or 'mentioned' by Dante as both autobiographical *narrator* and poetic *auctor* of the work. In particular, Arnold disputed that the *creative* intervention of the critic that flattened the allegorical dimension in favour of (ultra-)realism, rested upon a gross ignorance or – at least – misunderstanding of

> the essential characteristic of chivalrous passion in general, and of Dante's divinization of Beatrice in particular, misled by imagining this 'worship of the woman', as they call it, to be something which it was not, something involving modern relations in social life between the two sexes.
>
> (Arnold, 1863: 666)

Arnold invited to reconsider its place within the broader canon of works from the *stil novo* that sought to expound 'the variety of passions and the ways of understanding love' as a physical impulse and a demon (Mazzotta, 2014: 12). Ahead of his time, Arnold stressed the importance of the contextual element as the necessary step for reaching a fuller understanding of the workings of Dante's poetic genius appreciated in all its trans-historical and trans-cultural complexity of vision, signification and value. In rejecting Martin's oversimplifying attitude, Arnold advocated for a more responsible readerly behaviour, pushing readers to recognise that the *Vita Nuova* was, like the *Commedia*, characterised by allegorical realism in which 'the basis of fact and reality' is crucial but not absolutely predominant because 'the conditions of his art do not make it necessary' (Arnold, 1863: 668). Beatrice's real existence and the limited situations in which Dante saw, spoke, or 'felt her beauty, her charm' (Arnold, 666) are just enough to produce the passage from the outward to the inward life and the poetic metamorphosis of Beatrice into an immortal vision. This spiritual transformation which began when she was still 'a living woman' culminated when Dante's genius 'came to its perfection' as he began 'composing his immortal poem' in which Beatrice is finally 'a spirit altogether' (666). Here, the extensive reference to the conditions and purposes of art and to the definition of poetic genius establishes a foundational link between 'Dante and Beatrice' and his major pieces of literary criticism, thus placing Arnold's *dantismo* within a wider theoretical and methodological framework.

From the dialogic juxtaposition of annotations and reading lists, the history of Arnold's private *dantismo* emerges for the first time in Arnoldian scholarship as a consistent narrative that supports and completes the one carried out in the public dimension of his lectures, articles and essays on Dante. Altogether, both textual and epitextual productions revealed the historical relevance and cultural value of Matthew Arnold's marginal *dantismo* as one of the most significant examples of Victorian critical and proto-scholarly reception of Dante. The review is a central piece of evidence that demonstrates how Matthew Arnold exploited the Victorian literary periodical as an epistemological site for redefining the forms and modes of Dante criticism that paved the way to professional scholarship and institutionalised study.

Notes

1 In this regard, Zimmerman notes that the inclusivity was only apparent as 'the labouring classes were effectively expelled from the Romantic lecture room in an era when educating them was deemed dangerous, while middle- and upper-class women were welcomed but with stipulations about the nature of their participation'. Furthermore, 'their presence in numbers nevertheless seemed to pose a double threat to the cultural authority of the institutions and their literary lecturers: as auditors they could determine a lecture series' popularity, and as readers they wielded increasing power in deciding which writers and works would sell' (Zimmerman, 2019: 5).
2 Walter S. Landor (1840), 'Fine Arts', *Examiner*, p. 518; 'Portrait of Dante' (1841) *The Gentleman's Magazine: and historical review*, p. 73; 'The Bargello of Florence' (1847) *The Athenaeum*, pp. 1328–9; Henry C. Barlow (1857) 'Dante's Portrait in the Bargello at Florence', *The Athenaeum*, pp. 853–4.
3 As related in 'Publications of the Arundel Society', Layard's telling relies heavily on Kirkup's account *Quarterly Review* (1858), pp. 277–325.

The dynamics are retraced in R. Holbrook (1911) *Portraits of Dante from Giotto to Raffael: A Critical Study, with a Concise Iconography* (London: P L Warner).

4 Charles Lyell (1835) *The Canzoniere of Dante including the Poems of the* Vita Nuova *and* Convivio (London: John Murray). For a book-historical analysis of Rossetti's translation, see F. Coluzzi (2021) 'Rossetti Reconsidered: Dante's *Vita Nuova* and Its Paths to Canonization in Victorian Literary Culture', *Le Tre Corone: Rivista Internazionale di studi su Dante* 8, pp. 135–46. The forthcoming *Interdisciplinary Perspectives on Translation and Reception History: The Afterlife of Dante's* Vita Nova *in the Anglophone World* (Routledge, 2022) edited by Federica Coluzzi and Jacob Blakesley provides a comprehensive history of the translation and reception of the *Vita Nuova* in the English-speaking world.

3

The critic and the scholar: Christina and Maria Francesca Rossetti's Dante sisterhood

In Britain, Matthew Arnold's article in *Fraser's* marked the beginning of an exponential curve of 'positive study of the texts, documents and themes of Dante's works' (Caesar, 1989: 73) increasingly pursued as a public, professional occupation for individuals and newly formed learned societies. As much as the discovery of the Bargello Portrait had awakened the curiosity for the young lover of the *Vita Nuova*, the sixth-centenary celebrations of the poet's birth in May 1865 afforded the definitive stimulus to the widening field of Dante studies.

Native soil of the poet, Florence was the political site of the first communal festival for the newly unified country and the point of convergence of a transnational scholarly impetus encompassing Europe and North America. The participation found material realisation in an unprecedented production of literary, critical and scholarly works as well as of a 'weird and wonderful variety of materials used for souvenir images of Dante: from marble and bronze to ostrich egg' (Havely, 2011: 3). Henry Clark Barlow acting as a national correspondent did not hide his enthusiasm for the wealth of 'public lectures, readings, exhibitions and performances' nor his amazement for the popular 'merchandise on display' (3). In his report, he noted how

> programs of the festivities were published at all prices, from five centimes to a hundred. People who had anything to sell were proud to avail themselves of the Poet's patronage; placards bearing his name were stuck up everywhere; his medals and portraits filled the shop windows; and his sacred head was made to recommend barrow loads

of brooches, pins, and buttons. Whatever was said, or sold, or done, had a reference to Dante.

(Barlow, 1866: 7)

Bridging the geographical divide, Victorian newspapers and periodicals not only provided the foreign public with highly detailed reports of the undergoing events but also ignited the local critical debate with articles of literary, historical and biographical commentary on the latest published works. The centenary, in fact, had propelled the production of translations and commented editions; biographies, handbooks and thematic studies; popular adaptations and retellings for adult and young, general and specialised, middle-class and lower-middle-class English-speaking readership.

The analysis of the bibliographical records brings forth documentary evidence largely overlooked: the fact that many women relinquished their sheltered status of domestic readers and private admirers of the Florentine poet to assert themselves as public mediators of Dantean knowledge. Taking on this role were influential writers at the height of their careers such as Charlotte Mary Yonge, Margaret Oliphant and Christina Rossetti along with lesser-known authors like Claudia H. Ramsay, Maria Francesca Rossetti, Katherine Hillard, Arabella Shore, Frances Locock, and Eleonor Dujardin. Writing across a wide spectrum of genres, printed media and topics, their works ensured the continued reception and canonisation of Dante in high and popular British culture, often achieving critical recognition and success of sales. Thus far, the memory of their achievements has fallen prey to the gendered mechanism of historicisation perceptively unpacked by Dale Spender:

> When we are presented with an exclusively male literary tradition [...] this is not because women did not quite, could not get published or went un-acclaimed. Women qualified on all these counts. It was only later that they were disqualified. How do we explain the transition from prominence to negation? What does it mean when women who were esteemed in their own lifetime are later denied or dismissed?
>
> (Spender, 1989: 26)

Taking in Spender's cogent interrogative, the chapter discusses the issues at the heart of the modern reception of Victorian female *dantismo* and the gendered misconceptions that underlie past and present considerations. It then focuses on the Victorian poet Christina

Rossetti and her semi-unknown elder sister, Maria Francesca, who stand out as some of the most representative and well-documented examples of women *dantiste*. While the former engaged in matters of aesthetic criticism of Dante's poetry, the latter surged to the role of *lectrix*: scholarly interpreter guiding and administering the reading of the *Commedia* to the new, expanding British public. The chapter retraces the evolution of their *dantismo* from a condition of educational disadvantage and ancillary assistance within the Rossetti family to one of intellectual independence and public accomplishment within the Victorian literary marketplace and Anglo-American academic circles.

The gendered marginalisation of female *dantismo*: 1921–2011

By 1921, the year of celebrations of the sixth centenary of Dante's death, women *dantiste* had found ambiguous recognition in the pages of *The Tablet*, a Catholic weekly journal that had commissioned a two-part article on 'Dante Studies in England' by Azeglio Valgimigli, Lecturer in Italian at University of Manchester.

The first piece (24 September) discussed the assimilation of Dante into British literary culture from Chaucer's *Canterbury Tales* to the advent of Cary's translation. The second piece (1 October) mapped 'the astonishing diversity of the minds, the creeds, the interest' that fostered the emergence of a 'more careful school of criticism' and 'annotation, based upon ample knowledge and the most careful attention to details' (Valgimigli, 1921b: 435) advanced by Edward Moore, Paget Toynbee, Philip H. Wicksteed and Edmund Gardner, among others. The celebration of these achievements was preceded by a laconic discussion of ways in which 'the great Florentine has fared better at the hands of British women' (436). Brief and synthetic, the cursory round-up mentioned Elizabeth Barrett Browning's poetic appropriation of Dante in *Vision of Poets* and *Casa Guidi Windows*, the critical attempts of 'Francesca Maria Rossetti' and Mrs Phillimore's *Dante at Ravenna* along with other, more didactic interventions:

> Rose S. Selfe has given us 'How Dante Climbed the Mountain', a work dedicated to young people of both sexes. Emily Russell Gurney,

in 'Dante's Pilgrim's Progress', amply showed how Dante can be made the food for youthful minds. [...] Another publication in a simple style adapted for boys and girls is 'The Vision of Dante' by Elizabeth Harrison, illustrated by Walter Crane, and published by the Chicago Kindergarten College. The aim of the writer is to awaken in youth the horror of sin and to instil in them an intense yearning for virtuous actions.

(436)

Valgimigli's canon is dominated by gendered principles of evaluation. The survey accords greater attention to these contributions in virtue of their explicitly moralising intentions through which the authors were fulfilling the maternal and educational role that women imposed by societal conventions. For the more critical interventions, in fact, Valgimigli demonstrates condescension. This is patent in the misquotation of Rossetti's name and book title; in the definition of Miss Cotes' book topic – 'the plants and flowers in the *Divine Comedy*' – as a 'pretty subject which only a woman could treat with so much delicacy'; or in the elusive reference to Enriqueta Rylands as 'a woman here in Manchester who founded a library to which flocks of scholars from all parts of the world' (436). Similarly, the wording of the subheading that introduces the section replaces the notion 'study' used for the work of male *dantisti* is temporarily replaced by 'tribute' (436–7). The semantic shift exemplifies how the recently institutionalised field of British Dante studies remained 'most resistant to female infiltration in the area of high-prestige non-fictional prose' treating 'women's writings as a separate category, devalued by reviewers' (Mermin, 1993: 45) and altogether excluded from the canon.

Almost a century later, Anne Laurence surveyed 'the great burgeoning of popular works on Dante' (Laurence, 2011: 281) authored by women and published between the late 1850s and the turn of the century. The reconstruction purposefully excluded the works of 'women such as Mary Shelley, Elizabeth Barrett Browning, Christina Rossetti or George Eliot, with significant literary reputations' (281) to give prominence to the achievements of the multitude of non-canonical authors.

Unsurprisingly, translation stood out as one of 'the chief types of work in which women published on Dante' (Laurence, 2011: 281). The first was Claudia Hamilton Ramsay's translation of the

Commedia in *terza rima* (Tinsley Bros., 1862–63) followed by two versions of the *Convivio* by Elizabeth Pryce Sayer (George Routledge and Sons, 1887) and Katherine Hillard (Kegan Paul, Trench and Co., 1889), Caroline Potter's best-selling *Cantos* (Digby and Co., 1896; 1897; 1899) and Frances de Mey's *Vita Nuova* (George Bell, 1902). Equally popular were the creative retellings of famous episodes in Dante's bio-bibliography as well as the critical reversionings that appeared in the periodical press and in volume. The latter category included Charlotte Yonge's sixteen-part study in the *Monthly Packet of Evening Readings for the Younger Members of the English Church* (1863–65) on par with Margaret Oliphant's articles for *Blackwood's* (1867, 1886) and *Cornhill* magazines (1875). The former encompassed miscellaneous titles designed for the literary, moral and even religious instruction of Victorian readers. Some of these guided the English public on 'how to read Dante' like Arabella Shore's *Dante for Beginners* (Chapman and Hall, 1886), Alice Wyld's *The Dread Inferno: Notes for Beginners* (Longman, Green and Co., 1904), Marie Louise Egerton Castle's *Dante* (George Bell and Sons, 1907) and Marion Bainbrigge's *A Walk in Other Worlds with Dante* (Kegan Paul, Trench, Trubner and Co., 1914). In others, 'Dante was recruited as an aid to faith' (Laurence, 2011: 227), as in the case of Rose Selfe's *How Dante Climbed the Mountain* (Cassell and Co., 1887) and *With Dante in Paradise* (Cassell and Co., 1900), Emilia Russell Gurney's *Dante's Pilgrim's Progress* (Elliot Stock, 1893) and Marian Andrews's (née Hare, writing as Christopher Hare) *Dante the Wayfarer* (Stanley Paul, 1905). Among these works, Emily Underdown's *Dante Vignettes* (Elliot Stock, 1895) and *Stories from Dante* (Frederick Warne, 1898) as well as Mary MacGregor's *Stories from Dante Told to the Children* (T. C. and E. C. Jack, 1907) were storybooks designed for the instructive entertainment of young readers.

On a documentary level, Laurence's survey is a major advancement from Valgimigli's sketchy review, unearthing a greater range of authors and reconstructing the composition, publication and reception history of each work. The critical evaluation, however, is subtly veined by a similar scepticism about the nature of these interventions. Appraising them on the basis of the length of their 'publishing careers', Laurence found women's works 'the fulfilment of an enthusiasm rather than [the product of] either literary or academic aspirations', and thus inferior to the endeavours of male scholars who had 'made a life's work of Dante Studies' (Laurence, 2011: 285) like Henry Barlow, Edward Moore, Philip Wicksteed and Paget Toynbee.

Critically, this does not account for the historical and socio-cultural limitations that precluded women's access to the literary profession and academic scholarship in the Victorian period. Like most women entering the profession of letters, these writers faced severe ideological resistances as they 'confronted an almost entirely masculine literary establishment, from editors and publishers, readers through to publishers and reviewers' (Shattock, 2001: 3), a struggle exacerbated by their drifting away from the 'traditionally female literary mainstream' (2) circumscribed to fiction, didactic and religious writing to pursue the high-prestige literature such as Dante's poetry. Unlike them, the group of men mentioned in comparison entered the field as regular contributors of high-end periodicals (Barlow with the *Athenaeum*), academic and extramural lecturers (Moore at the Taylorian Institute and Wicksteed within the University Extension Movement) as well as full members of learned institutions (Toynbee as secretary of the Oxford Dante Society established and presided over by Moore). With minor differences, the path that led these men to the achievement of scholarly status, prestige and even income was smooth and highlighted by the acclaimed publication of their studies in general and specialised periodicals, major university presses and commercial publishers.

A non-negligible divergence lies in the fact these men had gained solid academic education pursued at the Universities of Oxford and Cambridge and University College London, institutions that, apart from strengthening their scholarly authority (with academic degrees displayed in the title pages of their books), provided the resources for the catalysation of their initial amateur interest into life-long scholarly commitment. They granted them access to library and manuscript collections, to funds for research travels, and to a widening international network of specialised scholars and publishers, as the following chapters will illustrate.

None of these institutions was accessible to the women who formed the first generation of *dantiste* in Britain. For the majority of them, the establishment of 'some excellent, highly influential secondary schools for girls came into being, as well as few non-residential, non-degree granting colleges' (Mermin, 1993: 51) in the 1840s and 1850s. The increasing opportunities to access university in the 1870s and 1880s came too late for them to benefit properly from it. In the rare instances in which they came to it, however, their academic education was not comparable to the one male students received, as this was conceived 'as aid to women earning a living and being good citizens, not as means of access to scholarly research' (Laurence *et al.*, 2000: 9). In most cases, women's reading and study of Dante emerged as a self-disciplined endeavour possibly initiated in schools and colleges that included Italian in their curriculum, but most commonly within the domestic space.

The biographical anecdotes in prefaces and encyclopaedic entries show that Victorian *dantiste* followed the common path of women's education. A good 'start might come from few years at a good school, a well-educated mother, a governess, a brother's tutor willing to let the sister sit in on lessons, or a cultivated father (most often a clergyman) who taught a daughter long with her brother or because he had no son' (Laurence *et al.*, 2000: 51–2). This was the case of Yonge, Selfe (daughter of Philip H. Wicksteed) and the Rossetti sisters for whom the access to high culture – particularly, the study of classical subjects and foreign poetry – 'came naturally and decorously as an inheritance from their fathers' (Mermin, 193: xiv–xvi). Others like Hillard, Oliphant, Shore and Wyld resorted to their own educational devices and for some, the scarcity of resources often became the impetus for their own critical endeavours. In her preface, Shore declared her intention to help 'others who were, as I had been in the position' as 'young and unadvanced readers' (Shore, 1886: vi) of Dante. In both cases, however, the lack of a structured academic education and the exclusion from the academy certainly 'hampered their ability to achieve the same level of expertise' (Johnston and Fraser, 2008: 244) on which male writers constructed their scholarly reputation and professional authority as interpreters of Dante in Britain.

This dynamic is reflected in Laurence's codification of women's work as an expression of *dantofilia* rather than *dantismo*: as 'the fulfilment of an enthusiasm rather than either literary or academic aspirations' (Laurence, 2011: 285). That is, it was the product of an amateur interest in the Florentine poet, largely based on 'fragmentary acquaintance' and a 'peripheral awareness' of his life and works that 'did not necessarily go far beyond the occasion on which they were expressed' (Caesar, 1989: 37) nor lead to any significant advancement in scholarship. While professional *dantismo* remained a male-exclusive affair, Laurence at least recognises that Victorian women writers gained a central role as primary agents of the 'popularisation' of Dante among 'an upwardly mobile, post-1870 Education Act population that was stirring the demand for non-specialist works on intellectual subjects' (Laurence, 2011: 301). Yet, the widening of the grounds of reception was achieved at the cost of turning Dante into 'a cultural product, pressing him into service in a wide variety of genres' (292) that channelled the educational, aspirational and recreational needs of men and women, boys and girls. Laurence's characterisation of these interventions as acts of 'exploitation' (281) through which women entered the literary profession to earn a living draws a divide between scholarly practice and popular literature.

The surge of the British interest in Dante offered a broad range of new possibilities and commercial opportunities for the professional woman author eager to enter the Victorian book market. Yet, it is also true that many of these writers hid their greater critical knowledge and scholarly aspirations behind self-derogatory tones and an 'aura of educational and edifying intent' (Mermin, 1993: xiv–xvi) in order to reach and command large audiences that were not used to listening to women discussing high-literature. From Ramsay and Hillard to Yonge, Oliphant and the Rossetti sisters, many used humbling tones to 'circumvent … the matter of literary ambition, vanity and self-exposure' and make them 'acceptable to the Victorian code of social conduct' (xiv–xvi). Behind this substratum, however, these works demonstrated the author's 'secure possession and employment of knowledge' determined by a substantial change in their readerly habits and practices – a transition from 'escapism', where 'the emotional element is more awake and more powerful than the critical' (Flint, 1993: 40), to systematic and analytic interpretative engagement aimed at the production of critical knowledge.

All things considered, however, my evaluation of the nature and scope of female *dantismo* rests upon the enlargement of 'the concept of scholarship beyond the recognised bounds of Victorian intellectual life and beyond that practised by men' (Laurence et al., 2000: 7) as well upon the overcoming of the ideological opposition between academic specialisation and popularisation of knowledge. Working from the margins of educational and scholarly institutions, Victorian women writers actively participated in the establishment of Dante studies as an area of academic specialisation through the pioneering practice of what I term as *popular dantismo*. This was a form of textual and critical, historical and biographical scholarship characterised by an unremitting concern for matters of intelligibility and didacticism that reflected in its scope Dante's authorial intentions of '*far intendere le sue parole a donna*', where *donna* synecdochically embraced common and learned readers. In doing so, women's works effectively unhinged previous preconceptions regarding the alleged inaccessibility of the Dantean oeuvre for wider fruition, and its exploitation as an instrument of social elitism and gendered exclusion.

The Rossetti sisters and the practice of popular *dantismo*

The Dantean sisterhood of Christina and Maria Francesca Rossetti is a paradigmatic example of a female interpretive readership developed under and in reaction to patriarchal influences. The synoptic analysis of their lives and works brings forth the major traits of continuity and discontinuity in the historical development of their serious study of Dante; in the ideological and methodological approaches underlying their individual practices of Dantean hermeneutics; and finally, in their relations with the male-centric tradition of family *dantismo*, embodied by their father Gabriele, Professor of Italian at King's College, as well as their brothers Dante Gabriel and William Michael, both of whom were Dante translators.

Paolo de Ventura observed that 'within the critical historiography of the Rossetti family, Maria's figure tells the story of an absence' (De Ventura, 2011: 18). The first-born of Italian scholar and political refugee, Gabriele Rossetti, and his wife, Frances Polidori, her existence has been overshadowed by the artistic and literary fame of her three siblings: the Pre-Raphaelite poet and artist, Dante Gabriel; the critic and family biographer, William Michael; and the poet, Christina. Neither photographed in the iconic portrait taken by Lewis Carroll on 7 October 1863 in the garden of the house at 16 Cheyne Walk, nor acknowledged in William Michael's genealogical dedication of his *Memoir*, the memory of Maria Francesca's life is consigned to brief sketches in her sibling's diaries and in family biographies (Waller, 1932; Weinstraub, 1978; Roe, 2011). To this day, De Ventura's introduction constitutes the first and only account offering a comprehensive bio-bibliographical reconstruction.

On the contrary, 'as historical personage and women poet' her sister Christina Georgina suffers from over-presentation, being the object of continuous critical attention for the 'prosaic ordinariness' of her public life and the 'interior ... emotional drama' that nurtured her works like *Goblin Market and other Poems* (1862), *The Prince's Progress* (1866), *A Pageant* (1881) and *The Face of the Deep* (1882) (Chapman, 2000: 20). The transformation turned her into a 'female icon' and 'mythologised figure', 'a disembodied and fetishized commodity in the literary and critical marketplace' (Chapman, 2000: 3) through the continued canonisation of her works as well as the recovery of her private notes and letters, manuscripts and unpublished drafts. Chapman sees a common trait of Victorian and contemporary biographism in the tendency to present Christina's intellectual life and 'thought processes' through gendered lenses as 'literal, feminine, and non-participatory in masculine literary tradition and masculine symbolism' (3). Such bias might explain the limited attention to Christina as a reader and a student, a critic and a re-writer of Dante. Initially experienced as 'a noxious feature of adult life' (3), Dante gave way to new opportunities for her educational and professional development as she began working as assistant editor of scholars (Alexander Grosart and Charles Bagot Cayley), writing Dante-criticism for British and North American periodicals and independently pursuing higher academic education through the cycles of Barlow Lectures at University College London.

The accounts of the sisters' early years reflect this bias. As a small girl, Christina was reputed to be both 'spirited and lazy', 'reading very little and only what hit her fancy' (Packer, 1963: 7) and more instinctively drawn to the inspired composition of poetry rather than the solitary study of literature. In turn, she 'admired Maria for qualities which she thought lacking in herself' like the natural inclination for scholarly pursuits and her 'ardently acquired stores of knowledge' (7). The eldest sister was the 'real prodigy' of the family. A 'precociously clever and thinking child ... who learned easily whatever was brought before her' (W. M. Rossetti, 1906: 18), Maria Francesca was 'the quickest and most indefatigable reader', and had 'a lively and active mind, eager to find something on which to exercise itself' (Waller, 1932: 171).

Both home-schooled by their Evangelical mother, Maria Francesca complemented the prescribed reading of 'the Bible, the *Confessions of St. Augustine*, *Pilgrim's Progress*, and edifying Victorian stories for children' (Weintraub, 1978: 6) with more 'masculine' studies. Waller recounts that 'when her brothers began to learn Greek at school, thus taking a step beyond her purview, Maria insisted on learning it by herself at home' (Waller, 1932: 171). Such vigorous appetite for high knowledge met with the approval and support of the family patriarchs. While her grandfather, Gaetano Polidori, allowed her daily access to the magnetising library within which she began to read and translate Euripides's tragedies, Homer's *Iliad* and Hesiod's *Theogony*, among others, her father Gabriele rebutted Victorian ideological prejudices against higher education. According to Jan Marsh, Rossetti commented: 'I am not afraid that too much application may injure her health for when voluntary application produces so much pleasure it cannot deny any harm; rather, it becomes food for mind, which in turn does the body good' (Marsh, 1994: 29).

Navigating the circle of patriarchal influence

By 1844, the seventeen-year-old Maria Francesca was admitted under strictly Ruskinian terms to her father's circle of *dantisti*. Her linguistic and Dantean expertise, in fact, served as an aid to men: she acted as reader, amanuensis and translator to her increasingly blind father or his circle of Dante-enthusiasts, starting with Charles Lyell. Although her name does not appear in the acknowledgement, she assisted Lyell in revising the translations for *The Lyrical Poems of Dante including the poems of the Vita Nuova and Convito* which included an expanded corpus of lyrics, taken from Witte's *Dante Alighieri's Lyrische Gedichte* (1842) and Fraticelli's *Opere Minori* (1834). Such collaborative experience had a lasting impact on Maria Francesca's principles and approach to translation. Lyell's influence, in fact, emerges when comparing the introductory notes to their respective works. In the preface to the collection, Lyell explaining that the 'object' of his endeavours was

> To assist the student in ascertaining this internal mystical sense has been my object; and with this view I have studied to make the translation correspond to the Italian with scrupulous exactness, line for line, and almost word for word; the outward and literal sense being the first indispensable step towards a right understanding of the interior sense concealed under an allegory.
>
> (Lyell, 1845: vi)

Thirty years later these very principles resonated in the declaration of method outlined for her *Shadow of Dante*:

> Not without regret, I sacrifice to faithful literality the pleasure of making readers ignorant of Italian acquainted with the exquisite ternary rhyme of the Commedia, so ably preserved in the translations by Mr. Cayley, the Rev. John Dayman, and the Rev. Prebendary Ford. The like faithful literality will be found to characterize my own rendering of passages from Dante's prose works; the blemish, as it would now by many be considered, of frequent tautology being by no means avoided. The principle of translation should, I think, be one thing, when an author and a style unique and immortal are to be set in living truth before living eyes; quite another thing when minds merely need to be enabled profitably and pleasurably to assimilate thoughts generated and originally expressed, it may even be with no distinctive force or grace, in a tongue not their own.
>
> (M. F. Rossetti, 1871: 6)

For De Ventura the 'choice of literality' also set out her distinct position within a *querelle* 'on the methodology of translation initiated by her own brothers' (De Ventura, 2011: 52) in the prefaces of their works: Dante Gabriel's *Early Italian Poets* (1861) and William Michael's blank verse translation of *Hell* (1865). While the former declared that 'literality of rendering is altogether secondary' (D. G. Rossetti, 1861: viii), approaching translation as a (re)creative art that allowed space for regular interferences of pictorial and emotional touches to the original, the other described his 'strenuous endeavour' to 'follow Dante sentence for sentence, line for line, word for word – neither more or less' (W. M. Rossetti, 1865: vii) in order to render the texts at their highest degree of readability and intelligibility for the English-speaking public.

In line with her position, Maria Francesca eventually discarded Dante Gabriel's *Vita Nuova* for her own literal renditions of the *libello* based on Fraticelli's edition and adopted Henry Longfellow's integral translation of the *Commedia* in blank *terzine*, at times complemented with William's own. In a short correspondence with the American scholar, Maria Francesca offered her 'little tribute of admiration' to Longfellow's work: 'I could not have conceived it possible to combine such fidelity with such wonderful grace and beauty, when translating into a language especially different in sources and in construction of the 30th Canto of the *Paradiso*, especially astonished me on reading over my own extracts' (M. F. Rossetti, 1871). Maria recognised that Longfellow's translation was the product of the synergetic combination of aesthetic sensibility (deriving from his work as a poet) with sound scholarship, and as such, it stood as the new reference text for British and American scholarship.

Even more than that of her brothers, Maria Francesca remained wary of her father's influence. Although she recognised in Gabriele, Professor of Italian at King's College London, a model of philological attitude and scholarly erudition, Maria Francesca was determined in her rejection of his highly idiosyncratic *dantismo*. Throughout her study, in fact, she kept her distance from his allegorical fanaticism that interpreted the *Commedia* as a reflection of the fear and hopes of Gabriele's own historical and contextual reality: a position taken to extremes in his essay on *Sullo Spirito Antipapale* (1832) and in the esoteric readings of the figure of Beatrice in his *Ragionamenti critici* (1842). Limiting his influence to general analytical practices, she forcefully preserved her critical independence, with only one exception: the interpretation of the dark wood and the three beasts as a political allegory, 'symbolical of the moral and political condition of Italy just before Dante's election to the Priorato, a state of anarchy rapidly lapsing, in his apprehension, into savagery' (M. F. Rossetti, 1871: 40).

Intimate collaboration: Christina's derivative *dantismo*

The Rossetti household represented a conducive environment for Christina's *dantismo*, through yet another male mediator: Charles

Bagot Cayley. In 1847, Cayley was one of the few pupils whom Gabriele Rossetti, by that time in failing health, still received at Charlotte Street. Here, Cayley 'sought instruction in Italian and aid in the study of Dante' (Cunningham, 1965: 40) and met Christina, who became increasingly interested in his project for a *terza rima* translation of the *Commedia* that was in four volumes between 1851 and 1855. According to William Michael's *Memoir*, the frequentation intensified towards the end of 1862 when the two became romantically involved to the point that Cayley proposed marriage in 1866, only to be rejected by Christina. From that point onwards, the relationship developed into friendship culminating with her nomination as his literary executor.

Although Christina had already been introduced to the family reading of Dante in her early adolescence, her mother's gift of a copy of Cayley's work for her birthday on 5 December 1866 sparked a more fervorous interest in the *Commedia*. The books, in fact, became treasured objects that she began to fill with extensive marginalia, pressed leaves and even a photograph of the translator himself. Denman and Smith advanced a romanticised interpretation of the notes as traces of affective responses; I see the stratified and codified repertoire of non-verbal reading signs, discursive annotations and interlinear glosses as material testimony of her developing Dantean scholarship.

These traces shed light on the personal mechanisms through which Christina established her own epistemological relationship with the text: either questioning or perfecting Cayley's translational choices. Similarly to Shelley's, Keats's and Gladstone's annotated copies, Christina's marginalia record the sedimentation of her textual knowledge and the formation of a critical spirit that she vehiculates through a series of corrective interventions, cross-textual references in the notes and alternative renderings of individual words and whole verses throughout the three *cantiche*. The range of signs inscribed 'in a firm, dark pencil' include 'the correction of punctuation, accents, spelling, proper names, and line numbers', which signal not only 'inconsistencies between the text of the volumes and the same text when cited in the Notes' but also advance suggestions for 'the improvement of diction, the correction of rhymes, the addition of lines' (Denman and Smith, 1994: 322). Possibly made in view of the publication of a second, corrected edition of Cayley's translation, these were more markedly intrusive alterations of the rhymes (altering words or even a single letter) done to redress any deviations from ternary rhyme pattern.

The intensive and intimate reading of Cayley's *Commedia* prompted Christina to write her first piece of Dantean criticism, published in the *Churchman's Shilling Magazine and Family Treasury* (1867). Titled 'Dante: An English Classic', the article was one of the five pieces that she had contributed to this High Church magazine between April and November 1867. These other interventions were religious and moralistic stories such as 'The Waves of this Troublesome World: A Tale of Hastings Ten Years Ago' (April and May 1867), 'Some Pros and Cons about Pews' (July 1867) and 'A Safe Investment' (November 1867). With the exception of the Dante article, these were all reissued in *Commonplace and Other Short Stories* (1870).

Jan Marsh suggests that what prompted Christina's critical intervention into the realm of public criticism was the anonymous review in *Blackwood's Magazine* published in June 1867 and later ascribed to the pen of Elizabeth J. Hasell, one of its regular contributors. Hasell's twenty-pages-long, double-columned article examined six *terza rima* translations of the *Commedia* published throughout little more than a decade: Cayley (1851–55), Brooksbank's *Hell* (1854), Thomas' *The Trilogy* (1859–62), Mrs Ramsay's *Commedia* (1862–63), Ford's *Inferno* (1865) and Dayman's *Divine Comedy* (1865). The piece denotes the expanding function that periodicals had as carriers of foreign texts and the importance they assigned to the review as a genre regarded as much a means of information management as a site for the theoretical formulation and practical application of discourses on modes purposes and strategies of translation. *Blackwood's Magazine*, in particular, encouraged the 'comparative evaluation of translations – the setting of several [renderings] of the same text side by side' as a 'novel tool' (Drury, 2015: 43) for educating the readers to a fuller, more insightful appreciation of foreign poetry.

In this case of 'Dante in English Terza Rima', the reviewer is assertively didactic as she stresses the importance of considering 'the intimate relation between sense and sound, between the meaning which animates the metrical structure which embodies and expresses it' (Hasell, 1867: 738). If the metre is the 'visible form', 'the evidence of design' and 'the mold in which' Dante 'cast' (738) his *Commedia*, the translator's primary responsibility should be that of linguistic preservation. On this account, the reviewer questions the primacy of Henry F. Cary as 'translator of Dante' and slams him as too simplistic in his choice of blank verse while applauding, in turn, the more recent efforts of those who sought to safeguard the source text in its entirety. Cayley and Dayman are joined together as 'incomparably the best terza rima translators of the "*Divina Commedia*"', both 'evidently ripe scholars' able to convey 'to the English reader Dante's thoughts in their majestic simplicity' (742) without a trace of any sort of creative antagonism. Although superior to most 'in intelligent appreciation and in vigorous expression of the meaning of the original' (754), the reviewer critiques Cayley's choices of diction and rhyme. While one combines 'archaic' and 'uncouth words', 'words of Latin origin, merely on account of their external resemblance' to the source, 'ordinary colloquialisms, and of technical words which poetry does not love' (748). The other is oftentimes problematic not only because 'he employs the same rhyme three or four times over one canto', but also because these are oftentimes the product of 'his daring experiments', 'more frequently grotesque than imperfect' (743).

From the pages of the *Churchman Shilling*, Christina Rossetti penned (and signed) a stern and punctual rebuttal of the shortcomings panned by the reviewer and advanced noteworthy considerations on the nature and cultural function of literary translation, conceived as an act of metaphorical reanimation – an act through which Dante, 'the venerable father of modern poetry', became 'a fellow-citizen' of English readers, fostering his literary canonisation and cultural nationalisation into the titular 'English Classic' (C. G. Rossetti, 1867: 200). Here, Christina's understanding of translation at once aligns with and even exceeds Dante Gabriel's, conceiving it as a means of appropriation and canonisation of Dante's poetry: 'as a strategy for the accrual of cultural wealth, a commodifying task through which a fresh nation' could be endowed 'with one more possession of beauty' (Drury, 2015: 45). At the same time, however, her theorisation responds to what Drury describes as 'incorporative impulse' (45) for it reasserts the power of English poetry and language, 'rich enough to lend itself to the sustained sonorous music of this metre' (C. G. Rossetti, 1867: 200).

Without ever mentioning the review, Christina's confutation tackles all the issues raised, beginning with the subtle defence of the translator's choice of diction by stating that 'to reproduce Dante in all fullness and subtlety of beauty would demand Dante's self'; the translator's 'occasional added grace may be condoned' (C. G. Rossetti, 1867: 200). She identifies the distinctive and long-lasting significance of Cayley's work not in that 'admirable translation itself', but in the 'volume of copious notes, at once learned, interesting and most elegant' contained in the fourth volume, which 'remain of high value to the student, let him adopt whatever version of the "Commedia" he will' (201–2). The notes are vehemently praised as a universal key to the 'keyless puzzle' of 'allegorical significations' classical and historical references that enabled English readers to achieve 'an adequate idea of the plan and working out of the "Divina Commedia" as a whole' (201–2). Despite valuing the critical paratext more than the translation, Christina ends her counter-review with a tableau of four juxtaposed passages of Cayley's English rendering to display his merits 'as a master of vigour and beauty, of pathos and philosophy' (202). Marking a reversion into the traditional Victorian modes of reviewing, I consider the showcasing of poetic rather than critical touchstones to be symptomatic of how, in the early days of her independent study of Dante, Rossetti was hesitant to fulfil 'the tradition of her race' (Rossetti, 1884: 566). Despite this, her rebuttal of the *Blackwood's* review 'was a small' but 'inestimable gift' (Marsh, 1994: 371) made to the afterlife of Cayley's *Commedia*, and a first expression of her scholarly proclivities.

Dante lectrix: Maria Francesca's *A Shadow of Dante* and the rise of scholarship

For Maria Francesca, the years between 1868 and 1871 was a period of silent preparation. Considering the inferences in William Michael's diary entries, it is possible that her decision of putting together a handbook to Dante and the *Commedia* derived from her experience as an in-house governess, reading, translating and teaching Dante to her young pupils. The book, however, drifted from the stereotypically feminine realm of pedagogical writing and children's literature and was aimed at the adult Anglophone readership that was spreading on both sides of the Atlantic.

On 1 December, Maria Francesca had the first draft of 'her book giving an exposition of Dante's Commedia', entrusting William Michael with the first task of reading and revisioning the manuscript before presenting it to the publishers. On 4 January, he 'began reading through, and making a few notes on' it, concluding that the book 'amply good enough to be published' and offering 'some chance of commanding a sale. It would certainly be a very suitable book for people to read and incentive and introduction of Dante in Italian' (W. M. Rossetti, 1977: 39). In February, the book was presented to William and Norgate (14 February) and Bell and Daldy (21 February), both of whom rejected it, and then accepted on 18 March by Rivington & Co.

While the title was an explicit tribute to that 'shadow of Dante' that her father Gabriele had evoked in one of his most *dantesque* poems (reinforced by the explicit dedication), Maria Francesca vehiculated her own originality through the smaller, italicised subtitle. This presented the volume as an 'Essay towards Studying Dante's life (the Poet), historical and sociocultural context (his World) and the Comedy (his Pilgrimage)'. More than a marginal addendum, the subtitle asserted a precise authorial intention: that of 'the essay as a form of her own', legitimately used by a female critic in defiance of the Victorian conservative patriarchal provisions that precluded it because it 'exuded experience, wisdom and contemplation, none of which fell within the province of women's expected behaviour' (Joeres and Mittman, 1993: 13). At once analytic and reflective, didactic but discursive, the *Essay* vehiculated the full range of her specialist knowledge adjusted to appeal to and to 'win the gaze of some who never looked upon the substance, never tasted the entrancement of this Poet's music, never entered into the depths of this Philosopher's cogitations' (M. F. Rossetti, 1871: 4).

Rossetti explained the purposeful prioritisation of the intellectual needs of first-time readers in a letter to Henry W. Longfellow, one of the foremost *dantisti* of her age, founding father of the Dante Society of America and author of an epoch-making translation of the *Commedia*. Dated 11 May 1871 and still unpublished, the letter is also one of the few surviving manuscript testimonies of Maria Francesca where she admitted that:

> My object is not to teach more to those who know much – an object for which I have no ability – but to teach something to those who know nothing. [...] It has long been a matter of surprise and regret to me that a book so truly elevating and ennobling as the Commedia should be confined in its use to decidedly literary people, while the poorest modern treatises on the mysteries of this life and the next find readers everywhere. And I hope both to have facilitated the studies of any who may use my little work as a study prefatory to that of the Commedia itself and also to have given such a summary and such extracts as may be durable for those who stop short in these, at least to profit as Christians by so transcendent an exposition of the free-will man and of life to come.
>
> (M. F. Rossetti, 1871)

Countering the slightly remissive tone of the letter, the introduction to *A Shadow of Dante* showcased the full breadth of Maria Francesca's scholarly voice. With rhetorical dexterity and a hint of irony, Rossetti manipulated the commonplace celebration of the universal grandeur of Dante's poetry to expose an inconvenient truth about 'the general ignorance of Dante in England', and the hypocritically elusive behaviour that generally derived from it.

> Like the Pyramids, again, he is known to all by name and by pictorial representation; must we not add, like them unknown to most by actual sight and presence. [...] Even of his fellow-linguists how many have read his great poem through? One of themselves has said it – few have gone beyond the Inferno; nay, most have stopped short at two passages of the Inferno – Francesca da Rimini and il Conte Ugolino. And of his fellow-cosmopolitans how many have read even so much? If in cultivated society we start him as a topic of conversation, how far is our interlocutor likely to sympathize with our vivid interest? How many young people could we name as having read Dante as a part of their education?
>
> (M. F. Rossetti, 1871: 2)

The volume opened with a chain of pressing questions that frames a sharp critique of the long-standing exploitation of Dante as a cultural commodity used as a topic of conversation as well as an instrument of social elitism within cultivated society. Similarly, the distinction between actual knowledge and knowledge by representation, the description of the approach of 'fellow-linguists' and 'fellow-cosmopolitans' all conveyed an oblique contestation of the sentimental and imaginative exuberances of nineteenth-century medievalism with its predilection and over-dramatisation of the tragic tales and gothic imagery of *Inferno*. The closing question ultimately shed light on productive practices of reading Dante as a source of literary and cultural, moral and spiritual education.

The study presented an innovative structure, with the critical discourse articulated over eleven chapters, with the first two ('Dante's Universe' and 'Dante's Life Experience') centring on a succinct yet substantial exposition of the historical and autobiographical context as well as the philosophical and literary imagery that informed the poem. The remaining chapters were entirely dedicated to the exposition of the *Commedia* 'in greater detail', following 'the course of his stupendous pilgrimage' and expounding 'the physical and moral theories on which his Three Worlds are constructed' (M. F. Rossetti, 1871: 5).

The division of the *cantica*-by-*cantica* analysis over eight chapters instead of the usual three served a two-fold purpose. For the reader, it facilitated the comprehension and elaboration of the information by relying on a slower, more calibrated learning pace. For the interpreter, it granted space for a multi-layered (thematic, linguistic and allegorical) analysis, even bringing forth specific interpretative interest for the iconic, spatial and spiritual topography of Dante's pilgrimage in the *Commedia*. Furthermore, the adoption of 'an eminently narrative approach to criticism' engendered 'a two-sided tale' between Dante's poetry employed for major passages and Rossetti's prose summary of minor episodes (De Ventura, 2011: 65).

As per Rossetti's design, the reader was thus engaged in a more direct encounter with the *Commedia* and introduced to Dante's minor works through a series of contextual and intertextual references embedded within the analysis of the poem. Throughout, the text (original or mediated) was accompanied by simple and didactic footnotes openly preferred to 'the glosses of commentators [...] bound up with the text' and often taking 'for granted in the reader a certain amount of preliminary knowledge and interest' (De Ventura, 2011: 4). Finally, the concise yet systematic paratext served as space for the didactic elucidation of the difficulties derived from the intertextual nature of the *Commedia*. The reference to a wide range of secondary sources ultimately demonstrates the foundational substrate of scholarly preparation and professionalism on which her didactic reading of Dante had been methodically built. Arguably, one of the decisive factors for the critical and commercial success of *A Shadow of Dante* was the fact that Rossetti derived her popular *dantismo* by shaping higher scholarship into narrative knowledge for the emerging English middle-class readers of Dante. The book set out a pioneering example of Dantean hermeneutics and traced a new path towards authorship status and scholarly recognition for the generation of Anglo-American women *dantiste* that would follow between the late 1870s and the 1920s. Carefully constructed, the paratext was a crucial hermeneutical instrument through which Rossetti could demonstrate the nature and the extent of the foundational substrate of scholarly knowledge upon which her critical discourse rested: a knowledge cultivated and conquered independently, away from the reach of the shadow of the Rossetti family *dantismo*.

Soon after its publication in 1871, *A Shadow of Dante* became a best-seller and marked its record tenth edition in 1913. In December 1871, William Michael reported that the publisher had informed 'Maria that the first edition of her *A Shadow of Dante* is now exhausted exactly six-months after the date of publication of the first edition: 500 copies sold in England, and 500 in America' (W. M. Rossetti, 1977: 179). Given this 'not insignificant success' (Rossetti: 179), the book was then reprinted in the same format by Rivington's in 1872 (2nd ed.), 1881 (3rd ed.), 1884 (4th ed.) and 1889 (5th ed.). Interestingly, however, the weight of the Rossettis' visual allegorism was eventually lifted from Maria Francesca's work on three different occasions. The first two were related to the American editions of *A Shadow of Dante*, issued by two prominent, Boston-based publishers. These were Roberts Brothers, the first to acquire copyright in 1872 (1st ed.) who then reissued it in 1886 (2nd ed.) and 1889 (3rd ed.), and subsequently Little and Brown, who specialised in imported titles and foreign nonfiction. The latter ultimately ensured the circulation and dissemination of Rossetti's handbook in the early decades of the twentieth century, in 1900 (1st ed.), 1904 (2nd ed.) and 1910 (3rd ed.).

The reception of the book is recorded from multiple perspectives – the domestic and the private, national and transnational – thanks to a broad-encompassing corpus of documentary sources produced by family members and acquaintances, biographers and reviewers. Within the Rossetti household, *A Shadow of Dante* was received as a 'piece of writing' that stemmed from Maria Francesca's 'enthusiasm' for Dante, while the family biographer R. D. Waller described it as 'the fruit of a lifetime's devotion' (Waller, 1932: 176). Undermining the professional seriousness with which the author regarded her work, Waller's comment also hinted at that burning religious spirit to which she eventually sacrificed, with much disapproval of her siblings, her scholarly ambitions. Within the family circle, it was Christina who recognised in it the clear signs of a 'knowledge far wider and deeper that could be compressed into its pages, eloquent and elegant' in its critical exposition and didactic qualities (C. G. Rossetti, 1884: 566). 'The fruit of a fine mind and a noble soul', she outspokenly vindicated the quality of Maria Francesca's study as a 'work of real weight', a 'really valuable and intellectual work', 'a masterpiece' that had to be 'brought within reach of both English and Italian readers' (566).

The harshest detractor was John Ruskin, the Victorian critic and close acquaintance of the Rossetti brothers. In a letter to his niece, Constance Hillard, written on 3 October 1877, he wrote an overtly caustic comment on Rossetti's book that was enjoying the commercial success of its second edition, and fast approaching its third:

> I write in haste to prevent you buying the 'Shadow of Dante' for me – It is (unless I mistake) a book by Rossetti's second sister – not Christina & I am sorry to tell you – very wrong and very [sic] – In fact, I can't think how you liked it – The poor girl knows (as she ought) nothing about much that Dante means & and [sic] has yoked her own evangelical nonsense into him. I mean, she knows nothing of revenge, lust, treachery & lots of things – & in that, is as she ought to be. But she is very conceited to think a girl can interpret Dante in such respects.
>
> (Ruskin, 1877)

Ruskin's spiteful words can be taken as one of the most representative – unmediated, unpolished and un-hypocritical – expressions of the critic's 'ideology of pure womanhood' and of the broader Victorian gendered prejudice against women's entering the male-dominated arena of high knowledge and culture. Ruskin's bitter comments questioned Maria Francesca's authorial authority and integrity as a socio-culturally acceptable interpreter of Dante's poetry: a 'poor girl' that claimed a place within the elitist circle of British *dantisti*. Claiming the right to interpret Dante despite having no direct and concrete experience of the 'outer world' represented in his poetry and characterised by 'revenge, lust, treachery & lots of things', she was essentially distracted from fulfilling women's 'proper cultural function' as 'helpmates and moral guardians' (Lloyd, 1995: 335) of their husbands and fathers.

In the year following its publication, *A Shadow of Dante* was reviewed on prominent British and American literary periodicals, penned by three of the most authoritative *dantisti* of their time. All favourable, the reviews differed in the way they made the patriarchal and familial heritage a centre of attention. The article published in the *Athenaeum* on 4 November 1871 was the one that stressed more insistently the author's eminent lineage and the derivative quality of her work. Later identified as Henry Clark Barlow, the reviewer opened with a glowing commendation of 'Rossetti's name as a household word of the *Divina Commedia*' following the publication of Gabriele's *Commento Analitico*, which had single-handedly

> formed an epoch in the history of Dante literature, and opened up to devout followers of the divine poet a new path for the exercise of their intelligence in the investigation of his recondite meaning [...]. is, and ever will be, held in honour by all who desire to fathom the deep things of Dante and to make his thoughts their own.
> (Barlow, 1871: 586)

'Mrs Rossetti's work', Barlow suggested, was the natural and inevitable product of a certain 'hereditary admiration', shaped in form and content under the influence of her father's scholarship (586). Despite its derivativeness, however, the reviewer recognises the innovative qualities of her interpretative approach to and didactic treatment of her subject as well as her original 'suggestions'. Barlow directed his enthusiastic praise towards Rossetti's 'intimate acquaintance with the whole of Dante's works' and the fact that

> in her explanations and description, [she] brings her knowledge in bear of the text in a most conscientious and instructive manner, and with an earnestness and force of words which, though concise, are

full of meaning and leave nothing more to the desires of those who weigh them well.

(586–7)

In November 1871, the *Saturday Review* praised the book for its highly didactic functionality, 'concise and lucid exposition' of Dante's life, his 'conception of the universe' (*Saturday Review*, 1871: 690) and the key narrative nodes of his poem. 'Miss Rossetti' stood out as a 'faithful guide and a lucid interpreter' of the *Commedia* for the way it brought

> into prominent relief its most important features and enable the student, by gaining acquaintance with the dominant conceptions which underlie the great poem and bind together its several parts, to understand it as a whole. [...] The result [being a] book, which is not only delightful in itself to read, but is admirably adapted as an encouragement to those students who wish to obtain a preliminary survey of the land before they attempt to follow Dante through his long and arduous pilgrimage.
>
> (690)

The review published in the *Academy* in December 1871 and signed by Henry Fanshawe Tozer, founding member of the Oxford Dante Society and author of an *English Commentary to Dante's Divine Comedy* (1901), forgoes the patriarchal shadow to expound the greater didactic nature of Rossetti's 'elegant volume' (Tozer, 1871: 551). The novelty of the work was not as much in the comprehensive and thoroughly illustrative content, but in its analytical modes of reading: 'a most interesting narrative' that provided an uncommonly unitary outlook over the *Commedia*, which contrasted a fragmentary knowledge and understanding of it – having 'become acquainted ... by means of selected passages' or 'deterred from proceeding proceed further by the intricacies of the poem' (552).

The most enthusiastic piece of commentary came from the other side of the Atlantic, and the pages of the *North American Review* in January 1872. There, James Russell Lowell, pioneer of American *dantismo*, proclaimed the book as 'by far the best comment that has appeared in English, and the best that has been done in England' (Russell Lowell, 1872: 147) – a work authored by 'a commentator who passes dry shod over the *turbide orde* of inappreciative criticism and opens for us his City of Doom with the divining-rod of reverential study' (147). Commending the cleverness of her choice 'of interpreting Dante out of himself, a method in which Germany reigned undisputed', Lowell exalted the scholarly quality of the 'comment' equally useful to Italian or English readers by providing to the former 'many suggestive hints' and to the others 'a travelling map in which the principal points and their connections are clearly set down' (148). With 'the refined enthusiasm of a cultivated woman and the penetration of sympathy', Rossetti's discourse possessed 'feminine softness with no lack of vigor or precision' as it expounded 'with surprising grace through the metaphysical and other intricacies of her subject' (148).

Despite its slightly gendered tones, Lowell's criticism was one of the rarest pieces of full appreciation of a woman's contribution to Dante studies of its time: one that did not confine the author to an 'ancillary status' deeming her 'marginal and effete' nor 'weigh down' the critical and commercial success (Russell Lowell, 1872: 148). While in Britain she was under the shadow of her family *dantismo*, Maria Francesca's work was well received among the members of the 'Dante Circle' – the modern Dante Society of America. From William Michael's account we know that on 7 May 1872 Longfellow himself had sent her 'a handsome letter regarding her A Shadow of Dante' (W. M. Rossetti, 1906: 196). Furthermore, we know that Lowell adopted it as one of the secondary sources for his Dante courses in Boston, and later her book was included in the Dante syllabus at Vassar College.

More concisely and less emphatically than Lowell, the anonymous reviewer of *The Nation* (later identified as J. R. Dennett) writing on 11 July 1872 stressed the timely significance of her contribution at a moment when the growing English-speaking public in both Britain and American is ever more in need of interpreters and mediators of 'Dante's intellectual medievalism', his 'lofty religious idealism and the narrow political intensity' (Dennett, 1872: 28) underlying his oeuvre. The attention to the paratext of notes, 'pictures and diagrams' as a literary and visual aid to comprehension, enhancing the already functional use of 'plain language' combined now with 'the poet's own words, now in a prose summary of her own, the course of his journey' (28). Along with this, the review pays particular attention to the way in which the volume meets the interests and needs of 'several classes of readers' (28): a public that encompasses not only the envisioned general audience but brings together a more stratified public, all of whom

> will welcome the book as a great assistance and a great means of pleasure [...] we believe they will nowhere else find in one volume so much help towards an understanding of the details of the poem, and at the same time towards getting into a mood of mind somewhere in the neighbourhood of sympathy with the poet's religious feeling and thought.
>
> (Dennett, 1872: 28–9)

By the time *A Shadow of Dante* was published, however, periodical reviews were no longer the only instrument for pushing the circulation and sales of a book nor for constructing the public reputation of its author in Britain. An even greater role was played, in fact, by the revived circulating lending libraries: commercial organisations that upon the payment of a weekly, monthly or annual subscription fee enabled access to impressive catalogues of fiction and non-fiction books to 'as wide a range of borrowers as possible' (Eliot, 2006: 133). Founded in London in 1842 by Charles Mudie, by the 1870s Mudie's Select Library had become 'the most important distributor of books for rent established in the Victorian period' ('Mudie's Circulating Library', 2011).

In January 1872, an advert placed in the *Athenaeum* included Maria Francesca Rossetti's *A Shadow of Dante* among 'some of the Principal New Books in Circulation at Mudie's Select Library', and together with 'several other works of acknowledged merit and general interest' (*Athenaeum*, 1872: 37). This was a crucial attainment that likely engendered a strain of productive effects on the commercial circulation, the popular reception, and the public recognition of the literary and scholarly authority of *A Shadow of Dante*. The appearance of Rossetti's title in print, positioned at the top of the third column of the list, meant, in fact, that the work on Dante 'conformed to the demands of Mudie's and its audience' and successfully won over his 'complex rhetoric of selection' (Eliot, 2006: 137). Consequently, the book, the author and her literary reputation deserved to benefit from both the economic and cultural power that Mudie's library exerted on the economics of the Victorian publishing market. As such, *A Shadow of Dante* was included in the bestseller list, presented and promoted among the library subscribers as a principal, high-class exemplar of nonfiction: a declaration of value that sanctioned the public reputation of Maria Francesca Rossetti as an authoritative Victorian author.

Furthermore, inclusion in Mudie's catalogue favoured the popularisation of *A Shadow of Dante* through direct sales, previously increased by the stock acquisition of a sizeable number of copies for circulation, but via the advantageous path of book-lending, thanks to which it expanded the reach of its national circulation and dissemination. Significantly, the listing of a Dante-related book in Mudie's makes us reflect on the role circulating and subscription libraries had in the dissemination of commercial *dantismo* at the turn of the century, as well as in identifying the place that commercial Dante studies came to occupy within the Victorian literary marketplace.

Christina Rossetti: Maria Francesca's heritage and the last contribution

After her sister's passing in 1876, Christina became her literary executor. She pursued both large and small-scale channels of distribution to ensure the re-circulation of *A Shadow of Dante* on both sides of the Atlantic, promoting and giving the book to writers, artists and intellectuals gravitating around the Rossetti family and the Pre-Raphaelite Brotherhood. Documentary evidence of this activity is held within her private correspondence exchanged with her brothers and niece as well as with Rivingtons, Roberts Brothers and Longmans, respectively the British and American publishers of Maria Francesca's masterpiece. To her correspondents, Christina presented *A Shadow of Dante* as 'really valuable and intellectual work', 'a book of real weight' bearing 'no insignificant touch of greatness' (C. G. Rossetti, 1997–2004). Two years after her death, Christina was discussing with Dante Gabriel the (remote) possibility of having the work translated in Italian by their cousin Teodorico. Similarly, in January 1890 she confessed to William Michael that 'having heard more about the "Beatrice Exhibition" in Florence, to commence in April', she thought of proffering *A Shadow of Dante*. Both plans sought to bring her sister's study to the Italian public, and to exploit the Exhibition, entirely dedicated to women's labours (*lavori femminili*) and celebrated on the anniversary of Beatrice's death, to establish her reputation as the foremost female interpreter of the Florentine poet.

Initially, Christina acted on behalf of her mother Frances, for whom she handled all small business communication, corresponding with Rivington's (3 November 1880) accepting 'with great pleasure' their 'proposal to issue, on the original terms, another 250 copies of "Shadow of Dante"' (C. G. Rossetti in The University of Virginia Press, 2006). Similarly, in February 1890, she corresponded with Thomas Niles regarding the improved royalties of the Roberts' edition of *A Shadow of Dante*, reaching £1. 1s. 7d., while also making known to him that '*here*', in Britain, the book was 'in its 5th edition. And to my thinking well deserves to be' (C. G. Rossetti in The University of Virginia Press, 2006). Finally, in March 1894 she was contacted by Longmans, Maria's other American publisher, regarding the issue of a cheaper '3/6 edition' to be included in their *Silver Library* series in light of what they reported to be 'steady request' for the book, even in its original, more expensive format. In this regard, she noted: 'I fully understand that the sale of the original is likely to suffer, but this is I think of little consequence set against the wider diffusion of a work which I earnestly trust is calculated to do good' (C. G. Rossetti in The University of Virginia Press, 2006). The new edition appeared in 1895 with a run of 1,000 copies.

Notably, the American editions also marked the definitive break from the family *dantismo*. Lifting the weight of Rossetti's visual allegorism, both Roberts Brothers (1872, 1886, 1889) and Little and Brown opted for a more neutral book design: a floral, neo-liberty motif on blue cloth for the Roberts, and brown-green cloth for the Little and Brown. Despite the gendered associations between women and flowers, the new designs freed the book from the lumbering shadow of her brother, Dante Gabriel, who had been commissioned by the first British publisher, Rivington, to 'design the binding, one with some of his wonted emblematic circles or the like' (W. M. Rossetti, 1906: 57). Such non-negotiable imposition sought to strengthen the popular appeal of the book as a recognisable Pre-Raphaelite artefact despite the intrinsic literary, scholarly and commercial value of Maria Francesca's independent contribution to Dante studies. The result was a dark red cloth binding with gilded decorations: the front cover presented an encircled lily of Florence in the centre, and on the opposite corners were bat wings and flames evoking *Inferno*, and angels' wings and a five-point star symbolising *Paradiso*. The text was complemented by four illustrated plates: a one-page portrait of Dante by D. G. Rossetti, and three foldable ink illustrations of Hell, Purgatory and Paradise.

Perhaps seeking to reinforce her self-taught knowledge of Dante largely grounded on the study of Cayley's notes and Maria's *Essay*, in 1879–80, at 48 years of age, Christina enrolled in the course of Barlow Lectures on the *Divina Commedia* taught by Charles Tomlinson, scheduled 'on Thursdays and Tuesdays at 3' at University College, London. Endowed by Henry Clark Barlow and inaugurated in November 1876, the course was the first public annual course on Dante to have been established within a British University, consisting of at least twelve lessons per year, free to both sexes and amply advertised in the *Times* and the *Athenaeum*. The *Family Letters* show that after that period Christina had become more conversant with more academic studies, such as Edward Moore's *Dante and His Early Biographers*.

Christina vehiculated the secured knowledge through two distinct projects: a work of poetry and a piece of periodical criticism. The first was a sonnet sequence titled *Monna Innominata*: a work of 'daunting length' which consisted of '14 sonnets, each one preceded by a double epigraph from Dante and Petrarch' and forming altogether 'a contemplative love letter possibly to a real person, but more importantly to Rossetti's poetic heritage, to God, and to the idea of love itself' (Roe, 2007: 59). The Dantean 'attributed yet untranslated quotations' are taken mainly from *Purgatorio* (nine), then *Paradiso* (four) and only rarely *Inferno* (one) while the 'secondary position' of those from the *Canzoniere* is 'structural illustration of his inferiority' (Roe, 2007: 70). In her study, Dinah Roe demonstrated how Rossetti's epigraphic use of the Dantean text was similar to Eliot's as the product of a close, intensive readerly practice through which the poet was able to reconfigure the Dantean discourse to her own creative ends.

Despite the deepening of her learning, Christina always remained sceptical about her own *dantismo*, regretting to have been 'all too late … sucked into the Dantean vortex' (C. G. Rossetti, 1908: 188) and feeling unable to match the 'permanent and worthy work' diligently produced by 'others of her own name' (C. G. Rossetti, 1884: 566–7). Commissioned by the editor of *Century Magazine*, Edmund Gosse, her second Dante article appeared in 1884. Entitled 'Dante: The Poet Explained out of the Poem', the piece opened on a celebratory overview of the Rossettis' achievements in the field of Dante studies within which Christina placed her contribution in a position of declared self-imposed *denouement*. The essential point of friction, she argued, was to be found in the almost diametrically opposite hermeneutic preconditions underlying their Dantean knowledge:

> I, who cannot lay claim to their learning, must approach my subject under cover of 'Mi valga ... il grande amore' ('May my great love avail me'), leaving to them the more confident plea, 'Mi valga il lungo studio' ('May my long study avail me').
>
> (566–7)

Voicing her own inner perceptions, this self-derogatory admission was somewhat paradoxical since Christina was, along with her father, the only one to have nurtured her amateur *dantofilia* not just within the private, self-regulated space of domestic learning but within the public dimension of institutionalised Dante teaching represented by Tomlinson's Barlow lectures. Despite the rhetorical denouement, however, the article is a significant undertaking in Dante criticism, critically and methodologically more complex than her first intervention. Spreading over eight pages in double columns, it consisted of a broad-reaching biographical account of Dante's life spanning his ancestry, education, encounter with Beatrice, marriage to Gemma Donati, political career and exile. Targeting the article to a non-specialist but learned readership, Christina reconfigured the model of narrative exegesis set out by Maria Francesca's in her *A Shadow of Dante* to construct a lively and engaging discussion in which the historical datum was directly inferred from selected passages from Dante's macro-text: from the *Comedy* (once again quoted in Cayley's translation over Longfellow's) to the *De Monarchia* and the *Vita Nuova*, complemented with secondary sources such as Boccaccio's *Trattatello* and Maria Francesca's *Essay*.

Notably, the decision to illustrate 'the poet out of the poem' enables Christina to put to the test her familiarity with Dante's entire oeuvre, and her ability to didacticise such content and make it fully accessible for a socially varied readership. While Jan Marsh judged Christina's treatment of the 'vexed question of Dante's love for Beatrice' as an 'unscholarly feminine response to the supposed plot of Dante's emotional life' she interpreted it in terms of 'present-day romantic love' (Marsh, 1994: 509). I find that the article bears extensive evidence of Christina's awareness of the greater, scholarly complexity of the issue and of the different trends in past and present exegetic traditions: 'esoteric interpretations of (unnamed) critics who saw in Beatrice "an impersonation rather than a woman"' (Marsh, 1994: 509) and in the *Divine Comedy* a concealed political meaning. Throughout, however, Christina remained faithful to her choice of not entering the dimension of scholarly hermeneutics on the grounds that 'so obscure a field of investigation is not for me or for my readers at least not for them through any help of mine' (C. G. Rossetti, 1884: 572). As Roe aptly pointed out, here Christina demonstrated herself to be interested, 'like her brother Dante Gabriel', in exploring

> the relationship of an artist to his muse, but this interest is troubled by two potential problems which can appear at the crossroads of the literary and the religious: misrepresentation and idolatry. Rossetti is attracted to the way Romantic imagination operates in the story of Dante and Beatrice but unsettled by Victorian secularization of the narrative.
> (Roe, 2007: 63)

Despite remaining a poet at heart, Rossetti's awareness of what is at issue in Dante studies still shines through her essays. While Rossetti's poetic instinct is to endorse the power of Dante's imagination, as a religious thinker reacting to perceptions of Dante in her day, she needs somehow to sanctify that imaginative impulse:

> For, taught by bitter experience in what scales to weigh this world and the things of this world, [Dante] bequeathed to future generations the undying voice of his wisdom, – a wisdom distilled in eloquence, modulated to music, sublimed by imagination, or rather subliming that imagination which is its congruous vehicle and companion
> (C. G. Rossetti, 1884: 573)

More than the interpretative path of her own, she encouraged those interested in 'fully entering into the mind of Dante' (C. G. Rossetti, 1884: 572) to engage with his oeuvre in its entirety and follow a *miglior guida*: her sister, Maria Francesca. The line of

Inferno XX – '*Se Dio ti lasci, lettor, prend frutto di tua lezion*' – used to bid her farewell to her readers in the words of Dante signals this transfer of knowledge under the same verse that Maria Francesca had chosen for the title page of her *A Shadow of Dante*. The verse was placed right under her name and, as per Christina's intention, had to remain the testament to the outer and democratic aims of her scholarly enterprise as one of the first and the greatest Victorian women *dantiste* in history.

4

'Everyman's Dante': Philip H. Wicksteed and Victorian mass readerships

The previous chapters have unpacked the phenomenology of Victorian *dantismo* from the privileged perspective of central figures in British literary, cultural and political history, such as William Gladstone and Matthew Arnold and Christina Rossetti. For Maria Francesca Rossetti and Philip Henry Wicksteed, the process of canonisation was halted by gendered and social factors. While the former was an enforced condition, Wicksteed deliberately pursued his *dantismo* down 'the unpretending paths of the Extension Lecturer and the Unitarian minister', who addressed a 'wholly different' (Herford, 1931: xxix) public of Sunday worshippers and evening students from the middle and lower classes.

The historical memory of Wicksteed's achievements survives in a full-length biography written by Charles H. Herford, and two entries in the *Oxford Dictionary of National Biography* and the *Encyclopedia Britannica*. Succinct and partial, the latter accounts fail to pursue the 'seemingly unrelated' paths that Wicksteed traced throughout his career as Unitarian minister and lecturer, translator and scholar (Herford, 1931: xxix). Born in Leeds in 1844, Wicksteed was educated at University College, London (1861–64; 1867, Gold Medal in Classics), and Manchester New College, Oxford (1864–67). In 1868, he married Emily Rebecca Solly and was appointed minister at Taunton (1868), then Dukinfield east of Manchester (1869–74), and finally at the Little Portland Street Chapel, London (1874–1900). Having joined the London Society for the Extension of University Teaching in 1887, in 1901 Wicksteed resigned from his ministry and settled with his family in Childrey (near Wantage) with the firm intention 'to concentrate on his lecturing, study, and writing' (Steedman, 2004). By 1918 he had given 'nearly three hundred extension courses' on an assorted range of subjects: from Aristotle, Dante and Wordsworth to drama, sociology and economics (Steedman, 2004). Such tireless activity became vital for his career as a published author.

Steedman in the *OXDNB* entry recognises that Wicksteed was 'perhaps best-known' among his contemporaries for his extensive work on 'Dante and on Dante's relationship to the thought of Aquinas', which encompassed popular titles such as '*Six Sermons on Dante* (1879) and the Temple Classics edition of Dante (1899–1906)' as well as 'more scholarly works' like *Dante and Giovanni del Virgilio* (1902), with E. G. Gardner, and *From Vita Nuova to Paradiso* (1922) (Steedman, 2004). Flattened into a succinct bibliographical catalogue, Wicksteed's studies on Dante are soon obscured by his work as a liberal economist, author of a critique of Marx's *Das Kapital*, *The Alphabet of Economic Science* (1888) and the *Essay on the Co-Ordination of the Laws of Distribution* (1894). *The Common Sense of Political Economy* (1910) is presented in Wicksteed's own words 'as the culmination of "my life effort to do something real for thought and life"' (Steedman, 2004). Yet, taken out of context, the heartfelt tones of the quote are strikingly misleading. They undermine Wicksteed's own perception of his life-long endeavours as one of the earliest and most prolific *dantista* in nineteenth-century Britain.

Published in 1931, Charles Herford's biography represents the best point of departure for reassessing the historical and cultural significance of Wicksteed's *dantismo*. A 'semi-domestic biographer', Herford combined literary professionalism with the 'incentive of a personal relation' with the man himself to whom he was united by a sincere friendship nurtured by common scholarly interests (Atkinson, 2010: 5). Similarly to Gladstone's biographer, John Morley, Herford's recovery of original documentary materials was facilitated by Wicksteed's family and friends keen to share with him their personal letters, photographs as much as his own diaries and notebooks.[1] Among these, Wicksteed's children Rebecca and Joseph became Herford's main correspondents invested, in turn, of a certain degree of decisional influence. Joseph's letters, in particular, offered a crucial insight into his father's 'habits of mind' and private reading:

Every authority he quoted [in his notebooks, letters or published writings] was one that had some time been independently interesting to him. He read Virgil or the Troubadours not that he might understand Dante better, but because if Dante had never written, he would have read or lived them. Dante, thus, became his companion and master in mutually interesting studies.

(Herford-Wicksteed Papers, 1 fol. 25)

The letter shows that Wicksteed conceived Dante (and his densely intertextual poetry) a 'companion' *and* a 'master': a source and a medium of knowledge able to stimulate in the reader a strong, sincere and productive intellectual curiosity that did not fall into the trap of idle intellectualism, but at the construction of new, disinterested and 'mutually interesting' knowledge (Herford-Wicksteed Papers, 1 fol. 25).

Apart from the family input, Herford's account of Wicksteed's life as *dantista* drew directly from their own twenty-year-long personal correspondence. On 28 May 1926, Wicksteed wrote to his 'Dear Herford' an accurate confutation of his description of 'Limbo as a definite place' that he had presented in a recently published article (Herford-Wicksteed Papers, 1 fol. 4). The booklet-style letter page is covered even in its extremities and margins with his counterargument: as a critique of sources detailing the philological and semantic process through which the word *limbo* came to be understood by Dante's readers and translators as a fringe, sphere or bay. Overall, the letter demonstrated his extensive knowledge of Dante's theological and Biblical sources with references to Paulus Orosius and the Old Testament, his familiarity with the Boccaccio who had 'perfectly understood' Dante's conception, and with Buti's commentaries on the *Commedia* (1–4).

A piece of a longer exchange, the missive documents the scholarly nature of their friendship, which relied on letters as carriers of knowledge and means of private, confidential formulation of a developing hermeneutical discourse. The chapter builds on Herford's biographical reconstruction to reassert Wicksteed's place in the history of British Dante studies through a comprehensive reassessment of his works. From preacher and Extension lecturer to translator and scholar of Dante, the chapter retraces and analyses the path that led Philip H. Wicksteed to become 'the most acceptable and accepted interpreter [of Dante]' in the eyes of 'the cultivated *laity* in England' (Herford, 1931: 92).

Preaching Dante: Wicksteed's *Six Sermons*

Originally, Wicksteed was drawn 'towards the Middle Ages of Dante and Aquinas and to the Aristotelian foundation on which Aquinas and through him Dante, had built' (Herford, 1931: 29) during his student years in London. What struck him the most was the way Dante 'had made the religion of his own time and country vocal for ours and for all others' by conveying in his verses 'the language of eternity … in the lineaments of a religion of time' (29). After an initial encounter, Dante's poetry was put aside as Wicksteed began his career as a Unitarian minister, first appointed in the southern countryside and later moving to the industrial north. It was only once he settled again in London that the early fascination was revived and turned into a prominent spiritual and scholarly concern.

The watershed event occurred in the autumn of 1874 when Wicksteed began his ministry of Little Portland Street Chapel, a 'sombre and unattractive place' that had become 'one of the focuses of spiritual religion in London' (Herford, 1931: 77). The appointment followed the retirement of James Martineau (1805–1900), Professor of Mental and Moral Philosophy and Political Economy in Manchester New College, Oxford, which Wicksteed himself had attended in his student days. Martineau was a leading authority of the Unitarian Church, whose 'soaring imagination and … impassioned religious genius Wicksteed sincerely revered' (80). The congregation that Wicksteed was inheriting had 'a very definite character' in itself, being

> chiefly composed of families descended from the early days of Unitarianism, bound together by intermarriage, common intellectual and religious tradition, and by common experience of the tempered kind of persecution. […] The sect was also a clan. Class differences, if they existed, were quite subordinate; the 'poor' were cared for, befriended and taught, but for the most part remained outside. The members were professional men, lawyers, university officials, with here and there a substantial shopkeeper from the neighbouring Oxford Street or Regent Street.
>
> (Herford, 1931: 80)

The choice of this young minister in his thirties was met with veiled scepticism and discontent. More than his 'inferiority in experience and power', the congregation critiqued the lack of 'the literary brilliance and exquisite diction, which clothed the spiritual intensity of his predecessor' that Wicksteed replaced with the rough but 'homely vernacular' used 'in addressing his Dukinfield working folks' (Herford, 1931: 80). Herford noted that even though 'he was willing to prune his style', Wicksteed refused to 'surrender the direct and simple address in which his strength lay' (80). Despite his best efforts and good disposition, it took more than five years for Wicksteed to legitimise his role in the eyes of his conservative, upper-middle-class congregation. The longed breakthrough occurred in the autumn of 1878 when Wicksteed delivered a series of six sermons on Dante in the ordinary course of his ministry. As Herford recounted,

> To the casual observer who read the announcement outside or who strolled in out of curiosity, the contrast between the setting and the subject was *extreme*. In this London backstreet, to this congregation of the rationalist and enlightened left wing of English Non-Conformity, the magnificent paradoxes of the medieval catholic poet were to be expounded, by a modern preacher, not chiefly as interesting literary matter, but in the service of moral and spiritual life, of religion.

(263)

For six consecutive Sundays, the sentiment of distrust and rejection was superseded by a sense of intellectual bliss for the way in which the young Minister was conveying his Protestant teachings through Dante's catholic verses. Drawing Dante and his poetry from 'that sheltered remoteness, that empty prestige' sealed by the aura of the medieval past, Wicksteed invited his congregation to discover the universal and 'enduring value' of his spiritual teachings 'in shaping and building up the soul of the modern man' (Herford, 1931: 261).

The success of the cycle of sermons established Wicksteed's public reputation as a Dante preacher. The key strength of his orations lay in their rhetorical and conceptual ability to transform the Florentine poet into 'a living concern' for 'the modern, educated and Protestant Englishman', persuading him that 'through the Catholic and medieval vesture of his thought' Dante's theological poetry penetrated 'the universal elements of all religion, and thus spoke, in his own great idiom, to universal man' (Herford, 1931: 268). Urging his congregation to move past the historical and confessional distance that only apparently separated their Non-Conformist modern age from Dante's medieval past, Wicksteed invited them to recognise 'the intimate kinship of all forms of religion' (261) powerfully expressed in Dante's universal language. This final claim reveals the essential continuity of Wicksteed's critical discourse on Dante: what had fascinated him the most in his youth eventually became the object of a more serious discourse on 'the varieties of the religious experience' (262), thus appealing to the intellectual eagerness for knowledge and culture, which traditionally characterised Unitarianism. Wicksteed did not manipulate Dante's theological message nor accommodate it to the needs of the present. Rather, it preserved its historical and cultural alterity so that 'the great medieval Catholic was medieval and catholic still; he had abated not a little of his paradoxes, nor a day of his six hundred years; and yet he was in their midst, their own' (263).

The sermons soon proved a very successful enterprise, replicated at the Free Christian Church, Croydon. The large public attending on Sundays was more variegated than expected: among 'the casual observers' (Herford, 1931: 263) there were also Dante enthusiasts eager to expand their knowledge and, from time to time, scholars interested in the way the minister had been teaching Dante's textuality through his preaching. In the summer of 1879 'at the request of many of [his] hearers', Wicksteed collected his six his sermons 'almost exactly as delivered at Croydon' (Wicksteed, 1879: v): the pocket-size volume was published by Kegan Paul and Co. In printed format, the volume was divided into five main chapters introduced by a short preface and followed by an appendix containing 'the substance of a sixth sermon' (vi): a hierarchical organisation that marks a significant shift between the verbal and written critical discourse on Dante.

In the first two chapters – 'Dante as a Citizen of Florence' and 'Dante in Exile' – the biographical account reads more as a 'tale' than an overview of Dante's troubled life, despite intending to also stir the public's attention for lesser-known works such as the *Convivio* and *Monarchia*. The following three chapters engage in a *cantica*-by-*cantica* preaching analysis of the *Commedia* conveying a vernacularised and inspiring elucidation of Dante's spiritual message. Although it cannot be excluded that the learned members of the congregation would be acquainted with Italian, the democratic use of English translations (personally authored by the minister) facilitated their encounter with Dantean textuality. Particularly interesting are the rhetorical features of the discourse and the way in which Wicksteed tends to annul any aesthetic or cultural distance with the poetic text by establishing continuous correspondences with the reader's everyday life as in the case of the fourth sermon-chapter on *Purgatorio* in which he passionately asserted that

> there is much in the Purgatory that seems to render it peculiarly fitted to support *our spiritual life* and *help us* in our *daily conflict* ... it is *nearer to us* in our daily struggles and imperfections, in our aspirations and our conscious unworthiness, nearer to us in our love of purity and our knowledge that our own hearts are stained with sin, in our desire for the fullness of God's light, and our knowledge that we are not yet worthy or ready to receive it ...; *nearer to us* in its deepest unrest of unattained but unrelinquished ideals, than either the Hell in its ghastly harmony of impenitence and suffering, or the Paradise in its ineffable fruition.
>
> (Wicksteed, 1879: 95)

Throughout, the risk of excessive personalisation is skilfully avoided as Wicksteed moves on to the description of 'the allegorical appropriateness of the various punishments' and 'the spiritual significance of the whole machinery' (Wicksteed, 1879: 93). Similarly, and most interestingly, in the sermon on *Paradiso* the predilection for the religious dimension is counterbalanced with what Wicksteed's titled as 'AN ATTEMPT TO STATE THE CENTRAL THOUGHT OF THE COMEDY'. Here, the preacher's spiritual use of the *Commedia* is superseded by the emergence of as critical and didactic interest for the wide-ranging study of Dantean textuality, which will characterise Wicksteed's activity as an Extension lecturer and Dante scholar.

As much as Arnold's transition from lectures to periodical articles, the new portable guise of the *Sermons* was a material change that enhanced the wider popularisation of Wicksteed's discourse on Dante. In 'allowing the publication of this little volume', the author wanted

> to let it take its chance with other fugitive productions of the Pulpit that appeal to the Press as a means of widening the possible area

rather than extending the period over which the preacher's voice may extend; and my only justification is the hope that it may here and there reach hands to which no more adequate treatment of the subject was likely to find its way.

(Wicksteed, 1879: v–vi)

The closing line of the paragraph encapsulates the unique character and ideology of Wicksteed's *dantismo*: a firm resolution that his hermeneutical efforts had to meet, first and foremost, the intellectual and material needs of non-specialist and possibly first-time readers of Dante's works.

The publication of the *Six Sermons* in their original form, still bearing evident traces of orality, also demonstrated Wicksteed's (and his publishers') strategic understanding of the Victorian sermon-publishing market. The 'most prominent aspect of Anglican and Dissenting religious observance', by the late 1870s the sermon was a popular form of religious production of which the Victorians were fond collectors but also avid 'users' (Ellison, 1998: 43–4). In linking his own work to such literary productions, Wicksteed intercepted the interest of a broadening readership. Dante was now in the hands of this new public of readers, Sunday worshippers 'for whom church attendance was an intellectual and aesthetic delight as well as a religious duty' (43); the sermon was also a practical, uplifting essay to be carefully studied by underlining passages, exploring references and annotating comments. Within these, Wicksteed combined oral colloquialism and literary refinement, practical life *exempla* and cultivated references to biblical or classical literature, emphatic, direct address and subtler rhetorical questions that captivated the public.

In cherishing rather than concealing the signs of the orality from the printed book, Wicksteed turned Dante into an object of common experience, private study and reflection, seemingly enhancing the ideological purpose of the *Six Sermons*. While the performative exposition of Dante's *exempla* from the pulpit produced a transient state of spiritual uplift among the congregation, the transposition to the written form facilitated a lengthier process of comprehension and interiorisation of the message, thus transforming the casual hearer into a serious reader of Dante. By stirring the intellectual curiosity for a comprehensive understanding of Dante, the volume influenced the demand for critical and scholarly knowledge. The *Six Sermons* came to be regarded and recommended as, on the whole, in spite of its immaturity and what he sometimes spoke of despairingly as "the trail of the preacher", the best introduction for English readers; not a substitute for the admirable *Dante Primer* later provided by his friend Gardner, but a general survey of the course which that book would help them to pursue.

(Herford, 1931: 265)

Although the *Six Sermons* were not a piece of mature and professional scholarship compared to his later works, they were soon recognised as the best point of departure for the serious reading of Dante and his *Commedia* by an expanding public. In the preface to the second edition (1890), Wicksteed himself humbly acknowledged the didactic value of his work and the different modes and levels of employments it fulfilled. They represented an accessible introduction about 'what the Comedy means' for 'those who go no further' as well as a practical and intelligible guide 'to approach its study from the point of view of *life*, rather than of literature and scholarship in the narrower sense' (Wicksteed, 1890: vi). Archival evidence suggests that Wicksteed's readers also included some of the most renowned Dante scholars of the period. Paget Toynbee, for instance, acquired the first edition of the *Six Sermons* for his own private Dante collection, kept cuttings of reviews in his records, and became more and more engaged with Wicksteed's activities both as a Dante scholar and lecturer. Similarly, a copy of the first edition was sent with the compliments of the author to Edward Moore: behind its basic rituality, this gesture could suggest that Wicksteed was seeking academic validation for his own work from the foremost authority of a newly institutionalised field of studies and, by extension, he was also recognising the existence of that national community of scholars of which Moore was a representative.

Apart from this (search for) scholarly endorsement, Wicksteed's *Six Sermons* won the appreciation of a broader British public as proven by the six, almost continuous editions printed between 1878 and 1905 by two different publishers, first Kegan Paul and later Elkin Matthews. What crowned his success was the ingenious adoption of the sermon to serve a two-fold, evolving purpose so that in the oral dimension Dante's textuality was used as a source of spiritual enlightenment, and then turned into an object of critical reflection and scholarly study by the written form.

Bringing Dante to the people: the University Extension Movement

The *Six Sermons* were 'the prelude to the years of brilliant exposition, interpretation and research that followed' (Herford, 1931: 268). In the mid-1880s, in fact, Wicksteed became progressively involved in the activities of the Extension Movement: an 'organised and functional education scheme' (Draper, 1923: 2) part of the broader educational reform of adult education that had been taking place throughout the country since the early decades of the century.

The request for higher knowledge among the middle-class public had led to the foundation of University College (1828), King's College (1831) – later incorporated as the University of London (1836) – Durham University (1832) and Owens College (1851). Liberal and non-denominational institutions specialised in the teaching of niche subjects such as modern languages, economy and history, the provincial universities produced a major shift in the public attitude towards the matter of access, forms and formative objectives of adult higher education. Their activities developed in parallel with the 1850s internal reform of the old, fossilised universities of Oxford and Cambridge, accelerated by state interventions. These led to the broadening of the conservative curriculum and the admission of Non-Conformists, Roman Catholics and non-Christian students to matriculate and graduate and later (with the Universities' Religious Tests Act, 1871) to take on professorships, fellowships and lay offices within these institutions.[2]

The most concrete steps towards catering 'more actively, and less exclusively' (Marriott, 1981:10) for the needs of the broader society were taken in 1857 when Oxford and Cambridge assumed responsibility for the central organisation of the Local Examinations system. In collaboration with provincial authorities, the system monitored the standard of secondary schools and promoted the educational improvement of the middle classes by administering annual examinations for school-leavers nationwide. Non-competitive, the examinations were designed as 'fair tests of average work' (Roach, 2008: 230) covering four subjects chosen among English, arithmetic, sciences, geography, outlines of British history, ancient and modern languages; the faith and religion paper remained optional. Students' success depended on their passing two out of the four sections of the exam and was marked by the award of certificates along with 'a title showing the connection of the possessor' to the old universities (230). In 1862–63, Emily Davies and the Langham Place reformers spear-headed a campaign for the admission of girls to Local Examinations, demanding equal standards of evaluation based on the same papers for both sexes, and not differentiated papers on the basis of girls' presumed capacities: a goal ultimately achieved in 1865.[3]

The establishment of the local or middle-class examinations, as they were often called, created the material and ideological conditions for the creation of the University Extension Lecture movement. Women's organisations, in particular, saw in the examinations 'a steppingstone to the equality of educational opportunity for women, including higher and university education' (Jepson, 1973: 35). Uniting into the North of England Council for Promoting the Higher Education of Women, these organisations launched in 1867 the very first course of itinerant lectures on literary, historical and scientific subjects taught on a voluntary basis by eminent lecturers from Cambridge and Oxford. By 1868, Manchester, Bowden, Liverpool, Birkenhead, Sheffield, Bradford, York, Leeds and Newcastle were setting up permanent centres with branches in smaller towns and rural districts. Cambridge was the first to set up a small-scale scheme of extramural teaching in the winter of 1873 when local lectures were first arranged in Nottingham, Leicester and Derby.

In the autumn of 1876, the newly founded London Society for the Extension of University Teaching established five metropolitan centres offering seven terminal courses. Once again, Oxford lagged behind. Inaugurated in 1878, the activities were suspended and then resumed in 1885 with the creation of twenty centres. The new universities also took an active yet minor part in the movement: while Durham was associated with Cambridge, the federal Victoria University, uniting with Owen's College, Liverpool University and Yorkshire College, Leeds, launched courses in Lancashire and Yorkshire. Ideologically, the movement responded to the educational needs of the industrialised nation and to 'the democratising urge to provide teaching of the highest standard to localities deprived of intellectual nourishment' (Marriott, 1981: 5). As such, it sought to act as an agent of cultural progress, social unification and mitigation of class conflict by extending and improving the provision of higher education to men and women of 'all classes', 'all ages, all degrees of previous knowledge', who were engaged in 'the regular occupations of life' (Moulton, 1890: 10) and could not access nor afford the complete resident degree courses. As for the Local Examinations, the translation of the ideological mission into practice depended on the initiative and enterprise of local committees formed by representatives of educational and social institutions, religious associations, co-operative societies, trade unions and workers associations, schools and colleges. The central universities confined themselves to the provision of teaching staff and the administration of final examinations.

The creation of a capillary system disseminated in provincial towns, rural districts and urban centres enabled the movement to penetrate within socio-culturally diverse communities and reach large and miscellaneous audiences of students. Since the early days, the middle classes represented the backbone of the movement. While elderly members of the clergy, professionals, businessmen and other wage-earning occupations were in regular attendance, the courses registered 'a marked predominance of women' (Jepson, 1973: 104) mostly attending in the morning and afternoon lectures but also taking part in the evening courses. A large fraction of the middle-class public consisted of secondary school scholars as well as secondary and pupil teachers: a datum demonstrating how 'the movement might "form a useful means of supplementing the otherwise imperfect provision"' of national education (109). Occasionally, Extension courses became integral to 'the regular curriculum of the school and given within its walls' (108). Furthermore, through the organisation of evening courses, the movement had also 'distinctly set itself to meet the needs of the Working Classes' (128). With the exception of a number of industrial areas in Yorkshire, Northumberland and Gloucestershire, however, their response was largely underwhelming – even among the female studentships. The main impediments to workers' participation were mainly financial and organisational, linked to 'shift work, overtime, fluctuations in trade' as well as to 'the expense of books and travel on top of the courses' (Rowbotham, 1965: 68), the material distance to class and free libraries. As Purvis pointed out in her seminal study, the situation for working-class women was particularly complicated by the curricula offered, the levels of literacy demanded, the solidly middle-class male ethos of university life and the ritual governing interaction between an elite male lecturer and a woman of the 'lower orders' would have been forbidden to all but the most determined of [them].

(Purvis, 1991: 110)

The movement proposed a liberal curriculum geared towards the development of 'faculty of thought rather than the power to absorb factual information' (Jepson, 1973: 216) through the study of literature, history, economy and art along with scientific and technical subjects. This led to an unprecedentedly wide offer of courses tailored to the specific demands of the local community and the financial resources of the centres.

To ensure a certain continuity and uniformity of learning as well as to the educational value of the experience, James Stuart – Trinity Fellow and pioneer of the movement – emphasised the importance of length, consecutiveness and coherence of teaching to engage students in a 'regular course of study extending over a period of two or three years' (Jepson, 1973: 288). Although the minimum length was fixed at twelve lectures, shorter six-lecture courses were also offered for new start-up centres in smaller and poorer localities. To limit their appeal as less-demanding alternatives to full-length courses, the Syndicates clarified their function as 'connecting link[s] between the more popular and the more serious kind of studies' that would 'as a rule, hinge upon a single book and aimed at encouraging [students] to read steadily and thoughtfully from week to week' (294). Along with traditional format, Extension records document that many centres also arranged courses of four, twelve and eighteen lectures.

Generally, the centres covered three main disciplinary areas: natural sciences, history and political economy (English and European) and literature and arts. The last category included a wide range of courses in ancient and modern languages and literatures, within which Italian was a subject almost exclusively vehiculated through the study of Dante, to the point that language classes were offered to facilitate the teaching. The records from the Oxford Centre show that among the lecturers employed on year-long contracts, Rev. S. Udny, associate to Magdalen College, delivered six-lecture courses ranging from a general overview of *Dante and His Art* and an *Introduction to Dante Based on the Study of* Purgatorio, both recommended to beginners, and a more advanced course titled *The Man and the* Commedia. William H. Draper from Keble College gave general courses on Dante of variable length of six, twelve and eighteen lectures. Mrs Paul Chapman, appointed for lectures in schools only, delivered at least three different courses: *Dante's Life and Works*, a general, six-lecture course, and *Outline of the* Divina Commedia and *The* Divina Commedia, which were described as 'more detailed courses on either of the three *Cantiche*', and illustrated by lantern-slides of the Botticelli drawings. Differently, Frederick York Powell (student and tutor of Christ Church) was employed for the Summer Meetings to teach a course of twelve 'special classes' on *Dante:* Vita Nuova *and* Inferno, in which the lecturer engaged in the reading and commentary of the two works, providing students with a list of passages to be specially considered for individual study at the end of each session. Powell's classes were the continuation of the three-lecture introduction (Dante's life and times, minor works, plan and purpose of the *Commedia*) taught by Wicksteed, the most prolific Dante lecturer of his generation with more than two hundred Extension courses delivered between 1887 and 1916.

Regardless of length, all courses had four fixed parts: the lecture, the weekly exercises, the class and the final examinations. The hour's lectures fulfilled a dual function, catering for the intellectual recreation of the general (and occasional) public and for the stimulation of the scholarly interest of committed students. Both would be equipped with a copy of the lecturer's syllabus: a thirty-to-forty-page-long handbook in demi octavo detailing the outline and content of the course, recommended bibliography and a list of questions for home study. Used synchronously, the syllabus supported students in 'following the lectures without distraction of taking notes' (Jepson, 1973: 263). Asynchronously, the textbook guided their independent reading and writing as well as peer discussions in between lectures. The limited book supply, however, impeded the individual study of many: an issue initially tackled with the provision of Travelling Libraries (1885) and then solved with the creation of the Book Union in 1898 that stirred plans for the set-up of a central library in the early 1900s. The class granted a more direct, personal and conversational exchange with the lecturer for those students who had been sending papers to him, clarifying doubts and issues arising during the week. The students' consistent production of written work held primary importance for the groundbreaking Extension method, where access to the final examinations and the award of the certificates was conditional to the submission of at least two-thirds of the weekly exercises throughout the term. This, along with the administration of tests by external examiners, ensured fairness of evaluation to all students.

The livelihood and socio-cultural impact of the courses chiefly depended on the lecturers employed. Initially, these were mostly young graduates from the ancient universities seeking to gain valuable teaching experience over a short (generally biannual) appointment. As the movement expanded and the staff began to be engaged at regular stipends, many decided to take on their role on a permanent, full-time basis and, at times, for more than one centre. Selection standards were severe. Candidates must hold a degree, along with producing evidence of their competence and public lecturing experience. If approved, they submitted a syllabus for a six-week course and arranged for trial lectures after which delegates would produce their report. Yet, the lecturers' duties went far beyond the effective delivery of the diversity of subjects offered. Scholarly distinction and competency in the subject were important, but not vital requirements as the movement favoured the dynamism of men 'of sound knowledge and many interests' over the 'mere knowledge' of the 'learned specialist' (Draper, 1923: 9). The ideal lecturer was a pragmatic and relatable figure, who could attract large audiences, inspire and support them through their learning experience, while also reminding them of the practical usefulness of the knowledge and the analytical and critical skills they were acquiring. By the 1890s, the lecturing staff also included women holding degrees in humanist and scientific subjects, following the creation of women's colleges at Cambridge (Girton, est. 1869; Newnham, est. 1871), Oxford (Somerville, Lady Margaret Hall, est. 1877) and London (Westfield, est. 1882; Royal Holloway, est. 1886).

In Philip H. Wicksteed, the London Society for the Extension of University Teaching, a voluntary organisation established in 1876 by the London University, found a match for its ideal lecturer: someone 'effective in attracting large audiences and, at the same time, securing a high degree of educational thoroughness' (Roberts,

1914: 7).[4] He was a young man in his thirties with strong academic credentials, a thriving career as a Unitarian minister experienced in addressing diverse audiences: from the working classes of the industrial north to the London middle classes, and with a growing reputation as a Dante interpreter. His art of preaching rested on the simple use of 'three faculties, the literary, the conversational and the illustrative', and the ability to answer the spiritual and intellectual demands of his congregations while respecting their socio-cultural 'variousness' (Herford, 1931: xv).

On 10 November 1887, Wicksteed was appointed Extension lecturer, at first without resigning from his ministry of the Little Portland Street Chapel. Although it was a practical decision common to most lecturers, for Wicksteed it also stressed the ideological continuity he saw in these two roles, as proven by the way he transformed the impersonal Extension classes into small 'congregations, by a fusion of documented scholarship unusual in any pulpit with a prophetic fire in any university' (Herford, 1931: 90).

Reflecting the movement's ideology, Wicksteed worked towards the development of an alternative academic discourse that would include those who had been kept so far at the margins of higher education, stirring in them the need 'to assume direction of their own intellectual lives' and 'become individual agents in framing an understanding of the world' (Rose, 2010: 12). Rephrasing Matthew Arnold's famous predicaments found in *Culture and Anarchy*, the knowledge Wicksteed 'fed' to his students was not 'an intellectual food prepared and adapted in the way they think proper for the actual condition of the masses' (Arnold, 1869: 48). Instead of teaching 'down to the level of inferior classes' to impress them 'with ready-made judgments and watchwords' (Arnold, 1869: 48), he seemingly embraced the educational mission of the Arnoldian man of culture.

The programmatic intent was to 'initiate' the Extension students 'in subjects', which 'for the most part were not yet taught' (Herford, 1931: 93) in canonical universities at that point in time, making him an apostle of equality – specifically, someone whose work sought 'to divest knowledge of all that was harsh, uncouth, difficult, abstract, professional, exclusive and to humanise it, to make it efficient outside the clique of the cultivated and learned, yet still remaining the best knowledge and thought of the time' (Arnold, 1869: 48). Such determination was epitomised in the choice of Dante as the subject of his inaugural two-part course of twelve lectures delivered in Wimbledon in 1887–88 and of the majority of the courses delivered between 1887 and 1918.

Wicksteed and the popular teaching of Dante

The *Six Sermons* had already proven that Dante's poetry was 'the kind of fictitious writing that could appeal to all powers of the mind (imagination, memory, reason, morality)' of modern generations of the Non-Conformist upper-middle class (Rose, 2010: 38). Most importantly, the *Sermons* had dexterously intercepted what Jonathan Rose describes as the 'transference of reverence from the Good Book to the Great Books' (34) among Non-Conformist readers and worshippers, which made them more open and receptive to literature and poetry.

Analogously, the success of the Extension lectures on Dante derived from Wicksteed's ability to channel the popular fascination with the Italian poet and capitalise on two contextual circumstances: the recognition of the civilising and instrumental value of literary knowledge and the developing habit of serious reading that were spreading among the middle and lower classes. Exploiting a (relatively) familiar topic, Wicksteed's Extension courses reflected the Arnoldian predicaments by setting forth a binding request for a methodical and engaged study of Dante's textuality. Understandably, however, the learning expectations set by the lectures were unlike those of the sermons. While the preacher invited the people in his congregation to immerse themselves into Dante's world and await an epiphany on his spiritual and moral message, the lecturer guided his students through the discovery of the texts through analytical reading, critical reflection and historical objectivity.

The Registers for the Extension Board show that between 1887 and 1916, Wicksteed worked for the four main Extension systems around the country: the London, Oxford, Cambridge and Victorian Universities. His extensive teaching engagement implied a continuous change of geographic and socio-cultural environments, ranging from traditional academic centres to northern industrial cities and southern countryside. Only rarely using official university spaces, such as the London University Hall, he held cycles of lectures in non-traditional educational spaces for high academic knowledge such as the Schoolroom of the Withington Presbyterian Church in Manchester. Reproduced on a national map, the list renders the extraordinarily vast geographical scope of Wicksteed's travels as an itinerant lecturer, and the parallel multiplication of the spaces in which the study of Dante was pursued by British men and women all around the country. Initially working for the London Centre, Wicksteed travelled to different boroughs: from Chelsea, Whitechapel, South Lambeth, Kew & Richmond and Notting Hill to Wimbledon and Greenwich where his teaching occurred mostly within dedicated learning spaces.

From the mid-1890s onwards the distances began to increase, and the perimeter widened to incorporate a rich variety of places. With the Oxford centre, the Dante lectures began to travel up and down the country, touching big and middle-sized centres such as Halifax, Birmingham and Reading with their peripheries, along with rural communities of the north, Harrogate, Bradford, and in the south Tunbridge Wells, Hove, Cranford Cliffs, Ramsgate. Around the same time, the work for Cambridge was concentrated in the north and specifically Yorkshire, touching his birthplace, Leeds, along with other centres such as Scarborough and York, Hull, Newcastle, and Nottingham. He only rarely extended to the south-west. The relatively shorter and occasional engagement with the Victorian Universities of Manchester, Liverpool and Leeds had Wicksteed teaching Dante for six consecutive cycles. He taught twice in Leeds at the Yorkshire Ladies' Council of Education (1895–96; 1897–98), an unequivocal sign of the sizeable presence of women of all ages among the Wicksteed Dante students, and then in Altrincham and Bowdon, Warrington, Withington and at the Victoria University of Manchester (1904–5). Similarly, the collaboration with the Liverpool Centre generally kept him within the city boundaries.

The time spent in each town varied on the length of the courses taught: from session courses of twenty-four lectures, terminal courses of ten or twelve lectures to short courses of five or six lectures. In both large and small centres, the lecturer made the request for the arrangement of his classroom to the Extension Committee of 'a large blackboard, chalk and duster' while he did not 'like any task or table between himself and the audience': a choice that is possibly a sign of his dialogic and non-hierarchical style of teaching (Oxford Records, 75).

Compiled by the lecturer and sold to students were booklets which constitute crucial documentary evidence for Wicksteed's teaching activities: from general courses (Wimbledon, 1887–88; University Hall, London, 1890; Ladybarn House, Manchester, 1903) to monographic cycles on the whole *Commedia* (London, 1890), on individual *cantiche* (*Purgatorio*, London, 1890; *Inferno*, London, 1894; *Paradiso*, Liverpool, 1904) or minor works such the *Convivio* (London, 1897). With minor differences, these were standardised booklets consisting of thirty-five to forty pocket-sized pages providing 'a detailed synopsis of each lecture, a list of appropriate books, hints for reading, and in some cases alternative subjects for Essays' (Harrison, 2009: 375).

The standard cover page, printed on white or even blue paper, showed the course title followed by the name of the lecturer and chronological coordinates, all written in bold letters. On its back, the syllabus presented the method of conducting lectures and classes: a brief overview of the content of the syllabus and the structure of the course, as well as peremptory instructions about the attendance to both lectures and classes, the submission of weekly coursework to the lecturer as a compulsory requirement to be eligible for the final examination and certificate. In some cases, Wicksteed supplemented these guidelines with inserted sleeves of paper in which he recommended his students 'to study this Syllabus carefully before and after the Lectures; but, as a rule, not to refer to it or try to remember it during the Lectures': a laconic notice that gives a clear sense of how the lecturer shaped their learning strategies while conditioning their classroom and home-study behaviour (Wicksteed, 1888).

Likewise, the *cantica*-specific courses were equipped with a lengthier and detailed introductory note setting forth their higher didactic requirements: those lectures, in fact, were designed for those 'who have already made some study of Dante' and thus 'a fair knowledge of the text of the "Comedy" (in the original or translation) and some acquaintance with the "Vita Nuova", the "De Monarchia" and the "Convivio" are expected' (Wicksteed, 1894: n.p.). The target public was a smaller group of returning Extension students who had previously attended and satisfactorily passed the examination for his general course on Dante. Notably, even at this stage Wicksteed valued the knowledge of Italian in a non-discriminatory fashion, as not 'essential to the intelligent following' of the lectures and necessary only for strictly academic purposes, required 'to gain the mark of "Distinction" in the final examination' (Wicksteed, 1887: 1).

Through the syllabus, Wicksteed also guided his students to the best books written on the subject of his lectures through the means of reading lists compiled for this purpose and placed either after the prefatory instructions or at the end of the syllabus. For his Dante courses, Wicksteed drafted commented bibliographies in which he provided extensive annotations detailing the content, the edition and price, the expected level of preparation for the student and the specific use of each book or essay recorded. In the Dante syllabi, the titles were generally ordered into variable categories. For his inaugural course in 1887–88, for instance, he distinguished between 'GENERAL', comprising handbooks and essay that would serve as an introduction to the study of Dante; 'EDITIONS', generally referring to a selection of original editions of Dante's minor works; and 'TRANSLATIONS' that included all major English translations of Dante's major and minor works (Wicksteed, 1887: 1). For the terminal course on *Purgatorio* given in Cambridge in 1901, Wicksteed marked a distinction between 'BOOKS' and 'Books of Reference'. The former were titles that *'every student* is expected to possess' (Wicksteed, 1901: 1–2; original emphasis), which included English and Italian editions of Dante's works, affordable handbooks such as Gardner's *Dante Primer* (1900) and also manageable Italian commentaries on the *Commedia*. The latter included a selection of specialist works and expensive editions supplied for consultation by the central library during the delivery of the course.

These bibliographies hold great documentary significance for they detail the set of scholarly resources Wicksteed used to bring the study of Dante out of the old, elitist circles and transform it into accessible knowledge[5] for the people of the middle and lower classes that had been so far either marginalised or excluded from the contemporary critical discourse. The aim was to offer the Extension students the opportunity to elevate their intellectual and cultural status of ingenuous (in the sense of amateur, fragmentary, largely acritical and impressionistic consumers) to serious readers of Dante.

Coincidentally, they also document the simultaneous process of professionalisation that Wicksteed was undergoing as a Dante lecturer and scholar: a growing dexterity with which he examined the scholarly sources, assessed their didactic potential, and ultimately chose them as suitable for the different intellectual needs of his students, from beginners to advanced. Concurrently, the bibliographies provide an authentic outlook on the status of British Dante scholarship at the turn of the century, a time in which it was still a specialism rather than a discrete and established academic discipline. Wicksteed's personal canon was grounded on four key titles from contemporary Anglo-American scholars: Lowell's essay on 'Dante' in *Among My Books* (1872), Symonds' *An Introduction to the Study of Dante* (1872), Wicksteed's earliest book of reference for the composition of his sermons, Wicksteed's own *Six Sermons* (1879), Church's 'Essay on Dante' (1888) and, finally, Gardner's *Dante Primer* (1900). Although presenting different hermeneutic, historical and textual modes of interpretation, these publications promoted rather didactic and openly democratic introductions to the critical study of Dante aimed at non-specialist readers. Remarkably, with the refinement of his teaching methodology, the use of those critical studies was 'kept strictly subordinate': the lecturer 'strongly recommended' all students of any level 'to get as quickly and keep as closely as possible to the text of Dante's own works' (Wicksteed, 1904c: 4) in translated or even, and most desirably, Italian versions.

The prominence of the textual approach in Wicksteed's teaching is most evident in the synopsis of the lectures, detailing the range of themes, topics, methodologies and textual approaches adopted and continuously refined throughout his thirty-year-long lecturing career. In the absence of the original transcripts for the Dante courses, the abridged summaries unearth the process through which Dante was turned into an object of study for Victorian middle- and lower-class students. Practical instruments of study, the synopses assisted their historical, critical and aesthetic discovery of Dante's life and poetry. Those from the introductory courses (1887–88, 1890, 1904) show that Wicksteed's primary concern was to educate students to develop a broad-encompassing critical understanding of Dante's entire literary production by learning to recognise 'the line of progress' which connects all his major and minor works into an 'organic' (Wicksteed, 1904c: 4) and non-hierarchical whole. This intention was reflected in the careful partition of the course contents. The introductory Dante module, for example, opened with a couple of lectures expounding Dante's place in the history of literature (I), his poetic models (II) and one general survey of his principles, purposes, instruments and methods (III). The ensuing lectures combined biographical reconstruction with literary criticism and separate accounts for each of his works as follows: the age of youth and the *Vita Nuova* (L. IV), Dante's exile and political activities: *De Monarchia*, *De Vulgari Eloquentia* and *Convivio* (V), *Letters* and *Quaestio* (IV), the *Divine Comedy*: as an allegory (VII), ethical system (VIII), cosmography and topography (IX), *Inferno* (X), *Purgatorio* (XI) and *Paradiso* (XII).

Differently, the monographic courses carried out a more minute study of the thematic and stylistic features of Dante's poetry, introducing students to the principles of textual criticism as well as engaging them in practical exercises in literary translation. The syllabi for the courses on *Purgatorio*, *Inferno* and *Paradiso* show that Wicksteed adopted a tripartite approach to the study of the *cantiche*. The synopsis of each lecture, usually focused on a group of two or three *canti*, is divided into three sections: (a) 'Notes and Suggestions for Analysis', a space for an introductory analysis of major themes, characters and motifs; (b) 'Translation of Cantos', paraphrastic translations containing glosses and interpretations, similar to those given in his *Six Sermons*; (c) 'Considerations on Special Points', providing a hermeneutical commentary on key passages, analysed in their stylistic and linguistic features through textual criticism. Finally, the synopses were complemented by the list of 'Questions' students were required to answer and submit to the lecturer on a weekly basis.

The list of questions given for weekly assignments and final examinations unveils Wicksteed's expectations in terms of learning objectives, critical refinement and the dialectical dexterity he envisioned for his students. The aim was to test not only their textual and contextual knowledge and analytical and translational abilities, but also their critical insightfulness: in relation to past criticism ('"The essence of Dante's genius is intensity." Discuss this statement') or independently produced ('Illustrate, from the original if you can, the qualities which make Dante one of the greatest poets of the world'; 'what do you take to be (a) the finest single line (b) the finest passage in the Divine Comedy? Justify your answers'). Interestingly, Wicksteed always featured a question inviting students to reflect upon their own learning experience ('what do you take to be the chief difficulties which confront one on beginning the study of Dante?') which concurrently allowed him to redirect and enhance his teaching strategy according to the learners' manifested needs.

Examined in their physical materiality, Wicksteed's syllabi are objects of knowledge conceived by the Extension scheme as a material support, affordable in price and accessible both in size and content, that would accompany and assist students in every phase of their study: before, during and after the lectures. Apart from some standardised features, every lecturer was free to design their syllabi in the way that would serve most effectively the proposed teaching purposes. In the introductory modules, the calculated use of different size, style and type of fonts was one of the ways in which Wicksteed directed the students' acquisition and assimilation of Dantean information by dividing it into memorable units of knowledge. Similarly, for the advanced courses, Wicksteed put together a number of tables of illustration to complement the information provided in the synopses with foldable schematics, generally relating to a character's historical lineage.

The syllabus for the 1890 course on *Purgatorio* shows that these technologies of knowledge also supported the lecturer's teaching in the form of a thick layer of manuscript annotations. These marginal commentaries and translations covered the blank left pages, surrounding the synopses with aspects to be further investigated or questions to be addressed within the classroom. Similarly, the intricate network of connections, relations and emendations shows that Wicksteed perpetually reshaped the content of the syllabus based on the response of his public. As such, the annotated syllabus is the closest thing we have to a consistent and intelligible transcript of his Dante lectures: a unique resource to penetrate and examine from a closer perspective the practices of critical and scholarly appropriations through which Victorian lecturers *and* students turned Dante into an object of study.

The Extension registers from the Oxford Centre show that Wicksteed's courses were attended by an average of sixty students per lecture and fifteen per seminar class, which fostered collaborative learning and open discussion among the class and with the lecturer himself. Although the effectiveness of the lectures was occasionally compromised by the students' unwillingness to submit weekly papers, the examination reports demonstrated that students had acquired 'good knowledge of the poem but were struggling with the Italian and the historical context'. Some candidates 'quoted well from the text' and offered evidence of independent study while some 'did not go beyond the notes from the lectures' (Oxford Records, 1906).

As he brought the study of Dante 'to the people', Wicksteed revolutionised British Dante scholarship. In the late 1880s, in fact, the study of Dante was pursued only by a restricted group of scholars and intellectuals organised in elitist circles such as the Oxford Dante Society, founded in 1876. Although open to all men and women upon payment of a fee, the Barlow Lectures on the *Divina Commedia* remained – at least in those early years – the privilege of the few because the commented reading of the poem was systemically delivered in Italian. Wicksteed's Extension courses, on the other hand, were always taught in English, a linguistic choice that not only broadened the range of the audience but effectively created a new category of Dante English-speaking middle-class readers.

Held within non-canonical academic institutions and in the presence of a wider public, the Dante courses 'grew both in comprehensiveness and in individuality' becoming 'less elementary, richer in examples of his singular power of lucidly expounding the abstruse matter of Dantesque philosophy and technique, thus more instructive to the Dante specialist' (Herford, 1931: 139). In a combined movement of evolution, Wicksteed built his reputation as a *dantista* at the same time as his students evolved into serious readers of Dante. Over the course of his twenty years of activity, the 'widely celebrated' lectures began to attract a category of 'hearers for whom from different, perhaps opposite, points of view, Extension Courses were in no way designed', as 'distinguished critics were allured by curiosity, maidservants invited by their mistresses, and both remained' (139).

Dante as a commercial commodity: the *Temple Classics*

A decade into his Extension teaching, Wicksteed recognised that in spite of the satisfactory attendance rates and their growing popularity, the lectures ran the risk 'of being water poured upon sand' as long as the original text was not 'easily and cheaply accessible with all legitimate aids, including the contemporary history and a literal prose version, to its intelligent interpretation' (Herford, 1931: 149). Much to the lecturer's despair even 'the well-to-do' who could afford the purchase were generally hesitant 'to lay out money in a book if it could be [...] otherwise secured' (151) by borrowing a copy from the central and university libraries affiliated with the Extension centres.

Victorian common readers were still struggling with the idea of books as instruments of knowledge to be materially possessed and actively used, rather than passively collected as untouchable objects of devotion. Acutely aware of the repercussions that this combination of factors would have on the impact of his teachings, in the late 1880s Wicksteed took the next step on his educational mission and decided to put to use his translating skills, developed during his ministry and systematically exercised with his Extension lectures.

Wicksteed's first published translation appeared in 1896: an abridged edition of Giovanni Villani's *Cronache*, a medieval history of the city of Florence written between the 1320s and the 1340s. In the introduction, Wicksteed stated that the book was conceived not as 'as a contribution to the study of Villani, but as an aid to the study of Dante', as all the passages translated from the first nine books were chosen because they contained references to 'Dante's works on which the text has a direct bearing, or towards the discussion of which it furnishes materials' (Wicksteed, 1896: xvi). The work was the result of a collaboration with his eldest daughter, Rose E. Selfe, who was responsible 'for the fidelity of the translation in detail, and for its general tone and style [and] the Indexes' and also '[saw] the work through the press' (Wicksteed, 1896: xvi). As editor, Wicksteed selected the passages, supervised and compared the translations to the original, and wrote the historical and bibliographical introduction for most volumes. The book enjoyed a success that spanned well beyond its contemporary public of students and scholars as it reached later generations of Anglo-American *dantisti*, affirming itself as a *unicum*: one of the only fairly extensive and accessible English translations of Villani's *Cronache* to date.

In 1898, Wicksteed introduced the British public to Karl Witte, the German philologist and *dantista*, whose foundational work on the textual criticism of the *Commedia* had strongly influenced the work of the forefathers of British *dantismo*, Henry Clark Barlow and then Edward Moore. Selected from the two volumes of *Dante-Forschungen: Altes und Neues* (1869–79), the *Essays on Dante by Dr. Karl Witte* (1898) was the result of yet another collaboration. This time with the American scholar, C. Mabel Lawrence: here Wicksteed was responsible for 'the biographical introduction, the translation of the Italian portions' of the work and 'the revision and editing of the whole' (Wicksteed, 1898: ii). In the same year, he drafted *A Provisional Translation of The Early Lives of Dante and of His Poetical Correspondence with Giovanni del Virgilio* (1898) which was 'not formally published' but rather 'issued to [his] pupils' as a cheap and convenient introduction to Dante's life (Wicksteed, 1898: 3).

In the late 1890s, Wicksteed joined Herman Oelsen, renowned *dantista* and author of *The Influence of Dante on Modern Thought* (1895), and Thomas Okey, scholar and later Serena Professor of Italian at Cambridge (1919), in the preparation of a scholarly six-volume edition of Dante's complete works. In the division of tasks, Wicksteed took on the editing and translation of *Paradiso*, *Convivio* and the Latin works; Oelsen worked on the 'revised text of John Atken Carlyle's 1849 version of the *Inferno*' (Havely, 2018) and Okey translated *Purgatorio*. Together, Okey and Oelsen undertook the *Vita Nuova* 'published along with *Early Italian Poets* in D. G. Rossetti's 1861 version, edited by Edmund Gardner' (Havely, 2018). The new edition presented the original text with a facing English translation, accompanied by marginal notes and closing commentaries as aids to comprehension.

The publisher, Joseph Malaby Dent, commissioned the whole project to be included in the successful series called *Temple Classics* he had recently begun publishing. Havely noted that along with Wicksteed, Okey and Dent were both 'a product of the autodidact culture that flourished among self-improving Victorian artisans' and 'working-class families' (Havely, 2018). Both self-taught in modern languages, their interest in Dante was deeply rooted in a shared interest in Italian language, literature and culture as well as a common involvement with the 'social settlement movement' that, similarly to the Extension movement, was bringing 'cultured thought [...] in touch' with the working classes (Havely, 2018).

The idea for the *Temple Classics* had come to Dent from his 'sound and at times ruthless business sense' for which he had 'recognized an enormous potential demand for cheap classics among self-educated readers', and which also happened to be 'out of copyright' (Havely, 2018: n.p.). Chronologically, the *Temple Dante* was the second undertaking that followed the 'immense vogue of the beautiful and scholarly Temple Shakespeare' (Herford, 1931: 150): a monumental edition in forty volumes, 'published at a shilling a volume and eventually selling 5 million copies' (Havely, 2018). The choice of Dante as the follow-up project in the autumn of 1896 signalled the continuity of the process of cultural appropriation through which Dante was being progressively assimilated to the national literary canon. From conception to final publication, the project took less than a decade (1896–1906) to be completed: a period during which Wicksteed fulfilled a range of different functions as translator and editor of the English text, curator of the commentaries, notes, concise essays or schematics included in each volume.

The *Temple Dante* was positively received by a large and varied readership, and particularly appreciated for its distinctive material features:

> when size and price (2s. for the leather, and 1s. 6d. for the cloth, copies) are taken into account, the most attractive cheap re-prints ever issued from a British press. [...] The book is small enough, and slim enough, and soft enough to lie easily in the pocket – the covers, though of strong green leather, are limp. The print is clear and pleasant to the eye, and the paper (though a trifle too thin) is sound, and agreeable to sight and touch. This thinness of the paper is indeed the only fault of these little books. It cannot be denied that to a certain extent it lets through the print from the other side.
>
> (*Spectator*, 1899: 2)

Addressed to 'the cultured or culture-seeking public, not primarily of scholars' (2), the *Temple Dante* served all of Wicksteed's ideological purposes: it had turned Dante's works into popular commodities affordable and accessible for either academic study or leisure reading. The selection of texts on which Wicksteed concentrated his energies tackled not the core of Dante's literary production, but rather the historical, critical and biographical margins identified with that range of secondary sources, which had so far appealed only to the 'narrowest circle of readers' (Wicksteed, 1922: vii). For Herford, such choices were motivated by the intention 'to expose the superficiality of the popular and even of the educated judgement, fortified by the crude sensationalism of illustrators like Doré, which emblematized Dante as the poet of *Inferno*, but ignored the *Paradiso* as a tissue of scholastic sermons' (Herford, 931: 152–3). In making the third *cantica* 'the first portion of the *Comedy* ... widely accessible' (Wicksteed, 1896: n.p.), Wicksteed tackled the common, prejudicial and hierarchical understanding of Dante's poetry by conveying sophisticated scholarly knowledge in the corpus of notes and arguments accompanying the translated text – a position reiterated by his limited participation in the Temple *Inferno* and *Purgatorio* and in his extensive involvement in the translation, editing and overall rehabilitation of Dante's philosophical and political works still largely unknown to the wider public.

Wicksteed's editorial note to his *Paradiso* illuminates his translational practices as he 'attempted first and foremost to satisfy himself as to the author's exact meaning, and then to express it (1) precisely (2) with lucidity (3) worthily (4) with as close adherence to the vocabulary and syntax of the original as English idiom allows' (Wicksteed, 1899: 416). Additionally, it expresses his personal expectations for the ultimate use of his translations 'taken only as a help to the understanding of Dante's words, not as a substitute for them' (417). Finally, it explains the use and nature of the 'Arguments': short introductory segments placed at the beginning of each *canto* designed 'to be helpful to the beginner as well as of interest to the more advanced student, as an attempt to facilitate the perception of the perspective, the articulation, and the wider significance of several portions of the poem' (417).

In 1903 Wicksteed published his translation of the *Convivio* complete with notes and two large appendices, which largely followed the text of Edward Moore's *Oxford Dante*. A year later, in 1903, Dent issued the volume of *Latin Works*, which included the *De Vulgari Eloquentia*, the *De Monarchia*, the *Epistolae* and the *Eclogues*. Of these, Wicksteed had already drafted provisional translations of Dante's letters and treatise on the Empire for his Extension students, issued respectively in 1896 and 1898. In this respect, particularly noteworthy is the fact that Wicksteed's translations of the *Eclogues* – two Latin poems written by Dante in 1319 to Giovanni del Virgilio, Professor of Latin at the University of Bologna – is still held by contemporary scholars as the standard reference edition, unsurpassed by the later translation authored by Wilmon Brewer in 1927.[6] For the Temple Dante, he also curated the notes on the arrangement and chronology of Dante's Hell for *Inferno* as well as the 'Arguments' and a note on the chronology of *Purgatorio*. Based on the evidence of the syllabi, all those critical interventions were revised and implemented versions of some of his Extension lectures and teaching materials. Wicksteed also worked on the last volume of the *Temple Dante* published in 1906, for which he provided the translation of Dante's *Canzoniere* printed together with the *Vita Nuova* translated and annotated by Okey.

The *Temple Dante* had a far-reaching impact on Dante's twentieth-century reception in Britain and the United States. According to Havely's reconstruction, Ezra Pound was 'thankful' for the material convenience of 'the Temple bilingual edition' because 'it saved one from consulting Witte, Toynbee, God knows whom'; Thomas S. Eliot found that it was of great help for puzzling out the *Commedia* and used it 'both early and late in his career ... with only a little modernizing, as the framework for the translations throughout his 1929 *Dante* essay' (Havely, 2014: 270–1).

Wicksteed's last act: the scholarly heritage

The study of Dante represented the pivot of Philip H. Wicksteed's intellectual life and the foremost preoccupation of his fifty-year-long eclectic career that saw him take on four hermeneutic roles, linked to one another. The trail of the Unitarian preacher and his sermons, in fact, resonated in the teachings of the Extension lecturer: a thirty-year-long engagement that presented him with both the necessity and the opportunity of becoming a Dante translator. Only once he had completed the educational mission of providing 'access for plain folks to the soul of Dante' (Herford, 1931: 313) through both lectures and translations, Wicksteed took on the robe of the traditional academic scholar, spending his final years working on two studies.

Dante and Aquinas was largely based on the series of lectures delivered for the Jowett Lectureship at the Passmore Edwards settlement in 1911 and published by Dent in 1913. Here, Wicksteed ventured into the realm of medieval philosophy and theology, a ground on which he confessed to being 'but a casual traveller' to the point of warning his readers that 'when references to other than the original form are given it implies, in various degrees, not only indebtedness, but dependence on the secondary authorities cited' (Wicksteed, 1913: ix). These served to enhance the current understanding of Dante's work by throwing out 'its distinctive features against the background of the accepted and authoritative exposition of the received philosophy and theology of his time, while at the same time enriching his utterances by relating them to the implications and presuppositions on which they were grounded' (viii). Although Wicksteed conceived the 'sketch of the scholastic philosophy, and especially of the teaching of Aquinas' as 'a disinterested and popular treatment of the subject free from all propagandist or polemical intention', the book engaged in an interpretative endeavour too abstract to grasp the 'interest, or at the lowest curiosity' (viii) of the large and socially varied public Wicksteed had been so far used to address and educate. Despite his best efforts, the book was not well received:

> If the Dante lectures won for Wicksteed hosts of potential friendships and not a few real and lasting ones, his devotion to the laborious discipline of Dante's master, Aquinas, did more perhaps to repel rather than conciliate. A Unitarian Thomist was bewildering or suspect to the orthodox of either order, a religious mongrel with whom the true-bred did not mate.
>
> (Herford, 1931: 134)

During that time, however, Wicksteed had found yet another way of establishing a critical interaction with the national and international communities of Dante scholars that would ultimately legitimise the academic value of his own contributions. Soon after the completion of the *Temple Classics*, in fact, Wicksteed began writing for the *Hebbert Journal* and the *Modern Language Review* book reviews of some of the most prominent publications in the field, including Edward Moore's *Studies in Dante – Third Series*, Michele Barbi's seminal edition of the *Vita Nuova*, Vincenzo Biagi's commentary on the *Quaestio de Aqua et Terra* and Charles Shadwell's English translation and edition of the same.[7] Apart from the balance between Italian and English scholarship, those reviews represented a crucial test bed for Wicksteed's expertise in textual criticism, philological and manuscript studies on which his critical account of such studies largely relied. Additionally, Wicksteed published a couple of original articles for *The Modern Language Review*: one, in 1916, entitled 'On the Disputed Reading in Dante's Epist. V 129,130' and the other, in 1921, on 'The Ethical System of the *Inferno*' on which he had lectured for the Extension Movement.[8]

Finally, in that same year, he also participated in the collection of essays *Dante. Essays in Commemoration 1321–1921*, edited by Paget Toynbee and published in honour of the Dante Sexcentenary, with an article on 'Dante and the Latin Poets'.[9] During this time he also became a member of the Manchester Dante Society, delivering lectures and participating in the monthly meetings. The year 1922 was the moment in which Wicksteed's variousness of hermeneutical efforts in the study of Dante found a point of unitary convergence in his last published word on Dante: the volume *From Vita Nuova to Paradiso*. The two long essays engaged in a systematic and comprehensive exposition of the ideological principle that had guided his work on Dante from the very beginning: the 'conviction that Dante's life and work were an organic whole, to which all merely fragmentary approach was futile' (Herford, 1931: 173). In a letter written in January 1921 to J. Lloyd Thomas, a fellow *dantista*, Wicksteed explained that his main purpose was 'to bring all Dante's work into relation with the "Visio Dei" at the end of Paradiso' (Herford, 1931: 173). Even at its higher scholarly stage, Wicksteed's educational mission was characterised by an essential unity of vision and continuity of form. The latest work was 'no mere summary of what he had said before' because it was 'a presentation, in many respects, new of the works especially of the *Convivio* and *Monarchia*, which, as ordinarily understood, were very indirectly related' (172).

Philip H. Wicksteed's work on Dante demonstrated how his preaching, teaching and translating activities gave origin to a form of *dantismo* that, in being scholarly and commercial, specialised and democratic at the same time, was able to redefine the conditions of the intellectual and material access to Dante and his works for the fast-growing, socially diverse public of general readers from the late Victorian period.

Notes

1 Although those materials were eventually returned to their owners, the *Herford-Wicksteed Papers* held in the library of the Harris Manchester College at the University of Oxford contain a sizeable body of authentic materials, particularly useful for illustrating Herford's process of selection and use of that vast array of resources for the construction of his biographical account.
2 For a broader outline of the nineteenth-century university reforms and Adult Higher Education, see R. D. Anderson, *Universities and Elites in Britain since 1800* (Cambridge: Cambridge University Press, 1995); S. Marriott, *A Backstairs to a Degree: Demands for an Open University in Late Victorian England* (Leeds: Department of Adult Education and Extramural Studies, University of Leeds, 1981).
3 For Emily Davies' and the Langham Place Group campaigns for women's education, see E. Davies, *The Higher Education of Women* (London: Alexander Straham, 1866); *Thoughts on Some Questions Relating to Women, 1860–1908* (Cambridge: Bowes and Bowes, 1910); E. Davies, *Emily Davies: Collected Letters, 1861–1875*, ed. by A. Murphy and D. Raftery (Charlottesville: University of Virginia Press, 2004); A. Rosen, 'Emily Davies and the Women's Movement 1862–1867', *Journal of British Studies*, 19:1 (1979), pp. 101–21; D. Bennett, *Emily Davies and the Liberation of Women: 1830–1921* (London: Andre Deutsch, 1990). For the history of women's education and Victorian feminism, see also M. Bryant, *The Unexpected Revolution: A Study in the History of the Education of Women and Girls in the Nineteenth Century* (London: University of London, Institute of Education, 1979); B. Caine, *Victorian Feminists* (Oxford: Oxford University Press,1992).
4 Compared to those established in Cambridge (1873) and Oxford (1878), the London Society was 'organised along slightly different lines: London University conferred degrees but was not a teaching body at this time, so the work of the Society was monitored by a Universities Joint Board, made up of three representatives from Oxford, Cambridge and London who recruited lecturers, organised courses, appointed examiners and awarded certificates' (Lawrie, 2014: 57).

5 These included A. J. Symonds, *An Introduction to the Study of Dante* (London: Smith, Elder and Co., 1872); Richard Church, *Dante and Other Essays* (London: Macmillan and Co., 1888); Edmund G. Gardner, *Dante* (London: J. M. Dent, 1900).
6 Wicksteed produced an additional edition of the *Eclogues* edited and translated in collaboration with Edmund G. Gardner and published by Constable in 1902. *Dante and Giovanni del Virgilio including a critical edition of the text of Dante's 'Eclogae latinae' and of the poetic remains of Giovanni del Virgilio*, trans. and ed. by Philip H. Wicksteed and Edmund G. Gardner (Westminster: Constable and Co., 1902); *Dante's Eclogues: The Poetical Correspondence between Dante and Giovanni del Virgilio*, trans. by Wilmont Brewer (Boston: Cornhill Publishing and Co., 1927).
7 These included: Philip H. Wicksteed, '"Treachery of Ciphers", Review of Moore's Studies in Dante, 3rd Series', *Hibbert Journal*, 2 (1904), pp. 634–6; 'Edward Moore, *Tutte le Opere di Dante Alighieri*', *Hibbert Journal*, 2 (1904), pp. 600–2; 'La Vita Nuova di Dante Alighieri per cura di M. Barbi', *Modern Language Review*, 3 (1908), p. 183; 'La Quaestio de Aqua et Terra di Dante Alighieri by Vincenzo Biagi', *Modern Language Review*, 4 (1909), 254–8; 'Dante. Quaestio de Aqua et Terra by Charles Lancelot Shadwell', *Modern Language Review*, 5 (1910), pp. 255–6.
8 Philip H. Wicksteed, 'On the Disputed Reading in Dante's Epist. V 129', 130, *Modern Language Review*, 11 (1916), p. 69; 'The Ethical System of the Inferno', *Modern Language Review*, 16 (July 1921), pp. 265–80.
9 Philip H. Wicksteed, 'Dante and the Latin Poets', in *Dante: Essays in Commemoration 1321–1921*, ed. by the Dante Sexcentenary Committee (London: University of London Press, 1921), pp. 157–88.

5

Academic networks: Dante studies in Victorian Britain

From the Romantic literary lectures through Arnold's lectures-turned-essays to Wicksteed's itinerant Extension courses, the nineteenth century amply demonstrated the highly teachable nature of Dantean textuality, now accessible to a vast and heterogeneous public of students with diverse levels of education, ability and interest.

Synchronous to these mechanisms of widening popularisation was the increasing specialisation of British *dantisti* who had turned the study of Dante into the sole and legitimate object of their 'creative research' and 'original' scholarship (Lubenow, 2015: 33). As much as the former phenomenon benefited from the 1860s university reforms that were bringing much-needed modernisation to the curriculum and to academic teaching practices, many felt quelled by the tyranny of examinations, which left little space for – and often undermined – the pursuit of knowledge for knowledge's sake. William C. Lubenow has argued that up until the early decades of the twentieth century, teachers and students interested in conducting original research gathered around the dining tables of clubs and modern learned societies. In this capacity, they

> formed interpretive communities within the universities, and without, which provided their members with the things that their colleges and courses of study could not provide: comradeship and mental as well as emotional stimulation [...] even those devoted to dining and drinking, contributed to the organization of knowledge by their creation of a culture of sociability.
>
> (Lubenow, 2015: 34)

Throughout the nation and the empire, the learned men (and more rarely, women) met in clubs and societies constituted as 'communities of practice' that actively fostered 'the discovery and legitimization of curiosity, originality, and objectivity' (34) through cooperative and, oftentimes, competitive work. Among the plethora of associations that came into existence during the century, there were those formed by 'small but productive group(s)' of *dantofili* who founded the three distinct Dante societies in the academic, political and industrial capitals of the country: Oxford, London and Manchester and their related university environments.

This chapter illustrates how these very societies vehiculated the individual efforts into a synergically coordinated activity – oriented towards the differentiation of the critical discipline from the broad field of medieval studies and the definition of its research interests, methodologies and social and cultural channels of communication. Despite their 'localised' specificity, each of these societies produced knowledge 'via transfer processes in cross-border networks' (Kirchberger, 2014: 3), establishing solid exchanges with their institutional counterparts in Germany, Italy and the United States. This was anticipated by (and eventually overlapped with) a marked intensification of 'informal contacts' (5) between individuals or smaller groups of scholars and enthusiasts through private correspondences, meetings, exchange of publications and even joined research travels. Initially configured as formal, highly hierarchical discipleship where prominent scholars acted patrons for younger researchers, these relationships progressively evolved into 'free and equal cooperation between scholars pursuing common research interests' (7).

In different forms and extents, the British Dante societies functioned as network structures that not only fostered 'intellectual companionship, trust and personal friendship' among all members (Kirchberger, 2014: 6). They also stimulated the 'gaining and exchanging of knowledge, skills and techniques, the pooling of complementary knowledge, the ability to access important material necessary for research as well as a desire to make the acquaintance of influential patrons and groups of researchers' (6). Their concerted action determined macroscopic changes in the modes of collective reading; positive reconstruction and collaborative interpretation of Dantean textuality as well as transformations in the practices of book-collecting and dissemination of scholarly and popular knowledge. As the Societies catalysed 'the cultural turn to academic literary studies' (Armstrong, 2013: 4), they also redefined the forms and practices of Dante studies as a specialised, document-oriented scholarly activity, one that was practised not only and no longer by generalist critics like Coleridge and Arnold, but by a growing cohort of 'practitioners who sought to give it an increasingly scientific rationale and methodology' (Atherton, 2005: 61–2).

This chapter draws on Lubenow's 'themes' of inquiry – 'the nature and character' of the society including their membership as well as the 'character' and 'manner' of their scholarly pursuits (Lubenow, 2015: 26) – the chapter demonstrates that the major advancements in Victorian *dantismo* came from the synergetic 'enterprise' of a group of highly motivated self-taught 'savants' and 'devotees' that gave shape and purpose to scholarly 'expertise' (Kargon, 1977: 79).

The Anglo-German connection and the emergence of the philological method

In his historiographical survey, Steve Botterill fixed the point of origin 'of a specifically British tradition of academic Dantology' in 1876, the 'year that saw the foundation of both the Oxford Dante Society and the Dante lectureship at University College London' (Botterill, 1993: 245–6). Both events were indirectly indebted to the personal and professional encouragement of Karl Witte, the foremost *dantista* in Germany, to Henry Clark Barlow and Edward Moore, respectively the endower of the lecture series and the society's founder and first president. For Barlow, this was a traditionally hierarchical 'relationship based on the teacher-pupil model' (Ellis, 2014: 25). Differently, for Moore, it reflected a 'more flexible idea of mutual exchange and collaboration' (37) largely developed over correspondence.

A young prodigy who could speak five languages by the age of nine (German, French, Italian, Latin and Greek), a Doctor of Philosophy by training and a jurist by profession, Karl Witte discovered Dante during his travels in Italy between 1818 and 1821. During this time, he began participating in the activities of the Roman-based Nazareni, collecting Italian editions and commentaries on the *Commedia* and delivering public exposition on *Inferno* for 'the circle of artists gathered in the house of Luigia Seidler in Rome' (Folena, 1967: 31–2). His rapid ascent to authority derived from a combination of attitude, self-promotion among the inner circles of Italian *letterati* and *dantisti*, and a precise intentionality oriented to the creation of a system of study applied to Dantean textuality, both individual and collective.

By 1824, in fact, Witte was advocating 'a return to the study of the earliest interpreters and commentators against the moderns' (Folena, 1967: 33) and concurrently setting forth a highly refined methodological approach, implemented in his pioneering critical edition of the *Commedia*. In 1865 he presented an unrhymed German translation of the poem in iambic metres, followed by critical editions of the *Monarchia* (Vienna, 1874) and *Vita Nuova* (Leipzig, 1876). In addition, he collected his vast corpus of critical notices, articles and essays in two volumes titled *Dante-Forschungen* (1869; 1879), a selection of which was later translated into English by Philip Wicksteed. As amply demonstrated by John Lindon and Giancarlo Folena, Witte's works reached beyond the German borders, widely appreciated by the Italian, British and North American scholarly communities as a foundational contribution to international *dantismo*.

Along with his solitary research, Witte was also the first to argue for the creation of a cultural institution devoted to the production, circulation and dissemination of Dantean knowledge within and beyond Germany. Two decades before the Società Dantesca Italiana and in symbolic conjunction with the Dante centenary, Witte established Deutsche Dante-Gesellschaft in Dresden in 1865 under the royal protectorate of the King Johann of Saxony (a Dante enthusiast himself, author of a well-received translation of the *Commedia* under the synonym of Philalethes). The foundational aim was to disseminate the knowledge and the public understanding of Dante's oeuvre in Germany through cooperation towards the correctness of the text of the *Commedia* and to the explanation of the same and other Dante's works; the creation of a Dante library to be established in Dresden; the issue of an *Annuario* for dissertations on Dante's works, speeches and reviews (Scartazzini, 1881: 25).

Titled *Jahrbuch der Deutschen Dante-Gesellschaft*, the first issue was published in 1865. The decision to fund the publication of a journal is historically significant not only because the *Jahrbuch* is still active to this day, but because Witte recognised the importance of *communicating* the discoveries and advancement made by the society to the wider world. Taking on the general editorship, Witte soon began writing to foreign correspondents inviting papers, reviews and articles thus forming to all effects the first transatlantic scholarly network for the historical, textual and socio-political reconstruction of Dante's life and oeuvre. Similarly, this led to the creation of a shared Dante collection filled with rare editions and translations bestowed from the private collection of members and bibliophiles or recent publications sent by scholars, either spontaneous or by invitation: a crucial space for centralising the perusal of both primary and secondary sources that were until then regulated by personal contact.

Initially, the German Dante Society consisted of a small group of German scholars such as the philologist Ekkehart Boehmer, Adolf Mussafia and F. X. Wegele. Shortly after, however, membership was opened to high representatives of the wealthy German aristocracy (whose generous donations ensured the survival of the institution until the late nineteenth century) while the presence of 'a handful of Italians among its members' was perceived 'as a threat to the Society's autonomy' (Lindon, 1989: 90–1). Such tension was ultimately resolved with the admission of other foreign honorary members from Britain and North America such as Henry C. Barlow and Henry W. Longfellow as 'counterweight to Italian influence' (90–1). The society grew steadily over the course of a decade (counting 90 members in 1867, and 137 by 1872) during which it gathered three times: first in Dresden (1865), then twice in Halle (1867 and 1877). Witte's death in 1883 marked the end of its nineteenth-century activities, even though the scholar F. X. Klaus tried to revive them with the help of the Società Dantesca Italiana at the turn of the century.

The later British Dante Societies saw in the *Dante-Gesellschaft* – the very first institution of its kind to be established on both sides of the Atlantic, anticipating almost two decades the Dante Society of America (1880) and the Società Dantesca Italiana (1888) – a model for the definition of the methodological approach, the coordination of internal activities and the paths of dissemination of their works. As for Witte, his *dantismo* grounded on the philological reconstruction of the Dantean text through the codicological examination of the manuscripts set forth a model that had a far-reaching impact on the modes of reading and studying practised by Henry Clark Barlow and Edward Moore. As we shall see, the Anglo-German connection produced a paradigmatic shift from aesthetic to textual and historical criticism in British Dante studies: one that laid the ground for its institutionalisation as a *disciplina nobile* that brought together philology, codicology, history, philosophy and literature.

Henry Clark Barlow and the challenge of textual criticism

Like Witte (and many of his countrymen and women) Henry Clark Barlow discovered Dante during his five-year-long sojourn in Italy begun in 1841 and divided between Florence, Rome, Naples and Milan. Initially, he directed his attention to the study and sketching of Italian architecture, sculpture and painting: a reminiscence of his earlier studies at the Royal Academy of Arts abruptly interrupted in 1835 and abandoned for a degree in medicine at Edinburgh. In the winter of 1844–45, Barlow was in Pisa where he decided to attend the popular lectures of Professor Silvestro Centofanti, whose discussion on the philosophy of history rested upon the use 'as his textbook of the *Vita Nuova* of the poet' (Barlow, 1868: 8).

Once discovered, 'the great Poet of Italy and Europe ... became the Doctor's Idol' to the point that 'the study and illustration of the Poet's work now took precedence over everything else' (Barlow, 1868: 8). This translated into the continuous reading of the *Commedia* constantly carried in his pockets, and a series of peregrinations to the places mentioned by the poet, ultimately culminating with 'a pilgrimage to Ravenna, the Mecca of all Dantophilists' (8) in October 1847. While in Florence, Barlow had become a close acquaintance of Seymour Kirkup who welcomed him in his home to consult his outstanding private Dante collection 'rich in early editions and boasting various manuscripts' and to discuss his research of 'the Dante relics still extant in Florence' or his most recent 'artistic collaboration in the lavish *Inferno* projected by Lord Vernon's edition of Jacopo Alighieri's *Chiose* to the Inferno' (Lindon, 2000: 125).

The circumstances of Barlow's first encounter with Witte were at once produced by and producers of a wide, transnational network of nineteenth-century Dante scholars from Germany, Italy and Britain. It is possible that Barlow's initial indirect contact with Witte came through Kirkup, who had known the German professor 'at least since 1831' but remained quite cold towards him as 'an incomparable, but mere, linguist' (Lindon, 2000: 128).

According to Lindon's documentary reconstructions, the introductory meeting with Witte occurred on 24 October in the professor's study in Halle. Once again, the visit was made possible by the mediation of yet another *dantofilo*, the illustrator Carl Christian Vogel von Vogelstein, who had recently completed a painting with ten episodes from the *Commedia* along with a portrait of Dante. After that occasion, Vogel became one of Barlow's most assiduous correspondents and promoters of his scholarly works in Munich and within the circles of German literati. During Barlow's two consecutive visits, Witte not only 'loaded' him with 'pamphlets, papers and maps' to further his private studies, but also recruited him within 'honoured roll of assistants' (Lindon, 1989: 79) collaborating with his monumental, thirty-year-long project: the first critical edition of the *Commedia*. Originally set out to reconstruct the text on the collation of more than 400 manuscripts, the professor's plan was ultimately scaled down as he 'resorted to the *pis-aller* of a "provisional" text' based on 'four manuscripts (Villani, Vatican, Rodd and Caetani) judged, from the evidence of the *Inf. 3*, to be outstanding authoritative' (Lindon, 2013: 438).

Barlow was assigned to the collection of the *varianti* of the *canto* from the manuscripts held at the British Museum, accessible to him thanks to Witte's personal letter of introduction to Panizzi, the librarian in chief. The task took several months to complete: 'the collations and a short accompanying letter in Italian occupy three sides of a large folded sheet ... bearing the postmark 27 May 1850' (Lindon, 2013: 80). In a letter to Vogel, Barlow defined the terms of his discipleship naming the professor as his 'spiritual Father in Dante' towards whom his 'heart turned with filial regard and affection' (79) because the possession of the 'Dante diploma' (84) – the letter to Panizzi – opened for him the doors to the consultation rooms of the British Museum. This would lay the foundations for a life-long collaboration with the 'Keeper of MSS, Sir Frederick Madden' who later began 'to submit Dante MSS to [him] before purchase for the Museum' (80), thus recognising Barlow's scholarly authority in the country. Initially, however, Witte's assignment gave impetus and direction to Barlow's studies, actively reconfiguring his amateur interest into a serious, professional(ising) occupation based on self-taught specialism in codicology and philology. Barlow's personal notebooks detail his analytical attention to the manuscripts, examined in their linguistic features but also their physical structure and material of the writing support, number of pages or folios, description of layout texts, script, binding, decoration and other features of their production.

After the satisfactory completion of the assignment, Barlow's activity of description and categorisation of the 'Dante manuscripts became increasingly important to him as an object of travel' (Lindon, 2013: 79) – an occupation that led him to visit libraries all over Europe and collect and study over 150 manuscripts over the course of four years, 1849–52, as well as during the following decade, when he returned to the codices in Florence (1865) and at the British Museum (1867). Relying on his advanced drawing skills, Barlow reproduced with minute accuracy the illuminated rubrics (opening and final), incipits and explicits, noteworthy lines or entire passages in the original scripts. These were interleaved with a detailed running commentary in which he combined aesthetic appreciation of the material artefact with the critical assessment of emendations and revisions, personal comments and discussion of the exegetical tradition. Disseminated among multiple, large and small, lined and plain notebooks, the research activity formed a descriptive catalogue of *codici*, editions and even translations examined that he routinely revised and expanded – as demonstrated by the thick layer of marginal annotations covering the borders of the pages. Either orderly transcribed in ink or disorderly traced in pencil, the personal papers document the intensification and diversification of Barlow's private study of Dante spread among notices and general remarks, lengthier dissertations and exegetical notes on Dante's works, life and times; commentaries and *chiose* to the *Commedia*; tables of allegories and metaphors; and diagrams and maps of the three realms of the afterlife.

These very notes provided the substance for the numerous studies published over the course of two decades thanks to a *sodalizio* with William and Norgate, publishers and book importers specialised in both British and foreign scholarly and scientific literature. With them, Barlow gave to the presses his *Remarks on the Reading of the 59th Verse of the 5th Canto of the* Inferno (1850); *Il Gran Rifiuto, What It Was, Who Made It, and How Fatal to Dante Allighieri, a Dissertation on Verses 58 to 63 of the 3rd Canto of the* Inferno (1862); as well as *Il Conte Ugolino e L'Arcivescovo Ruggieri: a Sketch from the Pisan Chronicles* (1862). His *Francesca da Rimini, Her Lament and Vindication; with a Brief Notice of the Malatesti* (1859) became one of Barlow's most popular and enduring contributions to Dante studies. In the study, the textual examination of the *varianti* of a line of *Inferno* V was followed by a compelling commentary on the *canto* as well as a ground-breaking interpretation of the figure of Francesca that stirred the interest of international scholars. As John Lindon argued, Barlow's continuous returns to the manuscripts of the *Commedia* did not seek 'to establish a new text, but revise the *vulgata* by trying to settle *ope codicum* the unresolved textual *cruces*' (Lindon, 2013: 437).

Published with a view to 'the approaching festival of Dante Allighieri', Barlow presented his *Critical, Historical, and Philosophical Contributions to the Study of the Divina Commedia* in October 1864: a 'laborious work' and 'the result of many years' research in the public libraries of Italy, France, Germany, Denmark and England' (Barlow, 1864: 2). According to his memoir, Barlow sent a copy of the book 'to all principal libraries of Europe' (Barlow, 1868: 17). In Italy, the work was well received and even awarded a silver medal of honour at the Mostra Dantesca organised by the Municipality of Florence. The *Contributions* unified and systematised the notebooks materials according to a two-part structure, beginning with the codicological analysis of the manuscripts of the *Commedia* grouped geographically, followed by a critical reading of selected passages based on the early commentary tradition. Despite Barlow's self-consciousness about the lack of the 'methodological manner', Italian scholars praised his textual approach adopting many of his 'proposed readings' and 'data for variants' (Lindon, 2013: 438) as in the case of Brunone

Bianchi in the fourth edition of his oft-republished commentary and Giovanni Scartazzini's pioneering edition of the *Commedia*. Barlow was invited to take part in the organisation of the 1865 Florentine Dante Festival as a foreign representative and correspondent of the festival. In this capacity, he documented his activities and later collated his notes in the volume *The Sixth Centenary Festivals of Dante Allighieri in Florence and at Ravenna*. The *opuscolo*, published in 1866 both in England and Italy, was a day-by-day record of the festival with detailed annotations of the people and the activities taking place like public discourses and lectures, the inauguration of the Mostra Dantesca, the assembly in Piazza Santo Spirito and the procession to Santa Croce. At the end of the celebrations, the King of Italy bestowed on Barlow the title of *cavaliere* of the order of SS Maurizio e Lazzaro for the prominent part he took in the promotion and organisation of the celebrations. Honoured alongside Lord Vernon and Seymour Kirkup, this symbolic investment was the means through which the British contribution to Dante studies, uniquely, received official recognition.

During these and the following decades, Barlow's network of scholarly correspondence and contacts grew exponentially with 'some 320 letters from upwards 100 correspondents, many of them notable figures in the history of Dante studies: Ashburnham, Boehmer, Emiliani Giudici, Kirkup, Laicata, Norton, the two Lord Vernon and Witte' (Lindon, 1988: 54). The German professor was no longer his sole authority of reference and the correspondence with him became more intermittent and often instrumental to either the promotion of recent publications or the intermediation of research favours. Witte's letters almost regularly contained the polite request to publicise his works within 'the rich English market' (Lindon, 1989: 86) with short notices and lengthier reviews in the periodicals of which Barlow had become a regular contributor: *Morning Post*, *Pantheon* and, most importantly, *Athenaeum*. Barlow penned thirty-four pieces (reviews and original articles) for the latter outlet, published between 1857 and 1872. Integrally transcribed by Lindon, the missives reveal that Witte sought to influence Barlow's reviewing practice, openly requesting him to comment and commend upon the ground-breaking nature of the 'sistema fondamentale della mia critica, cioe' di non ammettere neanche una parola del testo che non sia fondata sopra l'uno o l'altro' (Lindon, 1989: 87). Witte also voiced his concern for the unitary preservation and wider dissemination of Barlow's own miscellaneous writings on Dante and invited him to take on measures similar to his own:

> E' veramente un peccato che tanti articoli pieni di ingegno e di dottrina, abbiano a perdersi nei diversi giornali in cui furono stampati. Posso dire che la mia impresa di raccogliere in tal modo le mie cose sparse in non so quanti luoghi fu generalmente applaudita, e vi aggiungo che mi rincrescerebbe di non leggerne in qualche giornale il vostro giudizio.
> (Lindon, 1989: 103)

In his reply, Barlow voiced his resentment against 'the mercenary publishers [who] will have nothing to do with' the 'many manuscripts, the labours of years, which would make a literary fortune for their author if printed' (Lindon, 1989: 104). Despite having achieved a transnational reputation as one of the 'migliori o il migliore dei cultori delle cose Dantesche in Inghilterra' (89) and the general growing interest for matters of textual criticism, the publishers' reticence demonstrated that times were not ripe enough for the British *dantismo*. Towards the end of his life, Barlow published articles in the *Jarhbuch*, a short volume *On the Vernon Dante and Other Dissertations* – in which he had praised Witte's monumental work – and two more philological studies on the *Testi di tre canti della Divina Commedia tratti da codici conservati nella biblioteca del Museo Britannico* (1870) and *Seicento lezioni della Divina Commedia tratte dall'edizione di Napoli* (1875).

The ultimate, and most lasting, contribution came after his death when he bequeathed a 'sum of one thousand pounds in consols the dividends of which were to be applied in perpetuity to the delivery of a public annual course of lectures on the Divina Commedia, free to both sexes' (Lindon, 1977: 8). The decision had been in the making since the Dante Festival during which he had become 'well acquainted with the more fortunate state of continental Dante scholarship: intellectually, or at any rate philologically, more advanced and materially more favored' (Whiting, 1921: 173) than the British one. Determined to encourage the development of a national scholarly tradition in Britain, his course had to consist of at least twelve lectures per year and had to be advertised in the *Times* and the *Athenaeum* 'under the name of "The Barlow Lectures on the Divina Commedia"' (Lindon, 1977: 8), while the University College was responsible for appointing a lecturer on a three-year term, with the possibility of further re-election. Inaugurated in November 1876, the Lectureship was attended by a socially variegated audience intrigued by the public advertisements in newspapers and popular literary magazines and drawn by the open admission to the course for both men and women.

As the chapter will later demonstrate, the Barlow Lectureship played a pivotal part in the institutionalisation and professionalisation of Dante studies in Britain along with creating the space and the book heritage for the foundation of the London Dante Society. Despite this, Barlow's death in November 1876 represented 'the end of one era in English Dante studies, an era Barlow could be said to represent, and the beginning of another dominated by Edward Moore and the Oxford Dante Society: which held its first meeting on 24th of that month' (Lindon, 1989: 110). A fortnight before this occurrence, Moore had also dispatched his first letter to Halle, thus initiating correspondence that in effect had him taking over 'the role of English interlocutor to Witte about to be vacated by Barlow' (Lindon, 1989: 110).

Edward Moore and the institutionalisation of textual criticism

Born in Cardiff in 1835, Edward Moore was educated at Pembroke College, Oxford (1853–57) and elected to an open fellowship at Queen's College in 1858. Ordained in 1859, he became principal of St Edmund Hall in 1864, building the college reputation 'as a home of "true religion and sound learning"' (Armstrong, 1969: ix). A classical scholar by training and practice, Moore's teaching of Aristotle's *Poetics* and *Ethics* 'dwelt mainly on distinct points whether of language or subject matter, collecting and comparing authorities' with the aim of familiarising his students with 'the fruits of German classical philology from the past half-century' (Armstrong, 1969: ix). While the 'first push' towards Dante was perhaps the indirect result of a visit to Italy with R. G. Livingstone in 1863 in view of which they began learning Italian from De Tivoli, the then 'Taylorian Teacher' (ix), the serious scholarly impetus came from Henry F. Tozer.

Moore tackled the study of Dantean textuality 'with a scholarly habit and interests strongly influenced by his professional specialisation' (Lindon, 1989: 106), focusing on the philological analysis, emendation and reconstruction of 'Dante's *ipsissima verba*, whether in prose or poetry' (Armstrong, 1969: xiii). His approach rested on the systematic prioritisation of the manuscript authority and, similarly to Barlow, his travels to the continent were motivated by visits to libraries for manuscript collation. His studies on Dante ranged from the complexities of the chronology of the *Commedia* to crucial issues of textual, historical and philosophical criticism.

In 1889, the *Contributions to the Textual Criticism of the Divina Commedia* granted him a place 'in the front rank of living Dantistas' (Toynbee, 1921a: 28) for being the first British scholarly attempt at establishing the text of Dante's poem on a scientific principle and methodology. The result of laborious research that took him visiting libraries all over Europe – from Oxford, Cambridge and London to Rome, Florence, Milan, Paris and Berlin – the 700-page-long study opened with a critical account of the text of the *Commedia* touching upon questions of manuscript circulation, copyist issues and strategies, causes which have tended to produce variants. It then proceeded with the collation of seventeen manuscripts throughout the whole *Inferno*, followed by the discussion of about 180 passages throughout the poem collated in about 250 manuscripts. Although the collation of the seventeen manuscripts of *Inferno* in Oxford and Cambridge had been successfully completed, the sheer number of documents forced him to opt for the edition of a selected series of key passages throughout the poem. The volume was then concluded with five appendices on various points, including an essay by Tozer on the metre of the *Divina Commedia*. Despite his bespoke resistances, 'Moore clearly worked in conscious self-comparison (yet with a sense of superiority) to his English predecessor' (Lindon, 1988: 72). In his own *Contributions*, the latter's influence remained palpable 'in the study of *loci critici*' as both an expansion of his collations and enhancement of the critical perceptiveness in the 'discussions and proposals for emendations' (72).

During this time, Moore corresponded regularly with Witte, describing his own study as a complementary expansion to the latter's work, restricted to the collation and edition of four selected manuscripts. Particularly responsive to Moore's requests, Witte guided him during the design and the partial realisation of his project, warning him about the difficulties of such a vast enterprise. In spite of his persistent 'methodological uncertainty', the result was a pioneering work in textual criticism that remained unequalled for decades, and which acquired a paradigmatic function in Dante studies, so much so that in 1965 Giancarlo Folena was still considering it as 'the richest and most sophisticated work on the text of the *Commedia* done up to this point' (Lindon, 1988: 30–2).

The sign that time had changed was the comparatively different degree of appreciation that Moore's studies raised among reviewers and the widening circles of *dantofili* and *dantisti*. Whilst Barlow lamented how 'the result of [his] Dante publications in England has been so unsatisfactory that I do not wish to publish anymore' and that all he got 'in return from London Reviewers is abuse' (Lindon, 1989: 93), Moore's studies had been welcomed with 'admiring amazement' from the scholarly community and, even, the general public who later filled the ranks of the lecture halls at University College London. The *Contributions* were presented in the press as a work destined to become henceforth an indispensable aid to the comprehension of the *Commedia* to be used certainly 'not read in a day nor indeed in a good many days' but rather as 'a volume for the student to have at his elbow and consult as he goes along' (*Athenaeum*, 1889: 753). While British reviewers expressed a certain nationalistic pride for the achievement, Italian scholars applauded it as a timely intervention that 'perfectly aligned' with the foundational intent of the Società Dantesca Italiana: that of providing a critical edition of Dante's entire oeuvre. Following in the footsteps of Witte and the Italian textual tradition the work came to 'come essenziale punto di partenza o di riferimento per quanti avrebbero affrontato il piu' arduo problema della filologia testuale italiana' (Lindon, 1989: 72).

In the eyes of the Victorian public, the authoritativeness of Moore's (self-taught, like Barlow's) *dantismo* derived not only from his work, but from his institutional affiliation and prominent role at Oxford, as well as the reputation of his publisher, the

Cambridge University Press. Both in Britain and abroad, reviewers of his *Contributions* accorded particular attention to this datum, often establishing a direct inference of the value of the scholarly contribution as worthy in every respect of its press. Often detailing its publishing history, reviewers pointed out that the volume had been rejected as a bad investment by Oxford University Press, but quickly published by 'the press of the sister University' that could then take 'credit of publishing so important and valuable and aid to the correct understanding of a poem' (*Saturday Review*, 1889: 448). The press's decision to issue the 800-page volume at their own expense was interpreted by many as an endowment to Dantean research and textual studies, which reflected the broader change in university culture.

By the last decades of the century, Moore was the foremost authority in British Dante studies. Nationally and internationally renowned, he regularly published articles in the *Athenaeum*, *Academy*, *Saturday Review* and *Universal Review* as well as volumes such as *The Time References in the* Divina Commedia (1887) and *Dante and His Early Biographers* (1890) – both derived from his cycles of Barlow lectures in London – and a four-volume series of *Studies in Dante* (1896–1917). He was also invested with his institutional role(s) as a Dante lecturer: revolutionising the Barlow Lectureship at University College, London (1886–1909) as well as launching the Taylorian Lectures on Dante at Oxford in 1895. According to a press cutting from the *Academy* reporting the text of the 'Memorial presented to the Curators of the Taylorian Institution on Saturday, May 10', the lectureship was created to provide the 'opportunity ... for the systematic study of the works of Dante and particularly of the *Divina Commedia*' (*Academy*, 1895: 426). Moore was 'excellently qualified for such an appointment' given his work as 'editor of the Complete Works of Dante and author of several works bearing on Dante's history and writing' (*Academy*, 1895: 426). Perhaps to avoid any conflicts of interest, no mention is made of his crucial role as founding President of the Oxford Dante Society even though some of the twenty-eight members of the Congregation were also associates of it, including the Dean of Christ Church, Frances Paget, the President of Magdalene, T. H. Warren, Charles Shadwell and W. P. Ker among others. The Curators' response was positive, and Moore was appointed initially for 'one year' instead of the proposed three-year term, to deliver a course 'of, at least fifteen lectures' (*Academy*, 1895: 426).

The success of his course was such that Moore maintained the position for eleven years during which the study of Dante was to all effects institutionalised at Oxford, after twenty years of existence of the Oxford Dante Society, whose activities remained peripheral to the curriculum of the university. As a form of recognition to the Taylorian institution, Moore bequeathed his private Dante collection to its library. The 'precious library of books' counted 'circa 900 volumes by and about Dante' (Armstrong, 1969: xiv) published between the sixteenth and early twentieth centuries, minutely indexed in a set of pocket-sized address-books kept throughout his life. These were later reunited in a larger book, where the rare books were marked with a cross in red pencil. The collection included an extraordinary array of editions (Italian and foreign), commentaries and translations of Dante's works, critical essays and handbooks, either personally purchased or received as gifts: from Witte's seminal works to Moore's working copies of the *Tutte le Opere di Dante* and other nineteenth-century publications examined in this study, such as Philip Wicksteed's *Six Sermons on Dante* and the *Syllabus of Lectures on Dante* (1889); Maria Francesca Rossetti's *A Shadow of Dante* (1871); Arabella Shore's *Dante for Beginners* (1886) and Alice M. Wyld's *The Dread Inferno* (1904).

The delineation of Moore's individual achievements, however, is instrumental for understanding him as the central figure around which collective energies began to organise leading to the creation of the Oxford Dante Society and the publication of *Tutte Le Opere di Dante*: respectively, the first Dante Society to be established on British soil and the first integral critical edition of Dante's entire oeuvre ever published worldwide.

The construction of the paradigm: the Oxford Dante Society

On 24 November 1876 Moore hosted the inaugural dinner of the Oxford Dante Society in his private residence at St Edmund Hall. According to Moore's manuscript minutes, the meeting was attended by seven of the nine founding members: 'Sig. De Tivoli, Mr Kitchin, Christ Church; Mr. Cheyne, Balliol; Mr. Jackson, Exeter; Mr. Sayce,

Queen's; Mr. Livingstone, Pembroke' with 'Mr. Tozer, Exeter, and Mr. Laing, C.C.C. unavoidably absent' (Toynbee, 1920: 2). It was agreed that the foundational objective of the society should be that of 'stimulat[ing] and forward[ing] the study of the *Divina Commedia*' as well as 'encourag[ing] mutual inquiry as to critical, historical, and other points relating to [Dante's] works' and 'his age' (46).

As a knowledge-making institution, the society sought to bring order and discipline, structure and method to amateur endeavours through rigid criteria of organisation, participation and registration of its scholarly activities. To such intense scholarly commitment corresponded the strict exclusiveness of its admission policies. These prescribed a maximum of fifteen ordinary members with a small number of honorary members elected each year and a few occasional visitors admitted for the evening – all of which were men. On 14 March 1878 the members agreed that 'an explanation or illustration of some passage of Dante's works be included, whenever possible, in the programmes of the Society's Meetings', and that 'the Members reading Papers before the Society be requested, if possible, to inscribe a brief abstract or description of their Paper in a Book to be kept for that purpose by the Honorary Secretary' (Toynbee, 1920: 47–8).

Such intentionality is patent in the rigid, three-fold structure in which the society meetings were carefully organised to maximise the learning output deriving from the plenary conversations. Despite the collegiate spirit, Moore 'insensibly became the despot of the cleverest and most amiable Italian type' enforcing 'discipline' and 'pressure from above to induce members' (Armstrong, 1969: x–xi) to serious and productive engagement in its scholarly activities. Held once a term, the meetings opened with the members' reading of a paper or essay followed by a plenary commentary of two or three passages from Dante's works, one of which at least had to be supplied by the host. The evening closed with the exchange of news about recent Dantean publications, research trips and discoveries and communications to the society. On occasions, members participated in collection-encounters: on 25 May 1880, Moore exhibited two fifteenth-century manuscripts acquired in Rome, of the *Commedia* (c. 1400) and of the *Convivio* (1465).

The lists of presented papers and passages read show the far-reaching variety and sophistication of topics discussed, extending beyond the *Commedia* to encompass the *Convivio, Epistolae* and *Vita Nuova* and *De Vulgari Eloquentia, Quaestio de Aqua et Terra* and *Eclogae*. These tackled issues of transmission, editing and emendation of the manuscripts; ancient and modern commentary traditions; biographical and historical to discussions of the poetic, theological or political systems; and questions of translation and reception, influence and intertextuality. The interleaved abstracts testify to the perpetual refinement of approaches and methods, of structures and lexicon of their Dantean scholarship.

From the semi-private space of the society, the papers reached the (national and international) public sphere and wider dissemination on the pages of periodicals and specialised journals such as the *Athenaeum, Academy* and *Modern Language Review*. Often the discussions led to larger scholarly endeavours like Henry F. Tozer's *English Commentary to Dante's Divina Commedia* (1901) and Charles L. Shadwell's translations *Purgatory* (1892–99), *Paradise* (1915) and the edition of the *Quaestio de Aqua et Terra* (1909). The most prolific member of the society, however, was Paget J. Toynbee, who first joined as an occasional visitor, then became an ordinary member in 1895, and was ultimately elected Honorary Secretary in 1916. In two decades, Toynbee had contributed 31 papers and more than 40 passages for discussion, most of which were later published in the *Academy* and *Athenaeum*, to the *Modern Language Review, Annual Report of the Dante Society of America, Biblioteca storico-critica della letteratura dantesca, Romania* and *Giornale storico della letteratura italiana*. He also published full-length studies, such as the *Dictionary of Proper Names and Notable Matters in the Works of Dante* (1898), *Dante in English Literature from Chaucer to Cary* (1909), *Dante Studies and Researches* (1902) and *Dante Studies* (1921); translations and editions of Dante's works from the handbook *Dante Alighieri* (1900) and his edition of Henry Cary's *Vision* (1900) to the *Epistolae: Dante Alighieri Letters* (1920) – a reference work still current today.

Despite the rich variety of the members' scholarly achievements, Moore lamented in a letter to James Russell Lowell, founder of the Dante Society of America and honorary member of the Oxford Dante Society, that 'our Oxford Dante Socy., though I am sure a source of very great interest + profit to its Members + very great stimulates individual study, does not publish any of its Papers as you do' (Moore, 1889). Moore's regret poignantly demonstrates a certain desire – we don't know if personal or shared among the group – to burst the intimate (almost secretive) bubble of the society to make their endeavours known to the wider, international public through the means of an academic journal, like the German, the American or even the London Dante societies had successfully done. The existence of a journal would have not only created a new and more inclusive site for 'the intercourse of related minds' (Lubenow, 2015: 134) but also made more immediately evident the generative force of the society as a space for the formation and dissemination of original (even innovative) knowledge on Dante's life and works.

Although this proposal was never advanced nor pursued by the society, the size and range of scholarly works produced are still impressive if one considers that the Oxford Dante Society configured itself as an introverted society with limited membership: a small but industrious community of only ten ordinary members, 'subsequently enlarged to twelve' and eventually extended to 'reach the full number of fifteen' (Oxford Dante Society, 1920: 64). The majority were part of the Oxonian academic body and many were also members of the Anglican clergy, a datum which configured the society 'as the institutional expression of the virtual adoption of Dante by the Church of England, during the second-half of the nineteenth century' (Lindon, 1988: 40). Formed along the lines of the many Oxford dining clubs and coteries, the society originated from the gathering of figures of similar social standing and academic authority with 'intellectual and mental affinities' (Lubenow, 2015: 152). As was common at the time, the members 'had no common doctrine but their procedures, the processes by which they worked, created a climate of commensurability', that is, 'an intellectual and mental framework within which they would agree or disagree' (201). Throughout the first forty years of activity, the society brought together into intimate contact those individuals who had begun to turn the study of Dante into the primary object of their scholarly industry. Working within the physical but outside the academic perimeter of Oxford, the society 'supplemented the university formal arrangements' (78) – which did not offer courses on Dante – by creating opportunities for the pursuit of innovative research and the production of pioneering scholarship that laid the groundwork for the following generations.

Like for many other nineteenth-century clubs, societies and coteries, for the Oxford Dante Society 'membership' was a fraught thing' for which 'the culling and sorting, the blackballing and selecting, were complex' (Lubenow, 2015: 150). In order to achieve what Lubenow defined as an ideal 'calibration of their intellectual composition' (133), the founders set out strict membership criteria that could be expanded with a number of honorary members elected by the Committee and from whom they did not require any kind of direct contribution, neither papers nor passages read. Along with them, the society admitted two or three occasional visitors per meeting: 'strangers' who had to be introduced 'only by permission and [by] invitation of the Host for the evening' (Oxford Dante Society, 1920: 46).

The *Record* (Oxford Dante Society, 1920) shows that visitors included the Barlow lecturer, A. J. Butler, and William Michael Rossetti, while elected to honorary members were William Gladstone and John Ruskin (at the time Slade Professor of Fine Art at Oxford), in recognition of his work as 'the main agent in spreading Dante's popularity amongst the nineteenth-century *literati*' (Isba, 2006: 25). Along with them, the society reciprocated Moore's honorary membership within the Dante Society of America by nominating two of its three founders, James Russell Lowell and Charles Eliot Norton. Sporting the selected presence of British, North American and Italian scholars, the society became the centre of a transnational knowledge niche: a prototypical network of Dante studies fostering interaction among scholars as well as the learned institutions. In this regard, Marisa Boschi Rotiroti documented the involvement of the most eminent members of the Oxford Society in the activities of the Società Dantesca Italiana, founded in Florence in 1887 as

> a scientific organisation with three main goals: 1) accurate scientific research for a critical edition of the Commedia and of Dante's minor works; 2) the publication of a journal, the Bullettino, in which researchers reported the development of Dante studies in Italy and all over the world; 3) the sponsorship of the worship of Dante with the intention of maximum exposure.
>
> (Boschi Rotiroti, 2015: 48)

Recognising the growing role of British Dante studies, the Società welcomed Paget Toynbee, Edward Moore, Cesare Foligno and

William Warren Vernon as members and invited lecturers for the Lecturae Dantis.

Conceived as an exclusive space dedicated to the production and exchange of knowledge of and on Dante's works, the Oxford Society valorised its activities by enforcing academic rigour. Exclusive in terms of admissions, it demanded from its fellows a serious and proactive engagement: a binding request for scholarly professionalism that gave more precise contours to the figure of the professional *dantista* as distinct from the amateur *dantofilo*.

Monumental *dantismo*: the Oxford Dante

Contributing an article to the *Annual Reports of the Dante Society*, Paget Toynbee recalled how the occasion for a collaborative project came from York Powell, who proposed 'an edition of the whole works of Dante in a single volume' (Toynbee, 1926: 19). Presented on 17 June and accepted on 18 July 1892, the plan was brought to the society by Charles Shadwell on 22 November 1892, when he explained to the members

> the intention of the Clarendon Press to issue the complete works of Dante in one volume. The Society expressed a general approval of the plan, and willingness to render any help or advice that might be in their power. On the motion of Mr. Shadwell, the Principal of St. Edmund Hall, the Rector of Exeter, and Mr. Tozer were asked to represent the Society as a General Committee of consultation, assistance to be obtained from time to time from other Members of the Society in reference to special departments of the work.
> (Oxford Dante Society, 1920: 48)

Unanimously approved, the society created a General Committee presided by Edward Moore, who had gained international scholarly recognition through his monumental, Cambridge-published *Contributions*. Moore took on the responsibility of designing the volume, selecting editions, methodology and collaborators from within and outside the society. According to Armstrong's direct testimony, 'the division of labour, which the Society, not formally but actually, encouraged, made it possible for Moore to devote himself closely to aspects of Dante which particularly appealed to him'

(Armstrong, 1969: xii), while also giving definitive canonisation to the work of his German master.

Apart from the text of the *Commedia*, Moore's emendation of the text of the *Convivio* 'was undoubtedly the most important and most original contribution to Dante scholarship made by the *Oxford Dante*' (Toynbee, 1920: 22). A work of utmost difficulty given the 'innumerable corruptions of the MSS due to ignorant copyists, and on the even greater violence done to the text by the conjectural emendations of irresponsible editors' (Lindon, 1988: 72), both ancient and modern like Giambattista Giuliani. Notably, the reconstruction rested on 'two hitherto unutilized MSS' (22), the only two in England: one from the Canonici collection in the Bodleian and one he had personally acquired and kept in his private collection. For the text of the *Vita Nuova* and the *De Monarchia*, the volume resorted to Witte's pioneering work: respectively, on the Leipzig edition from 1876 and the second edition published at Vienna in 1874, of which Moore preserved chapter numeration to facilitate reference. Complementing these were Fraticelli's *texti recepti* of the *De Vulgari Eloquentia*, the Latin *Eclogae*, *Epistolae* and the *Quaestio de Aqua et Terra*. Finally, Moore entrusted the *Canzoniere* to York Powell: based on Fraticelli's text, he re-arranged the poems and numbered them consecutively so as to make them more convenient for reference, classing them in four divisions. Finally, Moore commissioned Toynbee for an updated version of his *Index of Proper Names and Notable Matters* to be added as an appendix to the volume.

What determined the fortune of the edition to the point of becoming 'the standard of reference, not only in Britain, but also throughout the Continent, and in America' (Lindon, 1988: 25) were its organisational features. The 'immense convenience' (25) of the *Oxford Dante* lay not only in the accuracy of the textual reconstruction, but in the systematic and compact organisation of the information as well as in the simplification of the whole system of references. The purpose of the volume was to act as a comprehensive work of reference that would make Dante himself, his Latin and vernacular oeuvre accessible at once to scholars, critics and even the wider general readership. As such, it offered itself as an alternative to the Giovanni Scartazzini's *Enciclopedia Dantesca*: an excessively elaborate work that exhausted 'the patience of the reader' burdening its 'Dante commentary, avowedly intended for beginners, with Hebrew and Greek words' (25) and confused the public with incongruous references to varying editions of the prose works.

Between 1894 and 1924, the *Oxford Dante* went through four editions, all internationally advertised and reviewed in major periodicals including the *Athenaeum, Academy, Bookman, Quarterly review, Dublin Review* and *Bullettino della Societa Dantesca Italiana*. Here, it was unanimously praised as 'the fruit of the best available Dante scholarship' (*Dublin Review*, 1895: 427), 'the most convenient edition of Dante's complete works – the first, it may be said, ever contained between two covers' (*Athenaeum*, 1894: 823), 'beautifully printed and as such an exceedingly moderate price' (*Academy*, 1894: 456).

For the Clarendon Press, the issue of the edition represented a great productive effort since the very first edition was printed in two ordinary paper editions (one leather- and one cotton-bound) at the cost of six shillings as well as an eight-shilling edition on India paper for which 'the thickness of the book (including the binding in each case) was reduced to less than half an inch: a veritable "edizione tascabile" of what had previously been unobtainable in less than four volumes' (Toynbee, 1920: 25). The 1,500 copies sold slowly, and the second corrected edition appeared in December 1897 with a more limited print run of 1,000 copies: by this time, the work had been widely adopted in both teaching and research activities.

The third edition issued in 1904 in 3,000 copies greatly benefited from the advances in textual criticism at the turn of the twentieth century. Despite its achieved monumental status, the *Oxford Dante* demonstrated its receptiveness of the work done by the transnational community of researchers, replacing altogether the old texts with 'the first-fruits of the Società Dantesca Italiana' (Toynbee, 1920: 26), Pio Rajna's edition of the *De Vulgari Eloquentia* as well as Friedrich Beck's critical edition of the *Vita Nuova* and the *Eclogae* edited by Philip H. Wicksteed and Edmund Gardner. Notably, because 'the plan of the Oxford Dante did not admit of an apparatus criticus, or of notes, in which attention could be drawn to corrections' (27), these macroscopic interventions were not immediately evident to readers. Yet, through them the historical and cultural value of the volume grew stronger, reflecting the state of Dante studies and the conditions of collaborative *dantismo* in Europe.

Five years later, in 1909, the Ashendene Press monumentalised the achievements of the *Oxford Dante* by producing a collectable, large folio edition with woodcut illustrations printed in a limited number of 111 copies, which 'faithfully reproduced the text of the 1904 edition', along with Moore's original *Proemio* to the first edition. With a 'full-page woodcut frontispiece and 8 text woodcuts by W. H. Hooper after Charles M. Gere', 'red, large initials designed by Graily Hewitt', the volume was valued as one of the 'three greatest fine-press books, alongside the Doves Bible and the Kelmscott Chaucer'. Finally, in 1924 the fourth and final edition curated by Toynbee saw much more comprehensive modification of the whole work, with the inclusion of Michele Barbi's *Vita Nuova* and Professor Santi's notes on the *Canzoniere*.

Undoubtedly, the *Oxford Dante* was a milestone for the relatively young history of the discipline in Britain as much as it was also hailed as the greatest achievement of modern Dante studies at an international level. Yet, it might have caused tension with the Italian scholarly community and the Società Dantesca Italiana that had been planning its own edition since its inaugural meeting. This project, however, took almost thirty years to complete: commonly referred to as the *Edizione Nazionale*, the volume was supervised by Michele Barbi and published in 1921 for the sexcentenary anniversary of Dante's death. The untimely appearance of the Oxford edition deprived Italian philologists of the scholarly supremacy and foundational scope that it claimed for both ideological and practical reasons, given that the majority of the Dante manuscripts was held in Italian, mostly Florentine, libraries. Nevertheless, as the true 'offspring of the Oxford Dante Society' (Toynbee, 1926: 27), the *Oxford Dante* stood as the enduring evidence of the pivotal part played by the society and its members (both *dantisti* and *dantofili*) and the first, paradigmatic and internationally recognised achievement of the developing tradition of British Dante studies.

Dante in the capital: from the Barlow Lectureship to the London Dante Society

The foundation of the Oxford Dante Society was not the only event that made the year 1876 a key moment for British Dante scholarship. In November, Barlow bequeathed a large sum of money for the creation of 'a public annual course of lectures on the *Divina Commedia*' (Lindon, 1977: 8) at University College London and a Dante collection within its library.

Lindon's reconstruction identifies Girolamo Volpe, Italian Master at Eton, as the first Barlow Lecturer appointed in May 1877: unfortunately, he fell ill shortly before the start of his course, in the spring of 1878. Charles Tomlinson was nominated as his replacement: a science lecturer from King's College, London, he had published a *terza rima* translation of *Inferno*, introduced by a lengthy essay on Dante's English translators (1877). Commencing on 25 April 1878, the fifteen-session-long course was carried out 'on six successive Thursdays and Tuesdays at three o'clock' (Lindon, 1977: 10). During these, Tomlinson deliberately adopted English as the vehicular language of his 'rather elementary but sound and informative' (Lindon, 1977: 10) *letture dantesche* so that they could be appreciated by a diverse public of students, scholars and auditors. In 1880, the Council elected Arturo Farinelli, 'a normalista from Pisa and a student of classical languages and comparative grammar at Florence' with a previous experience of delivering 'courses of "readings and interpretations" of Dante in London' (11). After the end of Farinelli's second lecture cycle in 1886, the Council began alternating his appointment with that of Edward Moore. Initially nominated for a first three-year tenure in 1886, Moore was re-appointed six more times teaching no less than seventeen sessions.

Although still relatively unknown outside Oxford, Moore's election marked a turning point for the Barlow Lectureship, reinforcing 'the position' the University College 'held for some decades as *inter alia* a leading centre for Dante Studies' (Lindon, 1977: 12). His designation was determined by a change in the politics of the institution which reaffirmed itself as 'an English lectureship for an English audience' grounded on the contention that 'much more benefit would be derived by the hearers if they were saved the double effort necessary for taking in a lecture in a language with which many of them were unfamiliar' (12). In choosing Moore over Farinelli the Council was seeking to increase the degree of accessibility of its Dante lectures for a wider range of audiences, thus circumscribing the use of Italian, which was seen as an obstacle to the dissemination of Dantean works and knowledge in Britain. Moore, however, defied all expectations by replacing the old cyclic approach desired by Barlow with a thematic analytical reading of selected passages from each *cantica*. Moore adopted this measure to introduce the audience to principles of textual criticism while conveying a wide-ranging representation of Dante's life, culture and poetry: a change of approach that was received sceptically by the public. As Moore 'emerged as the undisputed doyen of English Dantistas' (Lindon, 1977: 12), however, a growing number of students, fellow academics and Dante enthusiasts were drawn to London and enrolled in his annual course of lectures. Under his long tenure, the Barlow Lectureship grew to be one of the most important sites for the study and the popularisation of Dante's works in Britain, carried out by such prominent nineteenth- and twentieth-century *dantisti* as A. J. Butler, Edmund G. Gardner, and Cesare Foligno. According to a letter sent by Gardner to Herford, the Council had offered a lectureship position to Philip H. Wicksteed too.

Between culture and politics: the London Dante Society

In 1898 Barlow's Dante Collection at the College Library became the symbolic and material home of the London Dante Society. The foundation came after a few failed attempts, the first in 1892, promoted by Corrado Ricci, an Italian art historian and museum director with an interest in Dante, and a small group of his students. In 1894 the second attempt was publicly endorsed with an article in the *Athenaeum* by the then Barlow Lecturer, Charles Tomlinson, in which he postulated that the future society had to be physically linked to Barlow's material legacy as a fulfilment of his grand design for a British tradition of Dante studies. The library, which had been regrettably kept inaccessible to both academics and students at University College, would come to represent the heart of London *dantismo*. It was the ideal 'place of meeting for the members of the Dante Society' as well as the space 'where the Barlow lectures might be delivered, papers read and discussed, and an abundant store of books and objects of interest be ready at hand for reference or illustration' (Tomlinson, 1894: 792). The news was reported by local newspapers such as the *Liverpool Mercury* (1 November 1894), the *Manchester Courier* (3 November 1894) and then reached Scotland through the *Glasgow Herald* (21 November 1894), which stressed the importance of such an institution aimed at furthering 'the pious study and investigation' of the *Divine Comedy* among the already 'vast numbers of admirers and students of the Immortal Florentine in this country' through the means of 'notes, pamphlets and lectures' (*Glasgow Herald*, 1894: 5).

Tomlinson's pressing request derived from the success of the Barlow Lectureship, which had demonstrated that the capital city and its cultural milieu with the University College as its core needed a dedicated space in which to participate in the continuous process of rehabilitation and reception of Dante, started earlier in the century. However, Tomlinson's closing remarks sparked a public debate on the most suitable linguistic, rhetorical and even stylistic forms for the delivery of the Barlow Lectures and, by extension, the future readings of papers presented by the members of the society. The adoption of Italian, he argued, defied the general didactic purposes they both upheld for

> There are, I imagine, comparatively few English men and women who by their knowledge of the language are capable of deriving benefit from these lectures. [...] and I am informed that it has been a matter of complaint among students that an English lecturer is not more frequently preferred. It is true that the endowment is small, but I have reason to know that there are English Dante scholars who would gladly get up and deliver these lectures irrespective of the smallness of the fee.
>
> (Tomlinson, 1894: 792)

Just when the vast base of scholars and cultivated readers was rediscovering Dante, the use of the original language risked alienating the wider public once again. Notably, the very founder of the London Society, Luigi Ricci, defended the adoption of Italian and praised as exemplary the work of Napoleone Perini who at King's College was teaching 'the Italian text, accompanied by some simple explanations' which counteracted the highly 'confusing' studies that were proliferating in the English language (Ricci, 1908: v). For Ricci 'the imperfect knowledge of the Italian language shown by the majority of the writers' was one of the crucial causes of 'pitfalls on the path of Dante's commentators' (vi), unable to grasp the unmediated meaning of a word, a passage or a whole *canto* in its original form. Perini's lectures at King's College were the most commendable examples of good practice of Dante teaching because the lecturer would 'read to them its Italian texts' without 'loading or misleading their minds with his own surmises or personal opinions' (vi) after having expounded the argument of each *canto*.

The Tomlinson–Ricci debate epitomised the opposition between two types of British Dante scholars: those fighting for the preservation of the poetic and aesthetic value of the original language, and those demanding the democratisation and appropriation of Dante's poetry through the use of English. Adopted to make Dante's textuality more widely accessible to the broadening academic and non-academic public, English was also the language through which a new scholarly community was producing original contributions, developing innovative approaches and methodologies as an alternative to those formulated by Italian *dantisti*. By choosing English over Italian, the London Society and the Lectureship were shaping their own Dante discourse as much as the sister institution in Oxford had previously done with the edition of the emblematic *Oxford Dante*: recognising itself as *other* from the long-standing Italian tradition.

When the society was officially established in 1898 it became part of what Peter Clark described as a 'complex constellation of associations', 'clubs and societies for the improvement of learning and keeping up good humour and mirth' (Clark, 2000: 1–2) in the city of London since the 1720s, a system that grew to the point of becoming 'the most distinctive social and cultural institutions' of eighteenth and nineteenth-century Britain (2). For the Poet Laureate Alfred Austin – writing the preface to the second volume of *Lectures* (1904) – 'the object' and 'the use of a Dante Society in London' was that of a corrective antidote to the ignorance of 'our countrymen and countrywomen' who do not 'know of Dante and Dante's writings' (Austin, 1904: x). It came as a much-needed corrective to the stereotypical representations of the poet as one 'passionately in love with a Florentine girl he did not marry, and whom, when she was dead, he visited Hell, Purgatory, and Heaven in search of, and then described his experiences in a long and rather tedious poem' (Austin, 1904: x–xi).

While the Oxford Dante Society concentrated its activities to two to three dinner meetings a year, the life of the London Dante Society spread over multiple appointments for both formal and informal discussions on the historical and political, philosophical and religious, literary and artistic elements of Dante's oeuvre. The collaborative exchange was promoted through weekly meetings held every Friday afternoon during each year, except in the months of August and September, accompanied by free weekly readings from original works of Dante. These complemented the monthly public lectures given and chaired by fellow members of the organisation 'regularly graced by the presence of noble lords and ladies' (Gifford, 1956: 3). Such wealth of opportunities reflected the larger and more diverse body of membership, composed in large part of *dantofili*, and a small but consistent group of distinguished international *dantisti*. A copy of the *Annual Report* presented by Ricci in 1902 recorded that a total of '464 Members had already joined the Society since its Foundation', reaching 600 in 1906 to which they added an undefined number of 'study groups scattered throughout the United Kingdom' (Ricci, 1908: np). Thanks to a special fund raised from voluntary subscriptions of the members, the society created a Dante Library, which initially complemented Barlow's collection but progressively expanded with new acquisitions and donations. Reaching 2,000 volumes in the turn of five years, the Dante Library was a collective enterprise through which the society actively promoted the advancement of research and scholarship as well as reinforcing its cultural status through the formation and preservation of a book heritage of outstanding (material and intellectual) value.

Along with the library, it is possible that the members also funded the publication of three pocket-size volumes of society lectures issued for private circulation in 500 copies between 1904 and 1909. In the absence of minutes and records, the textual and paratextual content of the volumes provides crucial information regarding the composition and hierarchical organisation of the society, the range of topics discussed, the practices of reading and forms of delivery adopted by individual speakers. Showing date and place of delivery, the collected pieces were not polished articles, but authentic transcriptions in which all the characteristic features of the oral address were preserved such as the salutation incipit and the ritual expressions of gratitude towards the society. The indexes of the volumes document the broad variety of critical interventions as well as the socio-cultural and transnational heterogeneity of the community.

Founded by Luigi Ricci, the society was presided by Theodore Martin, who had risen to prominence thanks to the success of his translation of the *Vita Nuova*. The list of presenters included members of the Anglican clergy (the Bishop of Ripon, 'Dante'), historians (Thomas Hodgkin, 'Charles Martel') and British aristocrats and political figures (Count Plunkett, 'One of Dante's Illustrators – Pinelli'). Particularly notable was the presence of Arthur Serena, a key figure in Anglo-Italian diplomacy, who financed with £20,000/annum the foundation of four major chairs of Italian at English universities at Cambridge and Oxford (and later also at Manchester and Birmingham) as well as an annual gold medal for Italian studies. Significantly, the same appointments were created in Italy where Serena endowed a number of chairs of English in local universities.

Filling the ranks of the society both as speakers and members were also Italian political representatives, including 'Queen Margherita of Italy [...] mother of the present King of Italy', the King himself and 'his consort' (*Aberdeen Daily Journal*, 1902: 7). Along with them were the Ambassador the Baron de Renzis ('Dante'), the Italian Minister for Foreign Affairs, Sidney Sonnino ('Canto VI del Paradiso'), Guglielmo Marconi and Giuseppe Mazzini, who delivered a lecture titled 'Dante'. They were joined by professional Dante scholars and translators such as Edmund Gardner and Thomas Okey. The majority of *dantisti*, however, came from the Oxford Dante Society. These included Edward Moore, George Kitchin ('Dante and Virgil'), Charles Shadwell ('Notices of Siena in the *Divina Commedia*'), William W. Vernon ('The Great Italians of the *Divina Commedia*'), along with *dantofili* like William Gladstone ('Did Dante Study at Oxford?' [later published in *Nineteenth Century*]) and James Bryce.

The most distinctive feature of the London Dante Society regarded the admission and proactive participation of female members: figures that were traditionally excluded from all clubs, societies, unions, guilds and all other types of 'emphatically public' organisations. The 1909 Alphabetical List of Lecturers and Chairmen records twelve female members of high social and cultural standing as well as literary and scholarly merit. The Duchess of Sutherland (née Lady Millicent Fanny St Clair-Erskine) was a renowned society hostess and advocate for social reform, author, editor, journalist and even playwright, often publishing under the pen name Erskine Gower. Other members were Henrietta Russell, who was the Duchess of Bedford, and the Countess of Plymouth. Miss Camilla Croudace was a British supporter of education for women serving from 1881 to 1906 as Lady Resident at Queens College London, the first college to award academic qualifications to women in the country, established in 1848. Of Miss Schillington no evidence has been retrieved apart from a reference in the *School Magazine* of the Manchester High School for Girls, and her lecture to the society on 'Dante and Siena'. The society also welcomed prominent female novelists such as Magda Heinemann-Sindici, who joined the society with his father Augusto, poet and writer: her intervention, included in the third volume of *Lectures*, explored the topic of 'Dante as a Love Poet'.

The Anglo-American novelist, Pearl M. T. Craigie, was the only female lecturer to have two pieces featured in the volumes: the first on 'Dante and Botticelli' and the second on 'The Art of Portraiture: Dante and Goya', both of which were first reviewed and later published integrally in the *Academy*. Craigie was acclaimed on both sides of the Atlantic as a novelist and playwright, essayist and periodical contributor specialised in dramatic and art criticism, and during the early 1900s she 'lectured widely in England and Scotland' (OXFDNB). 'Brilliant' and 'learned' (OXFDNB), Mrs Craigie's two Dante lectures displayed her interest in the poet and in European art and classical culture, developed through her European travels and her curricular studies at University College London. Promised to the Dante Society in 1901, the first lecture was prepared during her stay in Florence in December. Warmly welcomed by the society, the lecture on Dante and Botticelli was also delivered in New York on 6 December 1905 at Columbia University before the students of Barnard College as part of her American lecturing tour.

The most insightful interventions in Dante textual and historical criticism came from Catherine M. Phillimore and Eleanor F.

Jourdain. By the time she delivered her lecture to the Dante Society, Phillimore had established her reputation as a literary scholar with a specialism in Italian history and literature (poetry, prose and drama) and as a member of the Dante Society of America and the London Dante Society. Her body of works included full-length studies and contributions to *Macmillan Magazine*, *Edinburgh Review*, *St Paul Magazine*, *Church Quarterly Review* and *National Review*. In 1887, these articles were reprinted with additions in *Studies in Italian Literature Classical and Modern*. The book was also published in Italy with a translation by Rosmunda Tonini. All her Dantean criticism tackled the most marginalised aspects of the poet's life and oeuvre, putting into question the choices of contemporary British commentators and essayists. In her *Studies*, she highlighted the unequal treatment suffered by *Paradiso* 'considered by Italian critics the greatest effort of Dante's mind' but 'so little appreciated by foreigners' thus conveying 'the impression that it is inferior to the preceding portions of the poem' (Phillimore, 1887: 2). The chapter was her attempt at explaining the general scope and plan of the *cantica* 'remov[ing] some of the difficulties which are to be encountered in the study of the "Paradiso" to give, if possible, a clue to the allegory which lies concealed in the poem, and thus to guide the reader to its manifold beauties' with the critical support of the 'best Italian writers and commentators of the subject' (2) such as the late Duca di Sermoneta, author of *Tre Chiose sulla* Divina Commedia. Similarly, *Dante at Ravenna: A Study*, her first (and only) full-length study of Dante published in 1898 focused on 'the closing years of the life of Dante ... his quiet exile at Ravenna' which is 'not so well known to the student' (Phillimore, 1898: 7). This was based on her own personal visits to Ravenna and the Romagna as well as 'research among such original sources of information' (viii) like the manuscripts found in Ravenna and Paris, the Bodleian and the British Museum highlighted by Corrado Ricci's *L'ultimo rifiugio di Dante Alighieri*. The London lecture largely derived from the book and continued to reconstruct the chronology and geography of the poet's exile, his occupations and friendships during this crucial and painful period of his life, which exerted a strong voyeuristic and sentimentalist appeal to Victorian readers.

Eleanor F. Jourdain was the most prominent female lecturer of the London Dante Society, who at the time was the Principal of St

Hugh's Hall. Having secured a place of study at Lady Margaret Hall, Oxford, in 1883, in 1886 Jourdain was one of the first women examined in the modern history school and the first woman to undergo a viva. She was placed in the second class. Following a short stint as secretary to Minnie Benson, wife of the archbishop of Canterbury, she took on the role of assistant mistress, first at Tottenham high school and then at Clifton high school. An activist of women's education, Jourdain was one of the founders of the Corran Collegiate School, Watford, a private boarding and day school offering a thorough education of the best type for girls of all ages, which attracted more than 100 pupils by 1900. In between these two roles, Jourdain began her Dante studies, publishing extensively in periodicals. It was during her summer holidays in Paris that she had the chance to pursue her research and further her investigation into the symbolism in Dante's *Divina Commedia*: a project that was first published in English (1902) and in French (1903), for which she was in 1904 awarded a doctorate by the University of Paris. The string of periodical publications was largely written for the *Expository Times*, an academic journal specialised in biblical and theological scholarship, starting with 'The Symbolism of the *Divina Commedia*' (1 November 1894), followed by 'Dante's Use of the Divine Name in the *Divina Commedia*' (1 April 1895) and 'The Women of the *Divina Commedia*' (1 July 1895). Notably, in that same month, Jourdain sent these very papers to William Gladstone, perhaps met at the society meetings, with a letter that reads:

> I venture to hope they may perhaps interest you, as some of the points raised in them have not, as far as I know, been treated before. I am wishing to publish these papers with others in book form. If, on perusal, you should feel able to say a word to me in their favour, I should feel most grateful from the help that an appreciation from a Dante scholar would be to me in the effort to launch the book.

Excluded from the Oxford Dante Society, whose statute did not accept female members, Jourdain took an active part in the life of the London Society as lecturer and Member of the Council. The topic of her lecture, in particular, sought to bring the book to the attention of a diverse audience of Dante scholars and amateurs in an attempt to demystify Dante. The somewhat ambiguous judgement of the *Saturday Review* found the work 'a very respectable review for beginners' yet 'not deserving of inclusion among experts' books' (*Saturday Review*, 1902: 587).

As a markedly extroverted and socially inclusive institution, the London Dante Society not only reflected but greatly benefited from the major reforms in women's higher education. Opened to female members and lecturers, the society played a central role in the formation of British women *dantiste* at the turn of the century.

Dante in the industrial north: the Manchester Dante Society

From the academic and political hearts of the country the interest in the study of Dante had spread to its industrial core: the city of Manchester, erringly seen 'as a modern metropolis shorn of cultural and aesthetic sensibilities' (Milner, 2013: 63). Throughout the nineteenth century, the city boomed for commercial and industrial wealth. With the population trebled by mid-century led by the expansion of the middle and working classes, the 'provincial' Manchester had become a vibrant urban hub and granted civic status in 1853. The cultural renaissance was furthered through to the proliferation of high-art institutions from the City Art Gallery, the Manchester Museum and Hallé Orchestra to the *Manchester Guardian* (a prominent daily newspaper) and a number of public libraries that neared 10,000 subscriptions in the turn of few years. Along with these, the city life was animated by the activities of a growing number of societies and clubs, leisure activities, people's theatre, most of which with a marked cosmopolitan reach.

The earliest and most long-lived of these was the Manchester Literary and Philosophical Society, a weekly gentlemen's club established by Thomas Percival in 1781 'with the object of promoting the advancement of education and public interest in any form of literature, science, arts or public affairs' (Manchester Literary and Philosophical Society, 2015). The society configured itself as an inclusive, socio-culturally diverse space of conversational encounters of lively minds sharing interests in a broad range of disciplines and topics, well represented by its 50,000-volume library and recorded in its eighty-three volumes of *Memoirs*. Donal Sheehan observed that the society not only engendered an 'atmosphere of intellectual curiosity unknown elsewhere in provincial England', but voiced 'continual demands for provincial university education, which culminated in the founding of Owen's College in 1851, and finally in the Victoria University Charter' (Sheehan, 1941: 519).

Similar and still active today, the Manchester Athenaeum (est. 1835) sought to foster educational reforms through the organisation of 'lectures and literary meetings, news and reading rooms and libraries' aimed at the 'mental and moral improvement of young men of the "intelligent middle classes"' (White, 1988: 88). Similarly, the Manchester Literary Club was created in 1862 with the 'stated aim' to 'provide a means of education and recreation by the reading aloud of original papers covering literary and related topics, and to give the opportunity for those interested in literature, but living outside the city, to "meet their Manchester friends"' ('Manchester Literary Club', 2020). Like the Literary and Philosophical Society, it welcomed a middle-class membership of businessmen and professionals of varying occupations, who were 'genuinely interested in literature as a humanising influence and as a source of true pleasure' (Swann, 1908: 7) and who enjoyed regular trips to places of interest. Observing such dynamics, Stephen Milner has argued that through the foundation and active participation in such institutions, the 'new industrial class' was expressing 'a high level of cultural discernment and civic pride in their roles as patrons of arts' while setting forth a constructive 'paradigm that fused capital accumulation with cultural production in a civic context' (Milner, 2013: 64).

Within this macroscopic process of 'cultural redemption' (Milner, 2013: 69), the projected institution of a Manchester-born and based society for the 'serious and severe' study of Dante in Manchester was 'a manifest sign of great culture and the great civil and scientific process' of the city that was 'prospering for work as well as wealth and material welfare' (Speight, 1957: 4).

In February 1900, J. B. McGovern expressed in two letters sent to the editors of the leading local newspapers, the *Manchester Guardian* and the *Manchester Courier and Lancashire General Advertiser*, his willingness to 'readily [...] lend a hand to set' a Dante Society 'afoot' in Manchester. This was a most necessary enterprise since 'the growing interest amongst us in matters Danteian' required 'guidance, the spur of emulation and the healthy friction of mind to mind' (McGovern, 1900: 3) to grow out of occasional amateurism into structured engagement. Set out as a space of collaborative scholarship, the Society's 'lectures, papers, readings from the Divine Comedy, "Vita Nuova," &c., discussion, criticism and the formation a library of Dante literature' would have furthered the study of Dante across the industrial metropolis and as a 'fitting complement to the admirable' (and intramural) 'Dante class at Owens College conducted by Signor Valgimigli' (McGovern, 1900: 3). Despite McGovern's enthusiasm, his proposed public gathering to discuss 'the appointment of a committee or council, election of president, scale of fees, unsectarian character of the society, institution of a magazine for insertion of notes, papers' (McGovern, 1900: 3) took place more than six years later.

The same newspapers recorded that the 'society for the study of Dante was formed in Manchester' on 13 September 1906, with a meeting held at the Grosvenor Hotel on Deansgate with a 'beautiful bust of the poet' ornamenting the room for the occasion (*Manchester Courier*, 1906: 10). Valgimigli, 'afterwards appointed honorary secretary', invited the conveners to reflect that the 'time' was 'very propitious' for the creation of such an institution not just because 'Dante studies' were 'pursued with great eagerness in England', but because it would have been the first Society to be born in the heart of the industrial North, based in Manchester: a city 'in the forefront of social, educational and literary movement' as well as 'the seat of a great University' and of the John Rylands Library (*Manchester Courier*, 1906: 10).

Channelling the Victorian revival of interest for the Florentine poet, the society was formed on the basis of a tripartite organism of institutional forces. First, the city of Manchester supported reforms of general and higher education for the middle and working classes through associations such as the Society for the Diffusion of Useful Knowledge, the Mechanics' Institutes and the Extension Movement. The Manchester University Settlement, in particular, brought 'the young, wealthy and educationally privileged to live amongst the urban poor ... a practical means of meeting some of the difficulties arising from the misunderstanding of class by class' (Rose, 1990: 138–9). Second, the Victorian University was itself a confederate institution established in 1880 and united the original Owen's College (1851) with the universities of Leeds and Liverpool. Like the city, its university was a major and strenuous promoter of liberal education and the modernisation of the curriculum. Since the 1860s, the university recorded a steady growth of the student body (400 day, 750 evening and 200 medical students) and an overall improvement of their performances in internal and external examinations. Parallel to this came also the growth of faculty, benefactors and investments in prizes and scholarships.

While the city and the university fostered a productive environment for the creation of the society, the conditions for its thriving development derived from the inauguration of the John Rylands Library in Deansgate on 6 October 1899. The neo-gothic building which 'enriched England with one of the most distinguished and the most perfect architectural achievements of this century' (Hodgson, 2012: 19) had been founded in memory of Manchester's first multimillionaire and owner of the country's largest textile manufacturing, John Rylands, by his wife Enriqueta Augustina Rylands. A committed philanthropist, Mrs Rylands was the 'controlling mind' of the project: 'no detail was too small, no expense too trifling to escape her attention' from 'the design and building of the Library' (19) to the formation, acquisition and organisation of its book-collection. As Elizabeth Gow aptly pointed out, although she self-effacingly described the institution as a 'private work' for which she never sought 'public recognition', Mrs Rylands regarded the library '"with pardonable pride as her great achievement"' (Gow, 2019b: 5) as a book collector, philanthropist and cultural entrepreneur: an enterprise for which she was awarded the Freedom of the City of Manchester.

The acquisition of rare books and manuscripts had begun even before the definition of the plan for the library thanks to an ever-expanding network of agents at her service all over the world. Initially conceived as a theological memorial library, the collection soon encompassed 'works in all departments of literature' (Rylands, 1902: 5) with manuscripts and rare editions 'in English, Latin, French, Hebrew and even Sanskrit' (Gow, 2019b: 7).

In 1892, Mrs Rylands purchased the largest and most refined 'Grand Tour private collection of early printed books in the world' (Milner, 2013: 73), that of the bibliophile Earl Spencer, for the price of £210,000. The acquisition, the first of that size and value by a woman book collector, marked a watershed moment not just in the history of the library, but also in the history of Dante studies in

Manchester. The Biblioteca Spenceriana at Althorp, in fact, 'contained at last eleven of the fifteen incunable editions of the text (printed before 1500) as well as the 1502 Aldine "vulgate" printed on vellum' that added to previous editions counted 'fourteen of the fifteen incunable editions' (74). In 1901 the purchase of the manuscript portion of the Bibliotheca Lindesiana brought two more Dante manuscripts: 'an exquisite Trecento Strozzi manuscript of Petrarch and Dante's Canzoni, which was consulted' by Witte and 'a copy of the *Divine Comedy* previously owned by Seymour Kirkup' (74).

The Dantean book-collecting continued in 1905 with the purchase of 'a Biblioteca dantesca wholesale from a Florentine book merchant, in all likelihood the famous publishing and auction house of Leo S. Olschki' (Milner, 2013: 75). The twenty-five-years-long labour of Count Giuseppe Landi Passerini, Head Librarian of the Laurenziana, founder and editor of the *Giornale Dantesco* and first Secretary of the Società Dantesca Italiana, the 5,000-book collection was rich in early editions of the original text. While the majority of Dante books went to form the library collection, Mrs Rylands kept aside as part of her own private collection held at Longford Hall a number of 'deluxe and private press editions, extra-illustrated books, autographs, fine bindings and illuminated manuscripts' (Gow, 2019b: 12). My research in the Rylands Archives revealed that these included the Ashendene Press's specimen pages on paper from Moore's *Tutte le Opere di Dante* as well as the Ashendene three-volume edition of *Lo inferno*, *Lo purgatorio* and *Lo paradiso di Dante Alighieri Fiorentino* (revised), published between 1902 and 1905. Printed on vellum and in large format, the volumes were decorated with miniature initials by Graily Hewitt and woodcutting by R. Catterson Smith based on the 1491 Venetian edition revised by Moore. These acquisitions were perhaps initially motivated by Mrs Ryland's bibliophile desire to enrich her personal library at Longworth Hall with a Dante section that had been missing at least until 1881. For Guppy (the head librarian), the private collection was put together with 'the library on a side, where it was but indifferently equipped' (Guppy, 1908: 355).

The result of these was an 'almost unrivalled' ('Gifts to the Library', 1906: 182) collection consisting of 'five manuscripts and nearly 6,000 printed volumes' divided between commentaries, editions and translations of Dante's works 'upwards of thirty different languages' (Speight, 1961: 175) including some Italian dialects. In her detailed survey, Speight noted that one largely undermined strength of the collection was the wealth of international nineteenth-century *Danteana* that Mrs Rylands was quick to acquire with the help of Mr Guppy and Count Passerini himself. The section ranged from studies, handbooks and biographies to 'pamphlets, offprints, reports of special events and in catalogues of exhibitions' relating to the 1865 anniversary celebrations as well as 'periodicals, reports and papers' (212) of various Dante Societies in Germany, Italy, Britain and the United States. The collection supported the activities of the Manchester Dante Society with a blurring the distinctions between private collecting and public (even popular) use. According to Mrs Rylands's philanthropic intentions, in fact, the John Rylands Library

> shall be of use in the widest sense of the word: for young students as well as for advanced scholars. It is not to be a mere centre for antiquaries and bibliographers, as its rich collection of early printed Books & M.SS. has led many, I find, to believe.
> (Rylands, 1896)

Even the 'principal treasures' had to be made accessible under due regulation to any persons who may be interested in them. On 1 January 1900, the library was finally opened to readers and visitors.

The amateur and professional interest in the study of Dante brought together 'Mancunians representing many different aspects of the life of their city' (Speight, 1957: 4). Along with Dr Louis Casertelli (Bishop of Salford and Lecturer in Iranian Languages and Literatures) and Sig. A. Valgimigli (University Lecturer in Italian), who were respectively elected to the positions of President and Honorary Secretary, the society elected Mrs Rylands as one of its Vice-presidents, and counted among its members political representatives (the Italian and the German consuls, Major J. Sington and Mr C. Collmann; the Councillor Godbert), clergymen (the Bishop Casertelli, and the Rev. A. Cossio, Rector of St Bede's College) and members from the 'world of industry and commerce' (4). These were joined by academics from the university (the Vice-Chancellor Prof. Hopkinson; Professors Herford, Conway and Tout from the Faculty of Arts, among others) and the curators of the John Rylands

Library and the City Library, Mr H. Guppy and Mr Sutton, who was elected Honorary Secretary of the society.

A surviving Membership Card and Statutes of the society sheds light on its scholarly undertaking as well as the organisation and administration of its activities. In line with its sister institutions, the Manchester Society pursued 'the promotion and encouragement of the study of Dante by means of Lectures, Papers and Discussions' led by ordinary members as well as guest lecturers, 'persons of distinction in the study and exposition of Dante'. Although membership numbers are currently unknown, the card shows that this was 'open to all applicants' of both sexes, upon the payment of an annual fee of five shillings and 'subject to the discretion of the Council'. Gathering at least six times during each academic year for regular meetings and lectures, the society normally hosted the latter in the grand Victorian setting of the Whitworth Hall, the grand neo-gothic ceremonial hall of the university opened in 1902.

The inaugural lecture took place on 24 November 1906, delivered by Lord Vernon with a paper 'The Contrasts in Dante' and the event 'drew a large audience and successfully launched the new society' (Speight, 1957: 5). In the concluding remarks, the lecturer praised the endeavours of 'the cultured city of Manchester – which I may be permitted to term the Athens of North England' (Vernon, 1906: 31). Most importantly, Vernon reminded the members that the only way the society could make a significant contribution to the field was to be 'a good and a permanent one – one that should be attended by those who really wanted to study Dante, and not only by audiences assembled to listen to an interesting discourse' (31). Thus, the encouragement was for them to claim for themselves the status of *dantisti*, serious and professional scholars rather than common amateurs. The address had an overall positive effect on the society that established itself as a space of study and discussion, showing 'the willingness ... to contribute papers, setting forth their ideas on various aspects of Dante for discussion with fellow members' (Speight, 1957: 5).

Throughout its existence, the society greatly benefited from the interventions of external lectures, fulfilling the foundational aim of securing 'the services of noted Dante scholars visiting the country' and the city. Among the local *dantisti*, the society hosted prominent figures A. J. Butler, E. G. Gardner, P. H. Wicksteed and W. Warren

Vernon, who was later elected an honorary member along with a number of foreign lecturers. In this regard, the society deliberated that 'if necessary, lectures might be given not only in English and Italian, but also in French, German and Spanish' (Speight, 1957: 4), thus admittedly configuring itself a space of international exchange and collaboration. Although the majority of invited speakers were men, the reports in the *Manchester Guardian* document the presence of female lecturers. In January 1908 the 'Principal of the Women's Hostel connected with the University', Miss E. L. Broadbend, 'directed the attention to those other women whose portraits appeared in the "Divina Commedia"' arguing that 'Dante's conception' and 'courteous sympathy [...] far transcended the usual conception of his age' (*Manchester Guardian*, 1908: 9). Similarly, the *Manchester Courier* reported that in December of the same year Mrs Paul Chapman had given a 'lecture on some of Dante's allusions in the "Inferno"': an intervention 'illustrated by excellent lantern slides selected with the view of explaining the many objects and places referred to in the poem' (*Manchester Courier*, 1908: 7).

In 1909, Mr Guppy arranged a large-scale exhibition of the Dante treasures, which were displayed in the Main Library from March to October 1909. Guppy's intentions were expressed in the preface to the catalogue, where he recounted that the exhibition was 'arranged in connection to the visit to the library of the members of the Manchester Dante Society, many of whom may be still unaware of the wealth of the material which is available' (Guppy, 1909: v). This event sought to encourage the members of the society to use such accessible treasures of Rylands for their studies and research. At the same time, it reinvigorated the civic pride of the urban community by bringing the wider public to discover 'something of the riches of the collections which have made the library famous in the world of letters, and which, at the same have helped to make Manchester a centre for the attraction to scholars from all parts of the world' (v).

Apart from its unparalleled range of sources, the Rylands Library also established a 'foundational link with Florence, Passerini and the activities of the Società dantesca italiana' (Milner, 2013: 76) vehiculated through the publication of reports from the society's meetings in the *Giornale Dantesco*. This introduced Manchester within the trans-European network that the Società Dantesca was creating through the organisations of lectures and conferences. Passerini's articles triggered the interest of an international scholarly community and members, and lecture transcriptions began to appear in print, particularly in the *Contemporary Review*, *English Review*, the recently created *Bulletin of the John Rylands Library*, *Tablet*, *Antiquarian* and *Rivista d'Italia*. Similarly, newspapers like the *Manchester Guardian*, the *City News* and the *Courier* 'recalled the interest of the local urban community', while *The Times* gave it national relevance by regularly reporting 'synopses of the lectures' (Speight, 1957: 6) and news regarding society activities. Surveying the history of the association for the society's twenty-first anniversary, *The Tablet* recounted that 'a good many of these reprints and the numbers of the reviews containing lectures and addresses delivered before the members of the Society were exhibited at the Exhibition at Turin in 1911 (foreign literary section)' and thanks to them 'the Society was awarded the Gold Medal for scholarly lectures' (*Tablet*, 1928: 21).

By the mid-1920s the fame of the Manchester Dante Society and the value of its scholarly endeavour had received international recognition. What distinguished it from the other Dantean institutions was the aspiration to animate the social life of the city and engage the broader local community of Manchester and the north. To do so, Milner noted, the society took part in a vast and diverse range of activities:

> From the talks given to such institutions as the Workers College in Chorley, and the Colonia Universitaria di Ancoats, to the tutorial classes in Salford, the lectures with the Ateneo di Leeds in the University Extension Lectures programme and tutorial classes which toured Wakefield, Brighouse, Castleford, and even Hebden Bridge in 1912. In April 1913 they even organised an outing to see the screening of Bertolini, Padoan and Liguoro's feature-length Dante's *Inferno* during its sell-out two week run at the Manchester Free Trade Hall.
>
> (Milner, 2013: 82)

Wicksteed's Extension courses on Dante were among these enterprises: in the fall and winter of 1903, in fact, the lecturer gave an introductory course of six lectures at Ladybarn Hall in Manchester, largely advertised in the *Guardian*. A significant stimulus to the urban promotion of Dante studies came from the cultural labour of the vast Italian community in Manchester: 'carvers, gilders, instrument makers and fine art dealers were at the forefront of bringing Italian culture to the region and were instrumental in establishing links with the city's libraries and institutes of higher education' (Valgimigli, 1932: 30).

For many, the 'chief cause of the success of the Dante Society' (*Tablet*, 1910: 24) was the Italian expatriate Azeglio Valgimigli. Arrived from Pisa in 1881, in 1882 Valgimigli began his career by teaching the only Italian class existing at the time at the Athenaeum Club: his classes were so successful that he not only added several others to the schedule, but also started an evening course for reading the poetic works of Dante. By 1883, he had expanded his activities to Clarke's College, Cheetham Hill, and the Municipal School of Commerce. In 1884, he became the first lecturer of Italian in the history of the Owens College, the future Manchester University, and later added 'an evening class for the reading of Dante' (10). In 1893 he was appointed lecturer in Italian at the newly established Royal Manchester College. Elected as Honorary Secretary of the Manchester Dante Society at the time of its foundation in 1906, he held the position for two decades during which he acted as the exchange channel with prominent British scholars such as Edward Moore, Paget Toynbee, Philip H. Wicksteed and Frederick Hasellfoot. Devoting himself to the mission of promoting 'Italian Studies' and 'Anglo-Italian friendship' (10), Valgimigli became a regular collaboration with the *Giornale Dantesco* directed by Passerini allowed him to pen reports of the meetings of the society as well as articles ('Il Culto di Dante in Inghilterra', 1898; 'La Forza Morale di Dante e Gli Anglosassoni', 1904) addressing the state of Dante's British reception, thus bridging the two scholarly communities. In appreciation of such strenuous endeavour 'in the cause of Italian literature, and more particularly in the study of Dante' (*Tablet*, 1910: 10) the society dedicated a night to the celebration of his work in July 1910.

Deeply rooted in the urban and industrial context of Manchester, democratically open to a broader membership, keen to preserve and valorise its foundational link with the Italian scholarly community, it played an important part in the enhancement of Dante studies in Britain. Throughout, the chapter has expounded at the historical and socio-cultural dynamics that fostered the rise of Dante studies as a critical discipline, and the establishment of research communities and cultural institutions such as the Oxford, London and Manchester Dante Societies. Sustained by the analysis of material evidence largely overlooked until this point, the reconstruction has filled a documentary gap in Dante reception history. Most importantly, it illustrated how the current scholarly tradition is the result of a binding relationship between scholars and enthusiasts whose collaboration furthered the development of the discipline through the synergetic and highly productive conflation of *dantofilia* and *dantismo*, individual study and collective cooperation.

Conclusion: From *grande amore* to *lungo studio*: rethinking the hermeneutic turn in Dante reception history

In October 1921, Azeglio Valgimigli wound up his two-part article for *The Tablet* by declaring that 'the last fifty or sixty years' had represented 'the golden age of Dante studies in England' (Valgimigli, 1921b: 435). In 1989, Michael Caesar concluded the introduction to his *Dante: The Critical Heritage* observing that by the late nineteenth century '"the age of synthesis" had passed and that of "analysis" had arrived' (Caesar, 1989: 73), revolutionising critical practices and approaches in Britain and all over Europe. In both cases, the identification of the hermeneutic turn in Victorian Dante criticism and scholarship marked the end point of the discourse: briefly surveyed in its macroscopic features, but not expounded in its greater complexity.

In this book, the Victorian hermeneutic turn represented not only the starting point but the central object of study: a key to broadening our current understanding of the greater pervasiveness of Dante's presence in Victorian literary culture, which is here seen as extending beyond the realm of creative appropriation into the wider dimension of interpretive criticism and academic scholarship. Through five selected and chronologically successive case studies, each emblematic of a specific phase and aspect of the phenomenon, *Dante beyond influence* has demonstrated that the study of Dante represented a transversal occupation accessible to and pursued by Victorian men and women of learning, coming from different social backgrounds and characterised by varying motives and approaches to the private pursuit and public use of their *lungo studio* of Dante.

The mapping of their distinctive readerly and annotating habits unveiled individual processes of inner acquisition and elaboration as well as of outer use and manipulation of Dantean knowledge. My study demonstrated that although approached in a serious and systematic, committed and purposeful manner, for Gladstone, Arnold and Christina Rossetti the *lungo studio* of Dante was pursued as a predominantly private endeavour, one externalised only on selected occasions – and through specific avenues of dissemination – with the programmatic intention to orient the wider discourse towards interpretive directions. This manoeuvring capability derived also from their secured position of literary, cultural and political authority.

Pushing the investigation beyond these canonical figures, I exposed lesser-known Victorians like Philip H. Wicksteed and Maria Francesca Rossetti for whom the study of Dante constituted their primary, professional occupation – for many, the lifetime opportunity through which many women and men self-fashioned their public identity and scholarly authority as popular mediators of Dante, meeting the intellectual interests and the material means of the middle- (and even lower-) class public. This book documented how towards the end of the century, the broadening of the readership was accompanied by the emergence of a large Victorian studentship base thanks to the creation of teaching institutions and courses within traditional and extramural universities. The historiographical reconstruction also showed that the multiplications of the spaces and opportunities for the teaching of Dante stirred an epoch-making process of discipline formation in Britain. Yet, the creation of professorship and lecture-cycles, library collections and curricular courses was the product not of self-governed interventions, but of concerted collaborative activities within newly formed, learned societies: networks of amateurs and professionals working towards the construction of national and transitional networks of knowledge production and dissemination.

The unification of these experiences was essential to provide a comprehensive reassessment of the cultural and historical dynamics underlying the emergence of the Victorian *dantismo* as a serious, systematic and positivist attitude towards Dante, and the definition of the *dantista* as a professionalised and professionalising figure, the specialised scholar. This interpretative attitude has been treated as complementary, but not opposed to Romantic and early Victorian *dantofilia*, understood as the amateur praxis of reading, commenting and translating Dante's works, common to celebrated poets and men of letters such as Coleridge, Shelley, Byron, Carlyle and, to a certain extent, Ruskin. Throughout this study, the terminological differentiation held a pragmatic rather than ontological value as it oriented the ideal reader among the vast array of contributors (academic scholars, intellectuals, men of letters, learned societies) and contributions (criticism, editions, translations, readings and commentaries) quoted throughout. Overall, this was not conceived as a dichotomised opposition between two incompatible approaches to Dante's textuality, but rather as the dialogical tension from which Victorian Dante scholarship emerged between the last decades of the nineteenth and the turn of the twentieth century. In conceptualising this transition or differentiation from amateur *dantofilia* to scholarly *dantismo*, however, I did not intend to convey what T. K. Heyck defined as 'a Whiggish interpretation' of the emergence Dante studies in Victorian Britain, which would

> argue that the production and support of serious thought has progressed from benighted and shallow world of the men of letters and amateur cultivators of science in the first half of the nineteenth century to enlightened and excellent conditions at the turn of the century.
> (Heyck, 1982: 10)

Instead, I argued that the transformation of Dante into an object of specialised study can be seen as an expression of what T. K. Heyck and Suzy Anger described as the substantial redefinition of the Victorian critical attitude towards the formation and organisation of scholarly knowledge; the reform and widening access to higher education; the revolutionisation of the publishing industry. By expounding the phenomenology of Victorian *dantismo* within and in relation to this broader socio-cultural context, *Dante beyond influence* has taken the representation of the phenomenon beyond the realm of productive reception. My book has sought to revaluate the margin as a productive material and socio-cultural condition in which new Dantean knowledge was produced and transmitted. It has redirected the attention onto agents, forms and materials of critical and scholarly reception that have been insofar largely marginalised from mainstream discourse.

The recovery of these long-lost experiences rested on the physical and methodological, with the use of the archive and library collection as the spaces in which the reception process can be seen materialising into an extraordinarily broad corpus of readerly and writerly objects. The papers and records document the transformation of Dante into the object of collaborative scholarship. The array of surviving articles and reviews, advertisements and press-cuttings attest concretely to the two-fold function of nineteenth-century periodicals. As Kathryn Prince argued about Shakespeare Victorian afterlife, for Dante too, 'periodicals and newspapers acted an important medium for the unprecedented popularisation of his works beyond the upper echelons of British society' (Prince, 2008: 20) through a miscellaneous body of reviews, articles and even poems of Dantean topic. An aspect largely overlooked in current reception scholarship, throughout the mid-Victorian age 'general audience weeklies and niche-audience trade magazines. specialist and non-specialist publications, cheap papers and expensive reviews' (Miller, 2016: 626–27) became key epistemological sites vehicular for the development of Dante criticism and scholarship, as 'crucial forum for discussion' (629) for a growing transnational network of *dantofili* and *dantisti*. Apart from being a hermeneutic instrument designed to educate the reader on how, when and (even) where Dante should be read, I have contended that periodicals were also key to promotion and commodification of Dante's works on the Victorian literary market along and in collaboration with publishers and booksellers. Responding to the intellectual needs of a new public of general readers, these publications determined a pivotal change in the approach towards Dante's life and works from their idealised monumentalisation to its concrete, commercial fruition.

Libraries and publishers' archives still hold more than one single book may explore. Much remains to be said in regard to the effective flow of books and sales, the publisher's exchanges with authors as well as their commissioning of original works, reprints and new editions. Broadening the geographical borders of the book, a further project would engage in a transcultural discourse in which the history and dynamics of the British nineteenth-century scholarly reception could be contrastively compared with their North American and Irish contemporary counterparts, examining the practices, forms and venues employed for constructing and creating Dantean knowledge. Similarly, these would need to reconsider to what extent the Victorian scholarly endeavour influenced the modernist literary, critical and scholarly reception of Dante, and whether this continuity would be traceable in the reading practices of Modernist readers of Dante.

Present and future projects share a common foundational intent, that of offering a more nuanced representation of what Daniela Caselli describes as the 'ubiquitous' presence 'of Dante' (Caselli, 2017: 91) in nineteenth- and twentieth-century literary culture: a presence that resonates not only in the verses and words of poets and novelists, but also echoes in the works of men and women critics, translators and scholars and which can be unearthed by following the material traces of their hermeneutic practices.

Bibliography

Manuscripts and archives

Eton

Eton College Library
Loo. I 14. *La Divina Commedia di Dante Alighieri*, ed. L. Pezzana (Venice: Gaspari, 1827).

London

British Library
Gladstone's Papers
Add MS 44503, f. 6.
Add MS 44689, ff. 209–211.
Add MS 44726, f. 24.
Add MS 44731, f. 139 v.
Add MS 44792, ff. 63–65.

The National Archives (UCL Special Collection)
Barlow Papers
BARLOW/1–97/17–23 (Unpublished works).
BARLOW/1–97/24–29 (Unpublished works).
BARLOW/1–97/30–44 (Manuscript essays and lectures).
BARLOW/1–97/45/1–46/3 (Commentaries).
BARLOW/1–97/47/1–53 (Commentaries).
BARLOW/1–97/54–62 (Commentaries).
BARLOW/1–97/91–97 (Festivals of Dante).

Manchester

Manchester Libraries

GB127.MISC/323/1–13 (Papers relating to the Manchester Dante Society, Manchester Libraries).

GB127.MISC/323/5 (William Warren Vernon's Letter to Sig. Valgimigli accepting the Honorary Membership of the Manchester Dante Society).

GB127.MISC/323/10 (Membership Card and Statutes of the Society, Papers relating to the Manchester Dante Society).

The John Rylands Library

MS. 1254, Letter from John Ruskin to Constance Hilliard, 31 October 1877.

JRL/6/1/3/6, E.A. Rylands, Letter to W. Linnell, 13 April 1896.

Archive of the University of Manchester

GB 133 DEM/1/2/1/3 (Papers relating to the Department of Extra-Mural Studies and Centre for Continuing Education).

Oxford

Harris Manchester College Library

MSS. Herford-Wicksteed 1–3 (Herford-Wicksteed Papers).

MSS. Wicksteed 1, 2 (Philip H. Wicksteed Papers).

Taylorian Library

GB 486 MSS. 18–20 (Papers relating to the Oxford Dante Society).

GB 486 MSS. 21–9 (Papers of Edward Moore relating to Dante).

Weston Library

GB 161 MSS. Toynbee (Paget Toynbee Manuscripts on Dante).

GB 161 MSS. Don. e.4–5 (Works of Paget Toynbee).

Oxford University Archives

Papers relating to the Oxford University Extension Lectures, tbd.

Balliol College

Letters from Maria Francesca Rossetti to Henry Longfellow.

Harvard

Houghton Library
James Russell Lowell additional papers
bMS Am 1483.
Moore, Edward, 1835–1916. A.L.s. to [ ]; Oxford, 18 Jun 1889. 1s.(3p.).

Printed sources

Works by Dante

Editions

Alighieri, D. (1822) *La Divina commedia col comento del Baldassare Lombardi*, 5 vols (Padova: dalla tipografia della Minerva).

— (1826–27) *La Divina Commedia di Dante Alighieri can comento analitico di Gabriele Rossetti: in sei volumi*, 6 vols (London: John Murray).

— (1827) *La Divina Commedia di Dante Alighieri, edizione formata sopra quella di Comino del 1727, per cura di Lorenzo Pezzana* (Venezia: Gaspari).

— (1843–50) *Delle Prose E Poesie Liriche Di Dante Allighieri, prima edizione illustrata con note di diversi*, ed. by Alessandro Torri (Livorno: np, Livorno).

— (1862) *La Divina Commedia di Dante Alighieri, edizione minore fatta sul testo dell'edizione critica di Carlo Witte* (Berlin: R. L. von Decker).

— (1873–87) *Opere minori di Dante Alighieri, annotato e illustrato da Pietro Fraticelli*, 3 vols (Firenze: Barbera).

— (1874) *Dantis Alligherii De monarchia libri III, codicum manuscriptorum ope emendatiper Carolum Witte* (Vindobonae: Sumptibus Guillielmi Braumuller).

— (1876) *La Vita nuova ... Ricorretta coll'ajuto di testi a penna ed illustrata da Carlo Witte* (Liepzig: n. pub.).

— (1893) *Vita Nuova di Dante Alighieri with Notes and Comments in English*, ed. by Napoleone Perini (London: Hachette and Co.).

— (1894) *Tutte le opere di Dante Alighieri nuovamente rivedute nel testo da E. Moore* (Oxford: Nella Stamperia dell'Università).

— (1895) *Tutte le opere di Dante Alighieri nuovamente rivedute nel testo da E. Moore con Indice dei nomi propri e delle cose notabili contenute nelle opere di Dante. Compilato da Paget Toynbee* (Oxford: Nella Stamperia dell'Università).

— (1895) *Vita Nuova di Dante Alighieri Fiorentino* (Oxford: Nella Stamperia dell'Università).
— (1897) *Tutte le opere di Dante Alighieri nuovamente rivedute nel testo da E. Moore con Indice dei nomi propri e delle cose notabili contenute nelle opere di Dante. Compilato da Paget Toynbee*, 2nd edn (Oxford: Nella Stamperia dell'Università).
— (1904) *Tutte le opere di Dante Alighieri nuovamente rivedute nel testo da E. Moore*, 3rd edn (Oxford: Nella Stamperia dell'Università).
— (1909) *Tutte le opere di Dante Alighieri nuovamente rivedute nel testo dal dottore Edward Moore*, ed. E. Moore (Chelsea: Folio Nella Stamperia Ashendeniana, Shelley House).
— (1924) *Tutte le opere di Dante Alighieri, a cura di Edward Moore, nuovamente rivedute nel testo da Paget Toynbee*, 4th edn (Oxford: Nella Stamperia dell'Università).
— (1995) *Convivio*, ed. by Franca Brambilla Ageno, 3 vols (Florence: Le Lettere).
— (2005) *La Divina Commedia*, ed. by Anna Maria Chiavacci Leonardi, 3 vols (Milano: Mondadori).

Translations

Alighieri, D. (1802) *Dante Alighieri: The Divina Commedia, Translated into English Verse, with Preliminary, Essays, Notes, and Illustrations*, ed. and trans. by Henry Boyd, 3 vols (London: Cadell and Davies).
— (1805) *The Inferno of Dante Alighieri*, trans. by the Rev. Henry Francis Cary 2 vols (London: Carpenter).
— (1814) *The Vision, or, Hell, Purgatory, and Paradise of Dante Alighieri*, trans. by the Rev. Henry Francis Cary, 3 vols (London: Taylor and Hessey).
— (1819) *The Vision, or, Hell, Purgatory and Paradise of Dante Alighieri*, trans. by the Rev. Henry Francis Cary, 3 vols (London: Taylor and Hessey).
— (1835) *The* Canzoniere *of Dante […] including the poems of the* Vita Nuova *and* Convito, trans. by Charles Lyell (London: John Murray).
— (1842) *The Poems of the* Vita Nuova *and* Convito *of Dante Alighieri*, trans. by Charles Lyell (London: C. F. Molini).
— (1844) *The Vision: or, Hell, Purgatory, and Paradise of Dante Alighieri*, trans. by the Rev. Henry Francis Cary (London: William and Smith).
— (1850) *The Vision, or, Hell, Purgatory and Paradise of Dante Alighieri*, trans. by the Rev. Henry Francis Cary, new and corr. edn (London: Henry G. Bohn).

— (1862) *The* Vita Nuova *of Dante, translated, with an introduction and notes, by Theodore Martin* (London: Parker, Son & Burn).

— (1862–63) *Dante's Divina Commedia: Translated into English, in the Metre and Triple Rhyme of the Original with Notes by Mrs Claudia H. Ramsay* (London: Tinsley Bros).

— (1865) *The Comedy of Dante Allighieri: The Hell, translated into blank verse by W. M. Rossetti, with intr. and notes* (London: Macmillan).

— (1865) *Dante Allighieri's Göttliche Komödie. Uebersetzt von Karl Witte* (Berlin: R. L. von Decker).

— (1865–67) *The Divine Comedy of Dante Alighieri*, trans. by Henry W. Longfellow (London: Routledge).

— (1867) *The New Life of Dante Alighieri*, trans. by Charles Eliot Norton (Boston: Ticknor and Fields).

— (1879) *The 'De Monarchia' by Dante Alighieri*, trans. by Frederick J. Church (London: Macmillan).

— (1887) Il Convito: *The Banquet of Dante Alighieri: Translated by Elizabeth Price Sayer with an Introduction Henry Morley* (London: G. Routledge and Sons).

— (1890) *Dante's Treatise 'De Vulgari Eloquentia': Translated into English, with Explanatory Notes by A. G. Ferrers Howell* (London: K. Paul, Trench, Trübner & Co.).

— (1899) *The Paradiso of Dante Alighieri*, ed. by Herman Oelsner and trans. by Philip H. Wicksteed (London: J. M. Dent and Co.).

— (1892–99) *The* Purgatorio *of Dante Alighieri: An Experiment in Literal Translation*, trans. by Charles L. Shadwell, 2 vols (London: Macmillan and Co.).

— (1900–2) *The Vision of Dante Alighieri. Translated by Henry Francis Cary. Revised, with an introduction, by Paget Toynbee*, 3 vols (London: Methuen & Co.).

— (1901) *The* Purgatorio *of Dante Alighieri*, ed. by Herman Oelsner and trans. by Thomas Okey (London: J. M. Dent & Co.).

— (1902) *Dante and Giovanni del Virgilio including a critical edition of the text of Dante's 'Eclogae latinae' and of the poetic remains of Giovanni del Virgilio*, ed. and trans. by Philip H. Wicksteed and Edmund G. Gardner (Westminster: Constable & Co.).

— (1903) *The* Convivio *of Dante Alighieri*, ed. and trans. by Philip H. Wicksteed (London: J. M. Dent).

— (1904) *The Latin Works of Dante Alighieri*, ed. and trans. by A. G. Ferrers Howell and Philip H. Wicksteed (London: J. M. Dent & Co.).

— (1904) *The* Purgatorio *and* Paradiso *of the* Divina Commedia *of Dante Alighieri*, trans. by Catherine Potter (London: Digby, Long & Co.).

— (1906) *The* Vita Nuova *and* Canzoniere *of Dante Alighieri*, trans. by Thomas Okey and Philip H. Wicksteed (London: J. M. Dent & Co.).
— (1909) *Quaestio de Aqua et Terra*, trans. by Charles L. Shadwell (Oxford: Clarendon Press).
— (1915) *The Paradise of Dante Alighieri: An Experiment in Literal Translation*, trans. by Charles L. Shadwell, 2 vols (London: Macmillan and Co.).
— (1927) *Dante's Eclogues: The Poetical Correspondence between Dante and Giovanni del Virgilio*, trans. by Wilmon Brewer (Boston: Cornhill Publishing and Co.).

Primary and secondary sources

Aberdeen Daily Journal, 'Editorial', 18 February 1902, p. 7.
Academy, 'A Dante Lecturership at Oxford', May 1895, p. 426.
Acheson, K. (2019) 'Introduction: Marginalia, Reading and Writing', in *Early Modern English Marginalia*, ed. by Katherine Acheson (London: Routledge), pp. 1–12.
Allan, D. (2010) *Commonplace Books in Georgian England* (Cambridge: Cambridge University Press).
Altick, R. (1957) *The English Common Reader: A Social History of the Mass Reading Public, 1800–1900* (Chicago: University of Chicago Press).
Anderson, R. D. (1995) *Universities and Elites in Britain since 1800* (Cambridge: Cambridge University Press).
Anger, S. (2011) *Victorian Interpretation* (Ithaca: Cornell University Press).
Armstrong, E. (1969) 'Edward Moore, 1835–1916', in Edward Moore, *Studies in Dante. First Series* (Oxford: Clarendon Press), pp. ix–xxii.
Armstrong, G. (2013) *The English Boccaccio: A History in Books* (Toronto: University of Toronto Press).
Arnold, M., 'Dante and Beatrice', *Fraser's Magazine*, May 1863, pp. 665–9.
— (1869) *Culture and Anarchy: An Essay in Political and Social Criticism* (London: Smith, Elder and Co.).
— (1880) 'The Study of Poetry', in *The English Poets*, 5 vols, ed. by Thomas H. Ward (London: Macmillan and Co.), I, pp. xvi–xlvii.
— (1882) 'Ecce, Convertimur ad Gentes', in *Irish Essays and Others* (London: Smith, Elder and Co.), pp. 109–39.
— (1902) *Matthew Arnold's Notebooks*, ed. by Eleanor M. C. A. W. M. Sandhurst (London: Smith Elder and Co.).
— (1952) *The Notebooks of Matthew Arnold*, ed. by Howard Foster Lowry, Karl Young, and Waldo Hilary Dutton (London: Oxford University Press).

— (1958) *Matthew Arnold's Books: Towards a Publishing Diary*, ed. by William E. Buckler (Genève: Librairie E. Droz).
— (1959) *Matthew Arnold's Diaries, the Unpublished Items: A Transcription and Commentary*, ed. by William B. Guthrie (Charlottesville: University of Virginia).
— (1960) *Essays, Letters, and Reviews by Matthew Arnold*, ed. by Fraiser Neiman (Cambridge: Harvard University Press).
— (1960–77) 'Preface to First Edition of Poems (1853)', in *The Complete Prose Works of Matthew Arnold*, ed. by Richard Super, 11 vols (Ann Arbor: University of Michigan Press), I, 1–15.
— (1978) *Unpublished Letters of Matthew Arnold*, ed. by Arnold Whitridge (Folcroft: Folcroft Library Editions).
— (1979) *Matthew Arnold, Prose Writings: The Critical Heritage*, ed. by Carl Dawson and John Pfordresher (London: Routledge & K. Paul).
— (1996–2001) *The Letters of Matthew Arnold*, ed. by Cecil Y. Lang, 6 vols (Charlottesville: University Press of Virginia).
Athenaeum, 'The Bargello of Florence', 25 December 1847, pp. 1328–9.
— 'The Vita Nuova of Dante', 8 February 1862, pp. 188–9.
— 'Dante's *Divina Commedia*', 5 March 1864, pp. 332–3.
— 'List of Some of the Principal New Books in Circulation at Mudie's Select Library', 16 January 1872, p. 37.
— 'Dante Literature', 15 June 1889, pp. 753–5.
— 'The Oxford Dante', 15 December 1894, pp. 823–4.
Atherton, C. (2005) *Defining Literary Criticism: Scholarship, Authority and the Possession of Literary Knowledge, 1880–2002* (Basingstoke: Palgrave Macmillan).
Atkinson, J. (2010) *Victorian Biography Reconsidered: A Study of Nineteenth Century 'Hidden' Lives* (Oxford: Oxford University Press).
Austin, A. (1906) 'Preface', in Dante Society, *The Dante Society Lectures*, 3 vols (London: 'Pall Mall' Press), II, pp. x–xviii.
Baker, W. (1977) *The George Eliot and George Henry Lewes Library. An Annotated Catalogue of Their Books at Dr. Williams's Library, London*. (New York and London: Garland).
Barlow, H. C. (1850) *Remarks on the Reading of the 59th Verse of the 5th Canto of the* Inferno (Privately printed).
— 'Dante's Portrait in the Bargello at Florence', *Athenaeum*, 1857, pp. 853–4.
— (1862a) Il Conte Ugolino e l'Arcivescovo Ruggieri: *A Sketch from the Pisan Chronicles* (London: Trübner and Co.).
— (1862b) Il Gran Rifiuto: *What It Was, Who Made It, and How Fatal to Dante Allighieri, a Dissertation on Verses 58 to 63 of the 3rd Canto of the* Inferno (London: Trübner and Co.).
— (1862c) 'Review of Theodore Martin's Translation of the *Vita Nuova*', *Athenaeum*, 8 February 1862.

— (1864) *Critical, Historical, and Philosophical Contributions to the Study of the Divina Commedia* (London and Edinburgh: Williams & Norgate).
— (1865a) *Critical, Historical and Philosophical Contributions to the Study of the* Divina Commedia (London: William and Norgate).
— (1865b) *Francesca da Rimini: Her Lament and Vindication with a Brief Notice of the Malatesti* (London: David Nutt).
— (1865c) *The Sixth Centenary Festival of Dante Alighieri in Florence and at Ravenna* (London: William and Norgate).
— (1866) *The Sixth Centenary Festivals of Dante Alleghieri in Florence and Ravenna by A Representative* (London, Edinburgh, Florence, and Turin: Williams & Norgate and Hermann Loescher).
— (1868) *A Brief Memoir of Henry Clark Barlow* (London: Privately Printed).
— (1871) 'A Shadow of Dante: Being an Essay towards Studying Himself, His World, and His Pilgrimage. By Maria Francesca Rossetti (Rivingtons)', *Athenaeum*, 2297 (4 November), pp. 586–7.
Beatty, H. M. (1914) 'A Century of Cary's Dante', *Studies: An Irish Quarterly Review*, 3:9, pp. 567–82.
Bebbington, D. W. (1993) *William Ewart Gladstone: Faith and Politics in Victorian Britain* (Grand Rapids: W. B. Eerdmans Publisher).
— (2004) *The Mind of Gladstone: Religion, Homer, and Politics* (New York: Oxford University Press).
Bell, E. H., 'Dante's *Vita Nuova*', *The Academy, 1869–1902*, 11 December 1880, p. 425.
Bell, M. (1898) *Christina Rossetti: A Biographical and Critical Study* (Boston: Roberts Bros.).
Le Belle Assemblée, or, Bell's Court and Fashionable Magazine Addressed Particularly to the Ladies, 'European Literature of the Fourteenth Century', 1 July 1838, pp. 50–5.
Bennett, D. (1990) *Emily Davies and the Liberation of Women: 1830–1921* (London: Andre Deutsch).
Berlin, J. A. (1983) 'Matthew Arnold's Rhetoric: The Method of an Elegant Jeremiah', *Rhetoric Society Quarterly*, 13, 29–40.
Blackwood's Edinburgh Magazine, 'On Public Lectures of Works Imagination at Literary Institutions', November 1819, pp. 162–9.
Boccaccio, G. (1833) *La vita di Dante Alighieri* (Firenze: per Ig. Moutier).
Boldrini, L. (2001) *Joyce, Dante, and the Poetics of Literary Relations: Language and Meaning in Finnegan's Wake* (Cambridge: Cambridge University Press).
Boschi Rotiroti, M. (2015) 'English Intellectuals in the Archives of the Società Dantesca Italiana', *Dante in the Nineteenth Century: The International Journal of Cross-Cultural Studies and Environmental Communication*, 4.1, pp. 45–52.

Botterill, S. (1993) 'Dante in the British Isles since 1980', *Dante Studies, with the Annual Report of the Dante Society*, 111, 245–61.

— (2005) 'The Trecento Commentaries on Dante's *Commedia*', in *The Cambridge History of Literary Criticism*, vol II, *The Middle Ages*, ed. by Alastair Minnis and Ian Johnson (Cambridge: Cambridge University Press), pp. 590–611.

Bradley, M. (2009) '"Annotation Mapping" and What It Means: Developing the Gladstone Catalogue as a Resource for the History of Reading', *Literature Compass*, 6, 499–510.

— (2015) 'Gladstone's Unfinished Synchrony: Reading Afterlives and the Gladstone Catalogue', in *Reading and the Victorians*, ed. by Matthew Bradley and Juliet John (Burlington: Ashgate), pp. 127–42.

Braida, A. (2004) *Dante and The Romantics* (Basingstoke and New York: Palgrave Macmillan).

— (2020) 'Mary Shelley in Italy: Reading Dante and the Creation of an Anglo-Italian Identity', *L'analisi linguistica e letteraria, Vita e Pensiero*, 17:3, pp. 107–18.

Brake, L. (1994) *Subjugated Knowledges: Journalism, Gender and Literature in the Nineteenth Century* (London: Macmillan).

Bryant, M. (1979) *The Unexpected Revolution: A Study in the History of the Education of Women and Girls in the Nineteenth Century* (London: University of London, Institute of Education).

Caesar, M. (1989) *Dante: The Critical Heritage, 1314(?)–1870* (London: Routledge).

Caine, B. (1992) *Victorian Feminists* (Oxford: Oxford University Press).

Camilletti, F., M. Gragnolati, and F. Lampard, eds (2011) *Metamorphosing Dante: Appropriations, Manipulations and Rewritings in the Twentieth and Twenty-First Centuries* (Wien: Turia + Kant).

Camilletti, F. (2019) *Portrait of Beatrice: Dante, D. G. Rossetti and the Imaginary Lady* (Notre Dame: University of Notre Dame Press).

Carducci, G. (1888) *L'opera di Dante* (Bologna: Nicola Zanichelli).

Carlyle, T. (1841) *On Heroes, Hero Worship and The Heroic in History: Six Lectures* (London: James Fraser).

— (1892) *Lectures on The History of Literature: Or the Successive Periods of European Culture delivered in 1838* (London: Curwen, Kane).

Cary, H. (1847) *Memoir of the Rev. Henry Francis Cary, M.A., Translator of Dante: With His Literary Journal and Letters*, 2 vols (London: E. Moxon).

Caselli, D. (2017) 'Dante's Pilgrimage in Dorothy Richardson', *Comparative Literature*, 69, pp. 91–110.

Chadwick, O. (1979) 'Young Gladstone and Italy', *Journal of Ecclesiastical History*, 10, pp. 243–59.

Chapman, A. (2000) *The Afterlife of Christina Rossetti* (Basingstoke: Palgrave Macmillan).
Chapman, A. and J. Meacock, eds (2007) *A Rossetti Family Chronology* (Basingstoke: Palgrave Macmillan).
Chester, N. (1895) *Dante Vignettes* (London: Elliot Stock).
Chiavacci, A. M., ed. (2005) *La Divina Commedia*, 3 vols (Milano: Mondadori).
Church, R. C. (1888) *Dante and Other Essays* (London: Macmillan and Co.).
Clark, P. (2000) *British Clubs and Societies 1580–1800: The Origins of an Associational World* (Oxford: Oxford University Press).
Coleridge, S. T. (1836–59) *The Literary Remains of Samuel Taylor Coleridge*, ed. by Henry Nelson Coleridge, 4 vols (London: Pickering).
— (1957–89). *The Notebooks of Samuel Taylor Coleridge*, ed. by Kathleen Coburn, 6 vols (New York: Princeton).
— (1987a) *The Collected Works of Samuel Taylor Coleridge*, ed. by R. A. Foakes, 16 vols (Princeton: Princeton University Press), V, pp. 401–2.
— (1987b) *Lectures 1808–1819 on Literature*, ed. by R. A. Foakes, 2 vols (London and Princeton: Routledge and Princeton University Press).
— (2003) *A Book I Value: Selected Marginalia*, ed. by H. J. Jackson (Princeton: Princeton University Press).
Collini, S. (1994) *Matthew Arnold: A Critical Portrait* (Oxford: Clarendon Press).
Colombo, D. (2011) 'Per l'edizione del Commento Dantesco dI Baldassarre Lombardi', *Rivista di Studi Danteschi*, XI, pp. 322–73.
Coluzzi, F. (2021) 'Rossetti Reconsidered: Dante's Vita Nuova and Its Paths to Canonization in Victorian Literary Culture', *Le Tre Corone: Rivista Internazionale di studi su Dante*, 8, pp. 135–46.
Connell, P. (2000) '*Bibliomania*: Book Collecting, Cultural Politics, and the Rise of Literary Heritage in Romantic Britain', *Representations*, 71, pp. 24–47.
Connell, W. F. (1950) *The Educational Thought and Influence of Matthew Arnold* (London: Routledge & K. Paul).
Cooksey, T. L. (1984) 'Dante's England: The Contribution of Cary, Coleridge and Foscolo to the British Reception of Dante', *Papers on Language and Literature*, 20, pp. 355–81.
Coolahan, M. L. (2020) 'The Cultural Dynamics of Reception', *Journal of Medieval and Early Modern Studies*, 50:1, pp. 1–12.
Cortese, R. (1981) *George Eliot and Dante*, unpublished PhD, University of Winsconsin-Madison.
Cotes, R. A. (1898) *Dante's Garden, with the Legend of the Flowers* (London: Methuen & Co.).

Crisafulli, E. (2003) *The Vision of Dante: Cary's Translation of the* Divine Comedy (Market Harborough: Troubador).
The Critic, 'Mr Martin's Dante', 1862, pp. 338–40.
Cunningham, G. F. (1965–66) *The Divine Comedy in English: A Critical Bibliography 1782–1900*, 2 vols (Edinburgh and London: Oliver and Boyd).
D'Israeli, I. (1795) *An Essay on the Manners and Genius of the Literary Characters* (London: printed for T. Cadell, Jr and W. Davies).
Dacome, L. (2005) 'Noting the Mind: Commonplace Books and the Pursuit of the Self in Eighteenth-Century Britain', *Journal of the History of Ideas*, 65, pp. 603–25.
Daily News, 'The Age of Dante', 22 April 1857, p. 2.
— 'Signor Nicolini's Lectures on Dante', 30 January 1860, p. 2.
Dante Society (1904–6) *The Dante Society Lectures*, 3 vols (London: Pall Mall Press).
Darnton, R. (1990) *The Kiss of Lamourette: Reflections in Cultural History* (London, Faber).
— (2000) 'Extraordinary Commonplaces', *New York Review of Books*, 20, pp. 82–7.
Daunton, M., ed. (2005) *The Organisation of Knowledge in Victorian Britain* (Oxford: Published for the British Academy by Oxford University Press).
Davie, M. (1994) '"Not an After-Dinner Relaxation": Gladstone on Translating Dante', *Journal of European Studies*, 2, pp. 385–40.
Davies, E. (1866) *The Higher Education of Women* (London: Alexander Straham).
— (1910) *Thoughts on Some Questions Relating to Women, 1860–1908* (Cambridge: Bowes and Bowes).
— (2004) *Emily Davies: Collected Letters, 1861–1875*, ed. by A. Murphy and D. Raftery (Charlottesville: University of Virginia Press).
Denman, K. and S. Smith (1994) 'Christina Rossetti's Copy of C. B. Cayley's *Divine Comedy*', *Victorian Poetry*, 32:2–4, pp. 315–38.
Dennett, J. R., 'A Review of Miss M. F. Rossetti's *Shadow of Dante*', *The Nation*, 1872, pp. 28–9.
De Ventura, P. (2011) 'Introduzione', in Maria Francesca Rossetti, *Un'ombra di Dante: ovvero un saggio per studiare l'autore, il suo mondo e il suo pellegrinaggio*, ed. and trans. by Paolo De Ventura (Lanciano: Rocco Carabba), pp. 9–71.
Donovan, R. A. (1956) 'The Method of Arnold's Essays in Criticism', *PMLA*, 71, pp. 922–31.
Doughty, O. (1953) 'Dante Gabriel Rossetti as Translator', *Theoria: A Journal of Social and Political Theory*, 5, 102–12.

Draper, W. H. (1923) *University Extension: A Survey of Fifty Years 1873–1923* (Cambridge: Cambridge University Press).
Drury, A. (2015) *Translation as Transformation in Victorian Poetry* (Cambridge: Cambridge University Press).
Dublin Review, 'Tutte le Opere di Dante Alighieri: Nuovamente Rivedute Nel Testo', April 1895, pp. 425–7.
Edinburgh Evening News, 'Mr Gladstone on Dante', 22 January 1884, p. 4.
— 'Mr Gladstone on Dante', 14 March 1896, p. 4.
Eliot, S. (2006) 'Circulating Libraries in the Victorian Age and After', in *The Cambridge History of Libraries in Britain and Ireland*, ed. by Alistair Black and Peter Hoare, 3 vols (Cambridge: Cambridge University Press), III, pp. 125–146.
— (2007) 'From Few and Expensive to Many and Cheap: The British Book Market 1800–1900', in *The Blackwell Companion to the History of the Book*, ed. by Simon Eliot and Jonathan Rose (Oxford: Blackwell), pp. 291–302.
Eliot, T. S. (1932) 'Matthew Arnold' in *Selected Essays, 1917–1932* (New York: Harcourt, Brace), pp. 346–56.
Ellis, H. (2014) 'Enlightened Networks: Anglo-German Collaboration in Classical Scholarship' in *Anglo-German Scholarly Networks in the Long Nineteenth Century*, ed. by Heather Ellis and Ulrike Kirchberger (Leiden: Brill), pp. 21–38.
Ellis, S. (1983) *Dante and English Poetry: Shelley to T. S. Eliot* (Cambridge: Cambridge University Press).
Ellison, R. H. (1998) *The Victorian Pulpit: Spoken and Written Sermons in Nineteenth-Century Britain* (Cranbury: Susquehanna University Press).
Ferris, I. (2004) 'Bibliographical Romance: Bibliophilia and the Book-Object', in *Romantic Libraries*, ed. by Ina Ferris, *Romantic Circles* (25 October 2004).
Flint, K. (1993) *The Woman Reader: 1837–1914* (Oxford: Oxford University Press).
Folena, G. (1965) 'La filologia dantesca di Carlo Witte', in *Dante e la cultura tedesca. Convegno di studi danteschi, 1965*, ed. by Lino Lazzarini (Padua: Tipi dell'Antoniana, 1967), pp. 111–39.
— (1967) 'La filologia dantesca di Carlo Witte', in *Dante e la cultura tedesca. Convegno di studi danteschi, 1965*, ed. by Lino Lazzarini (Padua: Tipi dell'Antoniana), pp. 111–39.
Foot, M. R. D. (1968–94), 'Introduction', in *The Gladstone Diaries*, ed. by M. R. D. Foot and H. C. G. Matthew, 14 vols (Oxford: Oxford University Press), pp. xix–xlviii.
Foscolo, U. (1917) *Poesie, lettere e prose letterarie / di Ugo Foscolo; scelte ed annotate per le scuole classiche da Tommaso Casini* (Florence: Sansoni).

— (1972) *Studi su Dante*, ed. by Giovanni da Pozzo, Edizione nazionale delle opere di Ugo Foscolo, 22 vols, IX.
Foster, K. (1965) 'Dante Studies in England, 1921–1964', *Italian Studies*, 20, pp. 1–16.
Fowler, A. (1979) 'Genre and the Literary Canon', *New Literary History*, 11, pp. 97–119.
Fraser's Magazine for Town and Country, 'The Vita Nuova of Dante', May 1862, pp. 580–94.
Fredeman, W. E. (1996) '"Woodman, Spare that Block": The Published, Unpublished, and Projected Illustrations and Book Designs of Dante Gabriel Rossetti', *Journal of Pre-Raphaelite Studies*, 5.1 (1996), pp. 7–41.
Friedrichs, H. (1896) *In the Evening of His Days: A Study of Mr. Gladstone in Retirement, with Some Account of St. Deiniol's Library and Hostel* (London: Westminster Gazette).
Gardner, E. G. (1899) *The Paradiso of Dante Alighieri*, ed. by Herman Oelsner and trans. by Philip H. Wicksteed (London: J. M. Dent and Co.).
— (1900) *Dante* (London: J. M. Dent).
Genette, G. (1997) *Paratexts: Thresholds of Interpretation*, trans. by Jane E. Lewin (Cambridge: Cambridge University Press).
Gentleman's Magazine, 'Historical Influences of the *Divine Comedy*', February 1900, pp. 167–76.
Gentleman's Magazine: And Historical Review, 'Portrait of Dante', January 1841, p. 73.
Gilson, S. (1995) *Dante and Renaissance Florence* (Cambridge: Cambridge University Press).
— (2018) *Reading Dante in Renaissance Italy* (Cambridge: Cambridge University Press).
Gifford, G. H. (1956) 'A History of the Dante Society', *Annual Reports of the Dante Society, with Accompanying Papers*, 74 (1956), 3–27.
Gittings, R. (1956) *The Mask of Keats: A Study of Problems* (Cambridge: Harvard University Press).
Gladstone, M. (1930) *Mary Gladstone, Her Diaries and Letters, 1870–1886*, ed. by Lucy Masterman (London: Methuen & Co.).
Gladstone, W. E. (1884) 'Lord John Russell's Translation of Dante's Francesca da Rimini', *English Review*, April 1884, pp. 1–16.
— (1892) 'Did Dante Study at Oxford?', *Nineteenth Century Review*, June, pp. 1032–42.
— (1930) *The Gladstone Papers*, ed. by A. Tilney Bassett (London: Cassell).
— (1968–94) *The Gladstone Diaries*, ed. by M. R. D. Foot and H. C. G. Matthew, 14 vols (Oxford: Oxford University Press).
Glasgow Herald, 'Our London Correspondence', 21 November 1894, p. 5.
Gottfried, L. A. (1963) *Matthew Arnold and the Romantics* (Lincoln: University of Nebraska Press).

Gow, E. (2019a) 'Feature Article: Enriqueta Rylands: A Study of Private Collecting and Public Philanthropy, 1889–1908', *Library and Informational History Group News*, Winter, pp. 2–4.

— (2019b) 'Enriqueta Rylands: The Private Collector of a Public Library', unpublished paper.

— (2020) '"Not Slothful in Business": Enriqueta Rylands and the John Rylands Library', in *Protestant Dissent and Philanthropy in Britain, 1660–1914*, ed. by Clyde Binfield, G. M. Ditchfield, and David L. Wykes (Cambridge: Boydell and Brewer), pp. 205–22.

Grafton, A. (1997) 'Is the History of Reading a Marginal Enterprise? Guillaume Budé and His Books', *The Papers of the Bibliographical Society of America*, 91, pp. 139–57.

Griest, G. L. (1965) 'A Victorian Leviathan: Mudie's Select Library', *Nineteenth-Century Fiction*, 20, pp. 103–26.

Guppy, H. (1908) 'In Memoriam. Mrs Enriqueta Augustina Rylands', *Bulletin of the John Rylands Library*, 1:6, p. 355.

Guppy, H. and John Rylands Library (1909) *Catalogue of an Exhibition of the Works of Dante Alighieri: Shown in the John Rylands Library, Manchester from March to October 1909* (Manchester: Sherratt and Hughes).

Hampton, T. (1990) *Writing from History: The Rhetoric of Exemplarity in Renaissance Literature* (Ithaca: Cornell University).

Harding, A. J. (2004) 'Coleridge's Notebooks and the Case for a Material Hermeneutics of Literature', *Romanticism*, 1, pp. 1–19.

Harrison, A. H. (2009) *The Cultural Production of Matthew Arnold* (Athens: Ohio University Press).

Hartley, R. A. (1990) 'Shelley's Copy of Dante', *Keats-Shelley Journal*, 39, pp. 22–9.

Hasell, E. J. (1867) 'Dante in English Terza Rima', *Blackwood's Edinburgh Magazine*, June 1867, pp. 736–55.

Havely, N. R., ed. (2011) *Dante in the Nineteenth Century: Reception, Canonicity, Popularisation* (Oxford: Peter Lang).

— (2014) *Dante's British Public: Readers and Texts, from the Fourteenth Century to the Present* (Oxford: Oxford University Press).

— (2018) 'Wider Circles: Popularizing Dante, from Temple Classics to Penguin Classics In Journey through Changing Landscapes' in *Literature, Language, Culture and Their Transnational Dislocations*, ed. by Carla Dente and Francesca Fedi (Pisa: Pisa University Press).

Havens, E. (2001) *Commonplace Books: A History of Manuscripts and Printed Books from Antiquity to the Twentieth Century* (New Haven: Yale University Press).

Hazlitt, W. (1930–34) 'Lectures on the English Poets', in *The Complete Works of William Hazlitt*, ed. by P. P. Howe, 21 vols (London: J. M. Dent), V, pp. 15–19.
Herford, C. H. (1931) *Philip Henry Wicksteed, His Life and Work* (London: J. M. Dent).
Hess, J. (2012) 'Coleridge's Fly-Catchers: Adapting Commonplace-Book Form', *Journal of the History of Ideas*, 73:3, pp. 463–83.
Hessel, K. (2016) 'The Romantic-Era Lecture: Dividing and Reuniting the Arts and Sciences', *Configurations*, 24, pp. 501–32.
Heyck, T. W. (1982) *The Transformation of Intellectual Life in Victorian England* (London: Croom Helm).
Hodgson, J. (2012) '"Carven stone and blazoned pane": The Design and Construction of the John Rylands Library', *Bulletin of the John Rylands Library*, 89:1, pp. 19–81.
Holbrook, R. (1911) *Portraits of Dante from Giotto to Raffael: A Critical Study, with a Concise Iconography* (London: P. L. Warner).
Hollander, R. (1983) 'A Checklist of Commentators on the *Commedia* (1322–1982)', *Dante Studies, with the Annual Report of the Dante Society*, 101, pp. 181–92.
— (2007) 'Dante and his Commentators', in *The Cambridge Companion to Dante*, ed. by Rachel Jacoff (Cambridge: Cambridge University Press), pp. 270–80.
Houghton, W. E. (1982) 'Periodical Literature and the Articulate Classes', in *The Victorian Periodical Press: Samplings and Soundings*, ed. by Joanne Shattock and Michael Woolf (Leicester: Leicester University Press), pp. 3–28.
Isba, A. (2006) *Gladstone and Dante: Victorian Statesman, Medieval Poet* (Royal Historical Society, London: Boydell Press).
Jackson, H. J. (2001) *Marginalia: Readers Writing in Books* (New Haven: Yale University Press).
— (2005) *Romantic Readers: The Evidence of Marginalia* (New Haven and London: Yale University Press).
— (2012) 'Coleridge As Reader: *Marginalia*', in *The Oxford Handbook of Samuel Taylor Coleridge*, ed. by Frederick Burwick (Oxford: Oxford University Press), pp. 271–87.
Jagger, P. J. (2007) *Gladstone* (London: Continuum).
Jennings, J. (1823) *A Lecture on the History and Utility of Literary Institutions* (London: Sherwood, Jones).
Jepson, N. A. (1973) *The Beginnings of English University Adult Education: Policy and Problems: A Critical Study of the Early Cambridge and Oxford University Extension Lecture Movements between 1873 and 1907, with Special Reference to Yorkshire* (London: Joseph).

Joeres, R. B. and E. Mittman, eds (1993) *The Politics of the Essay: Feminist Perspectives* (Bloomington: Indiana University Press).

Johnston, J. and H. Fraser (2001) 'The Professionalization of Women's Writing: Extending the Canon', in *Women and Literature in Britain, 1800–1900*, ed. by J. Shattock (Cambridge: Cambridge University Press).

Kargon, R. H. (1977) *Science in Victorian Manchester: Enterprise and Expertise* (Regno Unito: Manchester University Press).

Keats, J. (1958) *The Letters of John Keats*, ed. by Hyder Edward Rollins, 2 vols (Cambridge: Cambridge University Press).

King, R. W. (1925) *The Translator of Dante* (London: Secker).

Kirchberger, U. (2014) 'Introduction', in *Anglo-German Scholarly Networks in the Long Nineteenth Century*, ed. by Heather Ellis and Ulrike Kirchberger (Leiden: Brill), pp. 1–19.

Kirsch, A. (2008) *The Modern Element: Essays on Contemporary Poetry* (New York: W. W. Norton).

Klancher, J. (2013) *Transfiguring the Arts and Sciences: Knowledge and Cultural Institutions in the Romantic Age* (Cambridge: Cambridge University Press).

Kuhns, O. (1904) *Dante and the English Poets* (London: Bell).

Landor, W., 'Fine Arts', *Examiner*, 16 August 1840, p. 518.

Lau, B. (1994) 'Editing Keats's Marginalia', *Text*, 7, pp. 337–48.

— (1996) 'Keats and the Practice of Romantic Marginalia', *Romanticism*, 2:1, pp. 40–53.

— (1998) *Keats's Paradise Lost* (Gainesville: University Press of Florida).

— (2006) 'Analyzing Keats's Library by Genre', *Keats-Shelley Journal*, 65, pp. 126–51.

Laurence, A., J. Bellamy, and G. Perry (2000) *Women, Scholarship and Criticism C. 1790–1900*, ed. by Anne Laurence, Joan Bellamy, Gill Perry (Manchester: Manchester University Press).

Laurence, A. (2011) 'Exploiting Dante: Dante and His Women Popularizers, 1850–1910', in *Dante in the Nineteenth Century: Canonicity, Reception, Popularisation*, ed. by Nicholas Havely (Oxford: Peter Lang), pp. 281–301.

Lawrie, A. (2014) *The Beginnings of University English: Extramural Study, 1885–1910* (Basingstoke: Palgrave Macmillan).

Levine, P. (2002) 'Keats against Dante: The Sonnet on Paolo and Francesca', *Keats-Shelley Journal*, 51, pp. 76–93.

Lindon, J. (1977) 'One Hundred Years of Barlow Lectures', *Italian Studies*, 32 (1977), pp. 8–20.

— (1988) 'H. C. Barlow and His Contribution to Textual Criticism of the *Divine Comedy*', *Deutsches Dante-Jahrbuch*, 63, pp. 47–74.

— (1989) 'Henry Clark Barlow and Karl Witte: A Friendship in Dante, with Unpublished Letters', *Deutsches Dante-Jahrbuch*, 64, pp. 75–110.

— (1995) 'Gli apporti del metodo di Edward Moore nei primi decenni della Società Dantesca Italiana', in *La Società Dantesca Italiana, 1888–1988: Convegno Internazionale, Firenze 24–26 Novembre 1988* (Milan and Naples: Ricciardi), pp. 37–53.

— (2000) 'Dante "intra Tamisi ed Arno" (and Halle-am-Saale): The Letters of Seymour Kirkup to H. C. Barlow', in *Britain and Italy from Romanticism to Modernism: A Festschrift for Peter Brand*, ed. by Martin McLaughlin (London: Routledge), pp. 121–42.

— (2010) 'Notes on the British Contribution to the Nineteenth-Century Rise of Dante Studies: Edward Moore and the Text of the *Commedia*', in *Dante the Lyric and Ethical Poet: Dante lirico e etico*, ed. by Zygmunt G. Barański and Martin L. McLaughlin (London: Legenda, MHRA and Maney Publishing), pp. 227–35.

— (2013) 'Notes on Nineteenth-Century Dante Commentaries and Critical Editions', in *Interpreting Dante: Essays on the Traditions of Dante Commentary*, ed. by P. Nasti and C. Rossignoli (Notre Dame: University of Notre Dame Press), pp. 434–49.

Liverpool Mercury, 'Our London Letter', 1 November 1894, p. 7.

Lloyd, J. M. (1995) 'Raising Lilies: Ruskin and Women', *Journal of British Studies*, 34, pp. 325–50.

London Dante Society and L. Ricci (1908) *Annual Report Read at the Meeting of June 4th, 1908* ([London?]: [n. pub.]).

London Quarterly Review, 'The *Vita Nuova*, or New Life of Dante Alighieri', April 1903, p. 407.

London Review, 'Translations of Dante', 30 May 1863, pp. 585–6.

London Standard, 'Mr. Gladstone and Dante', 9 January 1884, p. 5.

Lowell, J. R., 'The Shadow of Dante, Being an Essay towards Studying Himself, His World, and His Pilgrimage by Maria Francesca Rossetti', *North American Review*, July 1872, p. 139.

— (1898–99) 'Dante', in *The Writings of James Russell Lowell*, 11 vols (Boston: Houghton, Miffin and Co.), IV, pp. 118–264.

Lubenow, W. (2015) *'Only Connect': Learned Societies in Nineteenth-Century Britain* (Woodbridge: Boydell Press).

Lyell, C. (1845) 'Preface', in *The Lyrical Poems of Dante including the poems of the* Vita Nuova *and* Convito (London: W. Smith), pp. v–vii.

Lyttelton, G. (1861) *Translations by Lord Lyttelton and the Rt. Hon. W. E. Gladstone* (London: Quaritch).

Macaulay, T. B. 'Criticism on the Principal Italian Writers. Dante', *Knight's Quarterly*, 2, 1824, pp. 207–23.

— 'Dante and Milton', *Edinburgh Review*, 1825, pp. 306–23.

Manchester Courier and Lancashire General Advertiser, 'Local Intelligence', 7 October 1846, p. 4.

— 'Mr. Gladstone and Dante', 22 January 1884, p. 8.
— 'Gossip of the Week', 3 November 1894, p. 2.
— 'Mr. Gladstone and Dante', 15 October 1895, p. 8.
— 'Dante Society', September 1906, p. 10.
— 'Dante Society', 18 December 1908, p. 7.
Manchester Guardian, 'Dante's Treatment of Women: A Discussion by the Society', 28 January 1908, p. 9.
Manchester Times, 'Manchester Royal Institution', 18 March 1854, p. 12.
Marsh, J. (1994) *Christina Rossetti: A Literary Biography* (J. Cape: University of Michigan).
Marriott, S. (1981) *A Backstairs to a Degree: Demands for an Open University in Late Victorian England* (Leeds: Department of Adult Education and Extramural Studies, University of Leeds).
Matthew, C. (1999) 'Gladstone and His Diaries', *Flintshire Historical Society Journal*, 35, pp. 167–75.
Mazzoni, F. (1996) 'William E. Gladstone a Giambattista Giuliani', in *Operosa parva per Gianni Antonini*, ed. by D. De Robertis and F. Gavazzeni (Verona: Valdonega), pp. 311–14.
Mazzotta, G. (2004) *Reading Dante* (New Haven: Yale University Press).
McGovern, 'A Manchester Dante Society', *Manchester Courier and Lancashire General Advertiser*, February 1900, p. 3.
— 'A Manchester Dante Society', *Manchester Guardian*, February 1900, p. 3.
Medwin, T. (1913) *The Life of Percy Bysshe Shelley* (Oxford: Oxford University Press).
Mercer, A. (2019) *The Collaborative Literary Relationship of Percy Bysshe Shelley and Mary Wollstonecraft Shelley* (New York and London: Routledge).
Mermin, D. (1993) *Godiva's Ride: Women of Letters in England, 1830–1880* (Bloomington: Indiana University Press).
Milbank, A. (1998) *Dante and the Victorians* (Manchester: Manchester University Press).
Miller, C. (2003) 'John Flaxman's Working Copy of Dante's *Divina Commedia*', *Italian Studies*, 58:1, pp. 75–87.
Miller, E. C. (2016) 'Reading in Review: The Victorian Book Review in the New Media Moment', *Victorian Periodicals Review*, 49: 4, pp. 626–42.
Milner, S. (2013) 'Manufacturing the Renaissance: Modern Merchant Princes and the Origins of the Manchester Dante Society', in *Culture in Manchester: Institutions and Urban Change since 1850*, ed. by Mike Savage and Janet Wolff (Manchester: Manchester University Press), pp. 61–94.

Moore, E. (1887) *Time References in the* Divina Commedia (London: David Nutt).
— (1889) *Contributions to the Textual Criticism of the* Divina Commedia, *Including the Complete Collation throughout the* Inferno *of All the Mss. at Oxford and Cambridge* (Cambridge: Cambridge University Press).
— (1890) *Dante and His Early Biographers* (London: Rivingtons).
— (1896–1917) *Studies in Dante*, 4 vols (Oxford: Clarendon Press).
Morley, J. (1903) *Life of William Ewart Gladstone*, 3 vols (London: Macmillan).
Mortimer, J. (1908) *Manchester Literary Club: Some Notes on its History, 1862–1908* (Manchester: Manchester City News Co.).
Mosk Packer, L. (1963) *Christina Rossetti* (Berkeley: University of California Press).
Moss, A. (1996) *Printed Commonplace Books and the Structuring of Renaissance Thought* (Oxford: Oxford University Press).
Moulton, R. G. (1886) *The University Extension Movement* (London: n. pub).
— (1890) *Address on the University Extension Movement* (Philadelphia: American Society for the Extension of University Teaching).
Nasti, P. and C. Rossignoli (2013) 'Introduction', in *Interpreting Dante: Essays on the Traditions of Dante Commentary*, ed. by P. Nasti and C. Rossignoli (Notre Dame: University of Notre Dame Press).
O'Connell, A. (2011) 'Dante's Linguistic Detail in Shelley's Triumph of Life', *CLCWeb: Comparative Literature and Culture*, 13:4, http://docs.lib.purdue.edu/clcweb/vol13/iss4/13.
O'Connor, A. (2012) 'Dante Alighieri from Absence to Stony Presence: Building Memories in Nineteenth-Century Florence', *Italian Studies*, 67 (3), pp. 307–35.
O'Gorman, F. (2012) 'Matthew Arnold and Rereading', *The Cambridge Quarterly*, 41, pp. 245–61.
Oliphant, M. (1876) *The Makers of Florence: Dante, Giotto, Savonarola and Their City* (London: Macmillan).
Owings, F. N. (1978) *The Keats Library: A Descriptive Catalogue* (Keats-Shelley Memorial Association: University of California).
Oxford Dante Society (1920) *The Oxford Dante Society: A Record of Forty-Four Years, 1876–1920* compiled by Paget Toynbee (Oxford: Printed for Private Publication).
Ozanam, F. (1840) *Dante et la philosophie catholique au treizième siècle* (Paris: Olivier Fulgence).
Parker, D. (1993) *Commentary and Ideology: Dante in the Renaissance* (Durham and London: Duke University Press).

Perini, N. (1908) *Lectures on Dante: Delivered to the Students of Italian at King's College* (London: Hachette).
Petroni, S. E. (1819) *La Divina Commedia. Nuova edizione corretta da S. E. Petroni*, 3 vols (London: Schulze e Dean).
Phillimore, C. M., 'Dante's *Paradise*', *St. Paul's Magazine*, April 1871, pp. 63–72.
— (1887) *Studies in Italian Literature, Classical and Modern* (London: S. Low, Marston, Searle & Rivington).
— (1898) *Dante at Ravenna* (London: Elliot Stock).
Pite, R. (1994) *The Circle of Our Vision: Dante's Presence in English Romantic Poetry* (Oxford: Clarendon Press).
Pollack-Pelzner, D. (2007) 'Revisionary Company: Keats, Homer, and Dante in the Chapman Sonnet', *Keats-Shelley Journal*, 56, pp. 39–49.
Powell, J. (1992) 'Small Marks and Instinctual Responses: A Study in the Uses of Gladstone's Marginalia', *Nineteenth-Century Prose*, 19, pp. 1–17.
Price, L. (2000) *The Anthology and the Rise of the Novel* (Cambridge: Cambridge University Press).
Prince, K. (2008) *Shakespeare in the Victorian Periodicals* (New York: Routledge).
Purvis, J. (1991) *A History of Women's Education in England* (Milton Keynes: Open University Press).
Quarterly Review, 'Publications of The Arundel Society', October 1858, pp. 277–325.
Raben, J. (1963) 'Milton's Influence on Shelley's Translation of Dante's "Matilda Gathering Flowers"', *The Review of English Studies*, 14:54, pp. 142–56.
Ramm, A. (1970) 'The Gladstone Diaries, Vols. i and ii by W. E. Gladstone and M. R. D. Foot', *The English Historical Review*, 85, pp. 591–3.
— (1992) 'Gladstone as a Man of Letters', *Nineteenth Century Prose*, 19, pp. 1–17.
Raven, J., H. Small, and N. Tadnor, eds (1996) *The Practice and Representation of Reading in England* (Cambridge: Cambridge University Press).
Raven, J. (2014) 'The Industrial Revolution of the Book', in *The Cambridge Companion to the History of the Book* (Cambridge: Cambridge University Press), pp. 143–61.
Ravinthiran, V. (2011) 'Dante and Shelley's Terza Rima', *Essays in Criticism*, 61:2, pp. 155–72.
Ricci, L. (1908) 'Preface', in *Lectures on Dante: Delivered to the Students of Italian at King's College*, ed. by N. Perini (London: Hachette), pp. v–xi.
Roach, J. (2008) *Public Examinations in England, 1850–1900* (Cambridge: Cambridge University Press).

Roberts, R. D. (1914) *Eighteen Years of University Extensions* (Cambridge: Cambridge University Press).
Roe, D. (2007) *Christina Rossetti's Faithful Imagination: The Devotional Poetry and Prose* (Basingstoke and New York: Palgrave Macmillan).
— (2011) *The Rossettis in Wonderland* (London: Haus Publishing).
Rose, J. (2010) *The Intellectual Life of the British Working Classes*, 2nd ed. (New Haven: Yale University Press).
Rose, M. (1990) 'Settlement of University Men in Great Towns: University Settlements in Manchester and Liverpool', *Transactions of the Historic Society of Lancashire and Cheshire*, pp. 143–4.
— (1995) *Everything Went On at the Round House: A Hundred Years of the Manchester University Settlement* (Manchester: Manchester University Press).
Rosen, A. (1979) 'Emily Davies and the Women's Movement 1862–1867', *Journal of British Studies*, 19:1, pp. 101–21.
Rossetti, C. G., 'Dante: An English Classic', *Churchman's Shilling Magazine and Family Treasury*, 2, 1867, pp. 200–5.
— 'Dante, The Poet Illustrated Out of the Poem, *Century Magazine*, 27 February 1884, pp. 566–73.
— (1908) *The Family Letters of Christina Georgina Rossetti: With some supplementary letters and appendices*, ed. by William Micheal Rossetti (London: Brown, Longham & Co.).
— (1997–2007) *The Letters of Christina Rossetti 1887–1894*, ed. by A. H. Harrison, 4 vols (Bloomington: University of Virginia Press).
Rossetti, D. G. (1861) *The Early Italian Poets from Ciullo d'Alcamo to Dante Alighieri (1100–1200–1300) in the Original Metres Together with Dante's Vita Nuova* (London: Smith, Elder and Co., 1861).
Rossetti, G. (1832) *Sullo Spirito Antipapale che produsse la riforma, e sulla segreta influenza ch'esercitò nella letteratura d'Europa e specialmente d'Italia* (London: Stampato per l'autore).
— (1834) *Disquisitions on the Antipapal Spirit which Produced the Reformation; Its Secret Influence on the Literature of Europe in General and of Italy in Particular*, trans. by Caroline Ward, 2 vols (London: Smith, Elder and Co.).
— (1842) *La Beatrice di Dante: Ragionamenti Critici di Gabriele Rossetti* (London: n. pub.).
Rossetti, M. F. (1871) *A Shadow of Dante: Being an Essay towards Studying Himself, His World, and His Pilgrimage* (London: Rivingtons).
— (1889) *A Shadow of Dante: Being an Essay towards Studying Himself, His World, and His Pilgrimage* (Boston: Robert Brother).
— (1901) *A Shadow of Dante: Being an Essay towards Studying Himself, His World, and His Pilgrimage* (London: Longman and Co.).

— (1904) *A Shadow of Dante: Being an Essay towards Studying Himself, His World, and His Pilgrimage* (Boston: Little and Brown).
— (2011) *Un'ombra di Dante: ovvero un saggio per studiare l'autore, il suo mondo e il suo pellegrinaggio*, ed. and trans. by Paolo De Ventura (Lanciano: Rocco Carabba).
Rossetti, W. M. (1865) 'Introduction', in *The Comedy of Dante Allighieri: The Hell, translated into blank verse by W. M. Rossetti, with intr. and notes* (London: Macmillan), pp. vii–xx.
— (1906) *Some Reminiscences of William Michael Rossetti* (London: Brown Langham).
— (1977) *The Diary of W. M. Rossetti, 1870–1873*, ed. by Odette Bernard (Oxford: Clarendon Press).
Rowbotham, S. (1965) 'Travellers in a Strange Country: Responses of Working Class Students to the University Extension Movement – 1873–1910', *History Workshop Journal*, 12, pp. 62–95.
Ruskin, J. (1843–60) *Modern Painters*, 5 vols (London: Smith, Elder and Co.), II, pp. 215–21 and 225–9.
— (1851–1853) *The Stones of Venice*, 3 vols (London: Smith, Elder and Co.)
— (1902) *Of Queen's Gardens* (London: Ballantyne Press).
Saglia, D. (2018) *European Literatures in Britain, 1815–1832: Romantic Translations: Romantic Translations* (Cambridge: Cambridge University Press).
Saly, J. (1965) 'Keats's Answer to Dante: "The Fall of Hyperion"', *Keats-Shelley Journal*, 14, pp. 65–78.
Saturday Review of Politics, Literature, Science and Art, 'Dante's Vita Nuova in English', October 1862, pp. 517–18.
— 'A Shadow of Dante', 25 November 1871, pp. 690–1.
— 'Dante's Divina Commedia', 13 April 1889, pp. 447–8.
— 'The Divine Comedy Again', 8 November 1902, p. 587.
Scartazzini, G. A. (1869) *Dante Alighieri: seine Zeit, sein Leben, und seine Werke* (Biel: Steinheil).
— (1881) *Dante in Germania* (Milano: Hoepli).
— (1896–99) *Enciclopedia dantesca: Dizionario critico e ragionato di quanto concerne la vita e le opere di Dante Alighieri*, 3 vols (Milan: U. Hoepli).
Scott, N. (1985) *The Poetics of Belief: Studies in Coleridge, Arnold, Pater, Santayana, Stevens and Heidegger* (Chapel Hill: University of North Carolina Press).
Scragg, B. (2000) 'Mrs Rylands and the Spencer Library', *Bulletin of the John Rylands University Library of Manchester*, 82:1, p. 217.
Shattock, J., ed. (2001) *Women and Literature in Britain, 1800–1900* (Cambridge: Cambridge University Press).

— (2002) 'Reviewing Generations: Professionalism and the Mid-Victorian Reviewer', *Victorian Periodicals Review*, 35:4, pp. 384–400.
Sheehan, D. (1941) 'The Manchester Literary and Philosophical Society', *Isis*, 33:4, pp. 519–23.
Shelley, M. Wollstonecraft (1987) *The Journals of Mary Shelley*, ed. by Paula R. Feldman and Diana Scott-Kilvert, 2 vols (Oxford: Clarendon Press).
Shelley, P. B. (1820) *Prometheus Unbound: A Lyrical Drama in Four Acts: With Other Poems* (London: C. and J. Ollier).
— (1821) 'A Defence of Poetry', in *Peacock's 'Four Ages of Poetry', Shelley's 'Defence on Poetry,' Browning's 'Essay on Shelley'*, ed. by Herbert F. Brett-Smith (Oxford: Blackwell), pp. 23–59.
— (1852) 'A Defence of Poetry', in *Essays, Letters from Abroad: Translations and Fragments*, ed. by Mary Wollstonecraft Shelley, vol. 1 (London: Moxon), pp. 3–48.
— (1926–30) *The Complete Works of Percy Bysshe Shelley*, ed. by Roger Ingpen and Walter E. Peck, 10 vols (London: Ernest Benn).
— (1964) *The Letters of Percy Bysshe Shelley*, ed. by F. L. Jones, 2 vols (Oxford: Clarendon Press).
— (1993) *The Prose Works of Percy Bysshe Shelley*, ed. by E. B. Murray (Oxford: Clarendon Press).
Sherif, A. (2017) 'Book Histories, Material Culture, and East Asian Studies', *Verge: Studies in Global Asias*, 3:1, pp. 35–53.
Sherman, W. H. (2008) *Used Books: Marking Readers in Renaissance England* (Philadelphia: University of Pennsylvania Press).
Shore, A. (1886) *Dante for Beginners: A Sketch of the* Divina Commedia (London: Chapman and Hall).
Sleeves, H. R. (1913) *Learned Societies and English Literary Scholarship in Great Britain and the United States* (New York: Columbia University Press).
Spectator, 'The Temple Classics', 11 February 1899, p. 209.
Speight, K. (1957) *Manchester Dante Society: A Short Account of the First Fifty Years* (Manchester: Morris and Yeaman Printers).
— (1961) 'The John Rylands Dante Collection', *Bulletin of the John Rylands Library*, 44, pp. 175–212.
Speller, J. L. (1977) *Christ, Faith and Language in the Religious Thought of Matthew Arnold* (Oxford: Oxford University Press).
Spender, D. (1989) 'Women and Literary History', in *The Feminist Reader: Essays in Gender and The Politics of Literary Criticism*, ed. by Catherine Belsey and Jane Moore (Basingstoke: Macmillan Education), pp. 21–34.
Straub, J. (2000) *A Victorian Muse: The Afterlife of Dante's Beatrice in Nineteenth-Century Literature* (London: Continuum).
Sturrock, J. (2006) 'Establishing Identity: Editorial Correspondence from the Early Years of "The Monthly Packet"', *Victorian Periodicals Review*, 39, pp. 266–79.

St Clair, W. (2004) *The Reading Nation in the Romantic Period* (Cambridge: Cambridge University Press).

Super, R. (1960–77) 'Preface to "Dante and Beatrice"', in *The Complete Prose Works of Matthew Arnold*, ed. by Richard Super, 11 vols (Ann Arbor: University of Michigan Press), III, p. 7.

Swann, J. (1908) *Manchester Literary Club: Some Notes on Its History, 1862–1908* (Manchester: Manchester City News).

Symonds, A. J. (1872) *An Introduction to the Study of Dante* (London: Smith, Elder and Co.).

Tablet, 'The Manchester Dante Society and Valgimigli', 1910, p. 24.

— 'The Dante Centenary', 27 August 1921, p. 7.

— 'The Manchester Dante Society: Twenty-First Anniversary', 7 January 1928, pp. 21–2.

Thompson, A. (1991) 'George Eliot, Dante and Moral Choice in *Felix Holt, the Radical*', *Modern Language Review*, 86:3, pp. 553–66.

— (1998) *George Eliot and Italy: Literary, Cultural and Political Influences from Dante to the Risorgimento* (Basingstoke and New York: Palgrave Macmillan).

— (2008) 'George Eliot's Borrowings from Dante: A List of Sources', *George Eliot George Henry Lewes Studies*, 44/45, pp. 26–74.

Times, 'Mr. Robert Wickham, late of No. 10', 24 May 1852, p. 2.

— 'Bombay by Steam', 18 June 1852, p. 1.

Tinkler-Villani, V. (1989) *Visions of Dante in English Poetry: Translations of the* Commedia *from Jonathan Richardson to William Blake* (Amsterdam: Rodopi).

Tipperary Free Press, 'Mr Wright's Lectures', 14 November 1849, p. 2.

Tognarelli, C. (2012) 'Il mito di Dante nelle opere del Carducci Giovane', *La Rassegna della Letteratura Italiana*, 116, 513–26.

Tomlinson, C. 'A Dante Society for London', *Athenaeum*, 1894, p. 792.

Toynbee, P. (1912) 'The Centenary of the Completion of Cary's "Dante"', *The Modern Language Review*, 7:3, pp. 326–9.

— (1926) 'The Oxford Dante', *Annual Reports of the Dante Society*, 42–4, pp. 19–44.

Toynbee, P. J. (1898) *A Dictionary of Proper Names and Notable Matters in the Works of Dante* (Oxford: Clarendon Press).

— (1900) *Dante Alighieri: His Life and Works* (London: Methuen & Co.).

— (1902) *Dante Studies and Researches* (London: Methuen & Co.).

— (1905) 'Chronological List of English Translations from Dante: From Chaucer to the Present Day', *Annual Reports of the Dante Society*, 24, pp. 1–107.

— (1909) *Dante in English Literature from Chaucer to Cary (1380–1844)*, 2 vols (London: Methuen & Co.).

— (1921a) *Britain's Tribute to Dante in Literature and Art: A Chronological Record of 540 Years (c. 1380–1920)* (Oxford: Oxford University Press).
— (1921b) *Dante Studies* (Oxford: Clarendon Press).
— (1926) 'Oxford Dante', *Annual Reports of the Dante Society*, 42–44, 19–44.
Tozer, H. F. '"A Shadow of Dante: Being an Essay towards Studying Himself, His World, and His Pilgrimage" by Maria Rossetti. 1871', *Academy*, 15 December 1871, pp. 551–2.
— (1901) *An English Commentary to Dante's* Divina Commedia (Oxford: Clarendon Press).
Trilling, L. (1952) 'A Great Instrument of Devotion', *The American Scholar*, 21, pp. 496–501.
Valgimigli, A. (1898) 'Il culto di Dante in Inghilterra', *Giornale dantesco*, 3, pp. 1–22.
— (1904) *La forza morale di Dante e gli Anglo-Sassoni* (Florence: L. S. Olschki).
— 'Dante Studies in England', *Tablet*, 24 September 1921a, pp. 393–5.
— 'Dante Studies in England', *Tablet*, 1 October 1921b, pp. 436–7.
— (1932) *La colonia italiana a Manchester* (Florence: Ariani).
Van Arsdel, R. and J. Don Vann, eds (2016) *Victorian Periodicals and Victorian Society* (Toronto: University of Toronto Press).
Vassallo, P. (2000) 'Keats's "Dying into Life": The Fall of Hyperion and Dante's Purgatorio', in *Challenge of Keats: Bicentenary Essays, 1795–1995*, ed. by A. C. Christensen (Amsterdam: Rodopi), pp. 206–17.
Vernon, W. W. (1906) *The Contrasts in Dante: A Lecture Delivered at the University on 24th October 1906* (Manchester: The University Press).
Villani, G. (1896) *Selections from the First Nine Books of the* Croniche fiorentine *of Giovanni Villani*, ed. by Philip H. Wicksteed and trans. by Rose E. Selfe (Westminster: Constable & Co.).
Waller, R. D. (1932) *The Rossetti Family: 1824–1854* (Manchester: Manchester University Press).
Webb, T. (1976) *The Violet in the Crucible: Shelley and Translation* (Oxford: Clarendon Press).
Weinberg, A. M. (1991) *Shelley's Italian Experience* (London: Macmillan).
— (2012) 'Shelley and the Italian Tradition', in *The Oxford Handbook of Percy Bysshe Shelley*, ed. by M. O'Neill and A. Howe (Oxford: Oxford University Press), pp. 444–59.
Weintraub, S. (1978) *Four Rossettis: A Victorian Biography* (London: W. H. Allen).
Westminster Review, 'Belles Lettres', April 1862, pp. 586–604.
— 'The Abbé Lamennais on Dante', 30 (1866) pp. 371–2.

Whiting, M. (1921) 'The Dante Sexcentenary of 1865', *Music & Letters*, 2:2, pp. 172–82.

Wicksteed, P. H. (1879) *Dante: Six Sermons* (London: C. Kegan Paul & Co.).

— (1887) *Syllabus of a Course of Lectures on Dante: Second Part* (London: Taylor & Francis).

— (1888) *Syllabus of a Course of Lectures on Dante* (London: Taylor & Francis).

— (1890) *Dante: Six Sermons*, 2nd edn (London: Elkin Matthews).

— (1894) *Syllabus of a Course of Lectures on Dante's* Inferno (London: Hampton and Co.).

— (1896) 'Prefatory Note', in G. Villani, *Selections from the First Nine Books of the* Croniche fiorentine *of Giovanni Villani*, ed. by Philip H. Wicksteed and trans. by Rose E. Selfe (Westminster: Constable & Co.), p. i.

— (1898) *A Provisional Translation of the* Early Lives of Dante *and of His Poetical Correspondence with Giovanni del Virgilio* (Hull: Elsom and Co.).

— (1901) *Syllabus of a Course of Twelve Lectures on Dante's* Purgatorio (Cambridge: Cambridge University Press).

— (1903) *Syllabus of a Course of Twelve Lectures on Dante* (Manchester: Victoria University Extension Lectures).

— (1904a) 'Edward Moore *Tutte le Opere di Dante Alighieri*', *Hibbert Journal*, 2, pp. 600–2.

— (1904b) '"Treachery of Ciphers" Review of Moore's *Studies in Dante*, 3rd Series', *Hibbert Journal*, 2, pp. 634–6.

— (1904c) *Syllabus of a Course of Twelve Lectures on Dante* (Manchester: Victoria University Extension Lectures).

— (1908) '*La Vita Nuova* di Dante Alighieri per cura di M. Barbi', *Modern Language Review*, 3, p. 183.

— (1909) 'La Quaestio de Aqua et Terra di Dante Alighieri by Vincenzo Biagi', *Modern Language Review*, 4.2, pp. 254–8.

— (1910) 'Dante. *Quaestio de Aqua et Terra* by Charles Lancelot Shadwell', *Modern Language Review*, 5, pp. 255–6.

— (1913) *Dante and Aquinas* (London: J. M. Dent).

— (1916) 'On the Disputed Reading in Dante's *Epist.* V' 129', *Modern Language Review*, 11, p. 69.

— (1921a) 'Dante and the Latin Poets', in *Dante: Essays in Commemoration 1321–1921*, ed. by the Dante Sexcentenary Committee (London: University of London Press), pp. 157–88.

— (1921b) 'The Ethical System of the *Inferno*', *Modern Language Review*, 16, pp. 265–80.

— (1922) *From* Vita Nuova *to* Paradiso: *Two Essays on the Vital Relationship between Dante's Successive Works* (Manchester: Manchester University Press).

Windscheffel, R. Clayton (2001) 'W. E. Gladstone: An Annotation Key', *Notes and Queries*, 48, pp. 140–3.

— (2003) *'Enlarging the Text': A Cultural History of William Ewart Gladstone's Library and Reading* (Unpublished doctoral thesis, University of Liverpool).

— (2007) '"Gladstone and Dante: Victorian Statesman, Medieval Poet by Anne Isba", Review of *Gladstone and Dante: Victorian Statesman, Medieval Poet* by Anne Isba', *The English Historical Review*, 122, pp. 1101–3.

— (2008) *Reading Gladstone* (Basingstoke: Palgrave Macmillan).

Witte, K. (1879) *Dante-Forschungen: Altes und Neues* 2 vols (Heilbronn: Gebr. Henninger).

— (1898) *Essays on Dante by Karl Witte*, ed. by Philip H. Wicksteed and trans. by C. M. Lawrence (London: Duckworth and Co.).

White, A. (1988) 'Class, Culture and Control: The Sheffield *Athenaeum* Movement and the Middle Class 1847–64', in *The Culture of Capital: Art, Power and the Nineteenth-Century Middle Class*, ed. by Janet Wolff and John Seed (Manchester: Manchester University Press), pp. 83–116.

Wolff, J. and J. Seed, eds (1988) *The Culture of Capital: Art, Power and the Nineteenth-Century Middle Class* (Manchester: Manchester University Press).

Wolff, J. and M. Savage, eds (2013) *Culture in Manchester: Institutions and Urban Change since 1850* (Manchester: Manchester University Press).

Wolfson, S. (2015) *Reading John Keats* (Cambridge: Cambridge University Press).

Woodhouse, J. R. (2000) 'Dante Gabriel Rossetti's Translation and Illustration of the *Vita Nuova*', in *Britain and Italy from Romanticism to Modernism*, ed. by Martin McLaughlin (Oxford: Legenda), pp. 67–86.

Woolford, J. (1982) 'Periodicals and the Practice of Literary Criticism, 1855–64', in *The Victorian Periodical Press: Samplings and Soundings*, ed. by Joanne Shattock and Michael Woolf (Leicester: Leicester University Press), pp. 3–28.

Yeates, F. A. (1951) 'Transformations of Dante's Ugolino', *Journal of the Warburg and Courtauld Institutes*, 14:1, pp. 92–117.

Zancani, D. (1998) 'Una biblioteca di cent'anni fa: la "Dante Collection" di Paget Toynbee (1855–1932)', *La Bibliofilía*, 100, pp. 495–12.

Zimmerman, S. (2019) *The Romantic Literary Lecture in Britain* (Oxford: Oxford University Press).

Online resources

Grant, A. H., 'Barlow, Henry Clark (1806–1876)', in *Oxford Dictionary of National Biography*, rev. by Alison Milbank, www.oxforddnb.com [accessed 6 May 2015].

Manchester Literary and Philosophical Society, *Our History*, www.manlitphil.ac.uk/our-history [accessed 30 October 2014].

'Manchester Literary Club', in *The National Archives*, www.http://discovery.nationalarchives.gov.uk [accessed 7 March 2020].

Morris, L. A. 'Keats Family Books in the Harvard Keats Collection' http://hcl.harvard.edu/libraries /houghton /collections /modern/keats.cfm [accessed 12 May 2019].

'Mudie's Circulating Library' (2011) *UCL The Bloomsbury Project*, www.ucl.ac.uk/bloomsbury-project/institutions/mudie.html [accessed 15 April 2017].

'Philip Henry Wicksteed', in *Encyclopaedia Britannica*, www.britannica.com [accessed 23 May 2016].

Roda, M., 'Baldassarre Lombardi', in *Dizionario Biografico degli Italiani*, www.treccani.it/ [accessed 10 September 2017].

Steedman, Ian (2004) 'Wicksteed, Philip Henry (1844–1927)', in Oxford Dictionary of National Biography, www.oxforddnb.com [accessed 23 May 2016].

The University of Virginia Press (2006) *The Letters of Christina Georgina Rossetti: A Digital Edition*, https://rotunda.upress.virginia.edu/ [accessed 20 June 2019].

Vatteroni, S. M., 'La collezione di Prose e poesie liriche di Dante Allighieri', in *La Biblioteca del Fondo Alessandro Torri, un protagonista della vita culturale dell'Ottocento pisano*, http://biblio.sns.it/en/collezioni/letteratura/torri/mostra/dantealighieri/ [accessed 23 June 2017].

Ward, L. (2016) 'A Translation of a Translation: Dissemination of the Arundel Society's Chromolithographs' (unpublished doctoral dissertation, The Australian National University) in Semantic Scholar, www.semanticscholar.org/paper/A-translation-of-a-translation%3A-Dissemination-of-Ward/eedd95ae0f904ef32644b98bca1eb9ff5dd47148 [accessed 20 June 2019].

Zweig, R. M. (1984) 'The Victorian Dante: Dante and Victorian Literary Criticism' (unpublished doctoral dissertation, College University of New York) in ProQuestDissertations and Theses Global, https://search.proquest.com/docview/303289310?accountid=12253 [accessed 14 April 2015].

Index

Notes: 'n.' after a page reference indicates the number of a note on that page; literary works can be found under the authors' names

Academy 9, 114, 170–1, 173, 178, 186
  see also periodicals; reviewers
Acheson, K. 6
adult higher education 154n.2, 156, 191, 201
  local examination system 132–3
  reform of 132, 137, 191–2
  women's 96–7, 133–5, 154n, 186–8
advertisements 203
  of Dante books 84, 116, 178
  of Dante lectures 73–5, 119, 167, 197
Albites, F. C. 72–3
Alighieri, Dante *see* Dante
Altick, R. 8
annotations
  as codification of critical discourse 5, 16, 47–9, 51, 93
  as commonplacing 64, 89, 104
  displacement of 10, 51
  as *marginalia* 6–7, 10, 14, 16, 21–2, 28, 37, 55n.3
  non-verbal marks 16, 44–5, 52
  practice in education 21–2
  as signs of critical engagement 31, 43–4, 48–54, 104
  in teaching syllabi 7, 145
  verbal marks 7, 14, 28–9, 31–2, 34, 53, 55n.2, 104, 142, 163, 165
annotators 9, 14, 31, 44, 68
  Christina Rossetti as 104–5
  John Keats as 28–9
  Percy B. Shelley as 29
  Philip H. Wicksteed as 145
  Samuel Coleridge as 24–5
  William E. Gladstone as 41, 45–53
Aristotle 56n.9, 124, 167
Arnold, M. 7, 10–11, 16, 22, 27–8, 59–66, 74–82, 84–9, 91, 123, 129, 138, 156, 158, 201
  commonplaced passages as touchstones 65, 77
  commonplacing practice 63–5
  'Dante and Beatrice' 11, 66, 80–2, 86–9, 121
  Dante and *grand style* 78–9
  Dante as touchstone 76–8
  lecture on 'The Modern Element in Dante' 75–6, 81
  notebooks 60
  and periodicals 80–1
  private reading of Dante 61–5
  reading lists 60–3

and Theodore Martin's *Vita
Nuova* 81, 86–9
Athenaeum 9, 85, 96, 113–4, 116,
119, 165, 167, 169–70,
173, 178, 181
see also Barlow, H. C.;
periodicals; reviewers;
Rossetti, M. F., *A Shadow
of Dante*

Balbo, C. 27, 53
Bargello portrait 82–3
Barlow, H. C. 7, 12, 82, 85–6,
91–2, 96, 113, 119, 148,
158, 160–9, 180–1, 184
and the Bargello portrait 82
Barlow Lectures on the *Divine
Comedy* 100, 120, 146,
167, 170, 175, 180–2
Dante collection 181–2
and the Dante Festival 165
and *Deutsche Dante-
Gesellschaft* 160, 166
disciple of Witte 162, 165–6
friendship with Kirkup 82, 161,
165
global connections 165
and the London Dante Society
181
research and publications 161–3
Barrett Browning, E. 93–4
bibliomania 17
and Dante manuscripts and
editions 17–8
Blackwood's Edinburgh Magazine
9, 67, 95, 105, 107
Boccaccio, G. 17, 27, 33, 41, 43,
46, 53, 85, 120, 125
book
history 6
as object 6, 10, 13
see also materiality
book-collecting
practices of 10, 34, 157
see also Gladstone, W. E.;
Rylands, E. A.
Boschi Rotiroti, M. 175
Botterill, S. 158

Boyd, H. 4, 23–4, 43
Braida, A. 24, 29–31, 56n.5, 56n.6,
57n.10, 58n.14
Brake, L. 80
British Library 23, 37
Bruni, L. 46, 50, 85
Butler, A. J. 15, 43, 175, 181, 195

Carlyle, J. A. 43, 67, 148, 201
Carlyle, T. 71–3, 75
Carroll, J. S. 15
Cary, H. F. 1, 43
The Vision 4, 8, 11, 45–7,
58n.14, 68, 70, 93
Arnold's copy of 61
Coleridge's copy of 24–5
Coleridge's support to 10, 20,
70–3
Gladstone's copy of 45–52
Keats' copy of 28–30
publishing and reception history 19–21, 106
Toynbee's edition of 173
Caselli, D. 204
Cayley, C. B. 100, 102, 104–7,
119–20
relation to Christina Rossetti
103–5
relation to Gabriele Rossetti 104
review of 105–6
translation of the *Commedia*
105–6
Chadwick, O. 14
Chester, N. see Underdown, E.
see also *dantismo*, female
Coleridge, S. T. 4, 16, 20, 22, 59,
70–1, 73, 75, 158, 201
marginalia 24–5
notebooks 23–4
notes for lectures on Dante 26
private study of Dante 22–6
see also commonplacing
practices; Dante, lectures on
commonplacing practices 22–3, 55n.1
George Eliot's 26–7
John Flaxman's 22–3
Samuel Taylor Coleridge's 22–6
see also Arnold, M.

Cooksey, T. L. 74
Coolahan, M. L. 6
Cornoldi, G. 40, 43
Cotes, R. A. 94
Crisafulli, E. 50, 58n.14

Dante
 1865 centenary 8, 91–3, 159, 165
 1921 centenary 93, 153
 biographies 9, 61, 68, 71, 74, 92, 128, 144, 148, 170, 194
 Boccaccio's *Trattatello* 27, 41, 43, 46, 53, 85, 120, 125
 collection (or library) 159, 171, 180–1, 184, 191, 193
  see also Gladstone, W. E.
 commentary
  modern tradition 15
  nineteenth-century editions
   published in Italy 16–17
   published in Britain 19, 44, 173
 exhibitions 91, 117, 194–7
 Extension courses on 136–7
  see also Wicksteed, P. H.
 handbooks 9, 142, 171, 194
 illustrations to the *Commedia* 23, 46, 119, 145, 179, 193
 introductions to 39, 44, 63, 73, 136, 142–3, 148
 lectures on 66–9, 72
  Carlyle's lectures 70–2
  Coleridge's *Lectures on the History of Literature* 70
  Foscolo's *Lectures on Italian Literature* 70–1
  Hazlitt's *Lectures on the English Poets* 69–70
  by Italian exiles 72–4, 183
  Schlegel's *Lectures on Dramatic Literature* 69
  see also Barlow, H. C., Barlow Lectures on the *Divine Comedy*; Taylorian Institution; Tomlinson, C.
 passages from the *Commedia* in anthologies 36

 societies *see* Dante Society of America; *Deutsche Dante Gesellschaft*; London Dante Society; Manchester Dante Society; Oxford Dante Society; Società Dantesca Italiana
Dante: references to works
 Convivio 3, 25, 30–2, 39, 73, 128, 141, 150, 153, 172–3, 177
  Extension courses on 144, 148
  translation of 95, 103
 Divina Commedia 3–4, 7, 16, 21, 23–4, 27–8, 30, 33–41, 43, 45–50, 52–4, 61–5, 68–75, 77–9, 87–8, 93, 95, 102–10, 113–14, 119, 125, 128–9, 131, 136, 146, 151, 159, 161–70, 172–3, 175, 177, 180, 188, 196
  Extension courses on 141–2, 144, 148
  object of study 10–11, 53
  translation of 4, 19–21, 28–9, 36, 44, 62, 70, 94–5, 102–5, 159
  see also Dante, commentary; Dante, handbooks; Dante, illustrations to the *Commedia*; Dante, introductions to; Dante, lectures on
 Eclogues 150–1, 155n.6
 Inferno 3–4, 19, 23–4, 27, 29–33, 35–7, 43, 49, 52, 56n.6, 57n.13, 61–2, 64–6, 70–2, 74, 109–10, 119, 122, 136, 141, 144, 148, 150–1, 153, 158, 161–2, 164, 168, 180, 196–7
  Extension courses on 136, 141, 144
  translation of 19–20, 24, 29, 37, 43, 68, 77–8, 105, 148, 150, 180
 Monarchia 34, 39, 43, 73, 120, 128, 141, 144, 150, 153, 159, 177

Paradiso 23, 27, 29–33, 35–9, 49, 52, 56n.6, 57n.11, 61–6, 72, 77–8, 103, 119, 124, 129, 141, 144, 153, 185, 187, 193
  Extension courses on 141, 144
  translation of 43, 148, 150, 173
Purgatorio 23, 27, 29–32, 38–40, 48, 52, 56n.6, 61–2, 64–5, 72, 119, 129, 193
  Extension courses on 141–2
  translation of 35–6, 43, 148, 150–1, 173
Vita Nuova 3, 24–5, 27, 34, 39–40, 62, 90n.4, 91, 103, 120, 136, 141, 144, 153, 159, 161, 173, 177–8, 191
  translation of 30–2, 43–4, 81–8, 108, 148, 151, 185
  see also Lyell, C.; Martin, T.; Norton, C. E.; Rossetti, D. G.
Vulgari Eloquentia, De 25, 27, 31, 34, 39, 73, 144, 150, 173, 177–8
Dante Society of America 108, 115, 160, 173, 175, 187
  Annual Reports of 173
  and Charles E. Norton 175
  and Henry Longfellow as founder of 108
  and James Russell Lowell 114–15, 173–4
dantismo 6, 18, 53, 60, 70, 80, 89, 93, 97–9, 103, 111, 119, 123–4, 130, 154, 169, 199, 202
  American 114
  British 15, 17, 33, 42–3, 55, 148, 166, 182
  commerical 12, 117, 154
  critical 80, 82, 89
  and *dantofilia* 12, 97, 199
  female 92–3, 98, 184–9
    conditions of development 96
    gendered attitudes 93–5
  German 161

popular 99, 111, 154
private 44, 60–1, 89
professional 98, 158–9, 169, 176, 179, 201–2
Rossetti family 11, 99, 111, 115, 118
public 53, 182
Victorian 6, 12, 123, 158, 201–2
dantofilia 12, 97, 120, 199, 201–2
Darnton, R. 6
Dartmouth Dante Project (DDP) 15
Dayman, J. 102, 105–6
De Ventura, P. 99–100, 102
Dent, J. M. 12, 20, 152
  Temple Classics 148–50
  see also Wicksteed, P. H., as editor and translator, *Temple Dante*
Deutsche Dante-Gesellschaft 159–61
  Jahrbuch der Deutschen Dante-Gesellschaft 159–60
  see also Witte, K.
Doré, G. 20, 150
Dublin Review 178

Edinburgh Review 4, 20, 57–8n.13, 69–70, 187
Eliot, G. 16, 22, 26–8, 55n.2, 94, 119
  see also commonplacing practices
Eliot, T. S. 59, 75, 151
Ellis, H. 158
Ellis, S. 82
Examiner 82–3

Farinelli, A. 180–1
Flaxman, J. 16, 20, 22–3, 27, 43
  see also commonplacing practices
Folena, G. 159, 169
Foligno, C. 175, 181
Foscolo, U. 4, 19–20, 46
  and *Edinburgh Review* 4, 20, 70–2
  lectures on Dante 70–1

Fraser's Magazine 9, 11, 62, 80–1, 84–6, 91
Fraticelli, P. 17, 27, 40, 53, 101, 103, 177

Gardner, E. G. 93, 142–3, 148, 181, 185, 195
  friendship and collaboration with Wicksteed 124, 131, 142–3, 155n.6, 178
Gentleman's Magazine 9, 82
Gittings, R. 29
Gladstone, W. E. 7, 10–11, 14–16, 21–2, 28, 33–54, 56n.9, 57n.11, 57n.13, 59, 61–2, 68, 104, 123–4, 175, 185, 188, 201
  annotation key 45
  annotation practices 44–52
  annotations to
    Cary's *The Vision* 49–50
    Comino edition 50–2
    Lombardi's edition 47–9
  comments in the diaries 35–7, 40
  Dante collection at St Deniol's 40–7
  Dante reading
    campaigns of 34–6, 38–41
    communal 39
    of secondary sources 35, 40–1
    solitary 34–5, 37–8
    as systematic study 47
  drafting papers on Dante 37–8
  library 14, 42–5, 47
  and *The Nineteenth Century* 52–4
  scholarly networks 34, 41, 57–8n.13
    and the London Dante Society 53
    and the Oxford Dante Society 41
  translations from Dante 36–7
Goethe, 76, 79
Guppy, H.
  and the Manchester Dante Society 193–6
  see also John Rylands Library
Gurney, E. R. 93, 95
  see also dantismo, female

Hallam, A. 35, 40, 83
Hartley, R. A. 31
Hasell, E. J. 105
  see also dantismo, female; periodicals, women contributors to
Havely, N. 2, 6, 14, 17, 148, 151
Hazlitt, W. 4, 67, 69, 73
  see also Dante, lectures on; periodicals
Herford, C. H. 123–5, 127, 150, 154n.1, 181, 194
Hess, J. 26
Heyck, T. K. 202
Hillard, K. 92, 95, 97–8
  see also dantismo, female
Hollander, R. 15–16
Homer 33, 42, 57n.9, 69, 76–7, 79, 101

Isba, A. 14

Jackson, H. J. 21–2, 24
Jennings, J. 67–8
John Rylands Library 12, 191–2, 194–7
  see also Rylands, E. A.
Jourdain, E. F. 44, 187–8
  excluded from Oxford Dante Society 188
  scholarship 187–8
  see also London Dante Society

Keats, J. 55n.4, 56n.4, 56n.5, 104
  reader of Dante 28–9
  see also annotators
Kirkup, S. 161–2, 165, 193
  discovery of the 'Bargello Dante' portrait 82–3, 89n.3
  see also Barlow, H. C.; Witte, K.
Kuhn, O. 74

Laicata, G. 53, 165
Landor, W. S. 28, 82

Laurence, A. 94–5, 97–8
  see also *dantismo*, female
lecture rooms
  admission to 71–2, 74
  geographical location of 70–4
    Marylebone Literary and Scientific Institution 72–3
    Willis' Rooms 71–3
    see also literary and philosophical societies
  within the Extension scheme 140–1
libraries 34, 41, 96, 163, 194–6, 201–3
  circulating 116
  Extension scheme's travelling 134, 136, 142, 147
  private 6, 17, 42, 61–2, 101, 193
  public 41, 94, 163–4, 168, 179, 189, 190–2, 198
  subscription 117
  see also Dante, collection; Gladstone, W. E.; John Rylands Library
Lindon, J. 159, 162, 164–5, 180
literary marketplace 16–20, 86, 93, 100, 117
literary and philosophical societies
  London Philosophical Society 70
  Manchester Literary and Philosophical Society 189–90
Lombardi, B. 17, 27, 43, 45–52, 54
London Dante Society 12, 53–4, 167
  female members 184–9
  formation and organisation of 181, 183–9
  lectures 183, 186–9
  linguistic *querelle see* Tomlinson, C.
  members 184–9
London Review 84
Longfellow, H. W.
  member of continental Dante societies 160
  and M. F. Rossetti 108–10, 115
  president of the Dante Society of America 108, 115

  as translator of the *Commedia* 103, 120
  see also Dante Society of America; Oxford Dante Society
Lowell, J. R. 143
  correspondence with E. Moore 173, 175
  review of M. F. Rossetti 114–15
  see also Dante Society of America; Oxford Dante Society
Lubenow, W. C. 156, 158, 175
Lyell, C.
  collaboration with M. F. Rossetti 101–2
  as translator of Dante 43, 82–3

Macaulay, T. B. 83
McGovern, J. B. 57n.13, 190–1
Manchester Courier 182, 190–1, 196
Manchester Dante Society 190
  contemporary societies of 189–90
  and Dante exhibition 196
  foundation of 190–1
  lecturers 195–6
  organisation of 194–5
  see also John Rylands Library; Rylands, E. A.; Valgimigli, A.
Manchester Guardian 189–90, 196–7
Marsh, J. 101, 105, 120
Martin, T. 81–8, 185
  Arnold's essay-like review of 86–8
  Barlow's review of 86
  favourable reviews of his *Vita Nuova* 83–5
  translation of the *Vita Nuova* 83–4
materiality 7, 15, 145
Medwin, T. 30
Milbank, A. 2, 82, 87
Miller, C. 23
Milner, S. 190, 197
Milton, J. 26, 33, 76–7, 79

Modern Language Review 152–3, 155n.7, 155n.8, 173
Moore, E. 12, 41, 44, 52, 83, 93, 96, 119, 131, 148, 150, 153, 158, 161, 167–77
 and Barlow 168
 Dante collection 171
 as Dante lecturer 169, 180–1
 Dante studies 168–70
 and Witte 169
 see also Oxford Dante Society, *Oxford Dante*
Morley, J. 35, 124
Mudie's Select Library 116–17

North American Review 114–15
Norton, C. E. 83, 165, 175

Oelsen, H. 148
Oelsner, H. 15, 57n.13
 see also Dent, J. M.; Wicksteed, P. H., as editor and translator, *Temple Dante*
Okey, T. 148, 151, 185
 see also Dent, J. M.; Wicksteed, P. H., as editor and translator, *Temple Dante*
Oliphant, M. 41, 44, 92, 95, 97–8
 see also dantismo, female; periodicals
Owen's College 133, 190–1
 see also Victoria University of Manchester
Oxford Dante Society 7, 12, 34, 41, 96, 114, 146, 158, 167, 173–6, 179–80, 184–5, 188
 exchange with other Dante societies 175
 formation of 170–1
 internal organisation of 172–5
 members contributions to 173–4
 Oxford Dante 176
  composition history 176–8
  publication and reception history 178–9
  and the *Edizione nazionale* 179

Panizzi, A. 72, 162–3
Passerini, G. L.
 Dante collection 193
 Giornale dantesco 196–7
 see also Manchester Dante Society; Rylands, E. A.
periodicals 4, 194
 as epistemological sites of Dante criticism 8, 55, 80–2, 85, 89, 92, 105, 119, 203–4
 women contributors to 95, 105–7, 120–1, 186–8
 see also reviewers; reviews
Petrarch, F. 33, 119, 193
Phillimore, C. M.
 as *dantista* 93, 186
 as lecturer of the London Dante Society 186
Pite, R. 24, 29–31, 50, 56n.5, 57n.10
Plumptre, E. H. 15, 41, 53
Potter, C. 44, 95
Prince, K. 8, 203

Ramsay, C. H. 92, 94, 98, 105
 see also Divina Commedia, translation of; *dantismo*, female
reading 22, 93
 history of (Dante) 18–19, 24, 27, 30, 32, 59, 61–2, 104, 201
 modes and practices of 3–7, 10, 25, 30–1, 60–1, 67, 86, 100, 110, 114, 124, 131, 139, 146, 161, 181, 201, 204
 aloud 39, 172, 182
 annotated 8, 10, 13, 21–2, 28–9
 see also annotators; commonplacing practices; Gladstone, W. E.
 close 69–71
 communal 39, 157, 172, 182
 extensive 22–3, 34
 see also Gladstone, W. E.
 intensive 22–3, 34, 53, 100–1, 105

reading public 97
re-reading 23–4, 28, 30, 35–6, 38–9, 51–2, 55, 64–5
solitary 39, 100, 124, 161
reception 1–3, 14, 60, 83, 85–6, 90n.4, 92, 98, 111, 116, 173
aesthetics 2
critical 60, 202
definition of 6, 8, 23–4, 26
history of Dante's 1–3, 5–6, 9, 10, 13–14, 19, 22, 46, 70, 89, 95, 151, 182, 198–9, 203
popular 116
productive 2, 202–3
scholarly 13–14, 54, 89, 202–3
Renaissance 15, 189
reviewers
periodical 4, 9, 18, 63, 73, 81, 84–6, 94, 96, 105–6, 112–13, 115, 169–70
women as *see* Hasell, E. J.
reviewing
puff 82–3
Victorian modes of 107, 165
reviews 1, 9, 11, 20, 62, 68, 83–6, 89, 95, 105, 107, 113–16, 131, 152–3, 160, 165, 189, 197, 203
Ricci, C. 181, 187
Ricci, L. 182–5
Rivera, A. G. 72–3
Roe, D. 119, 121
Romantic period 2–3, 15, 21, 28–9, 31, 33–4, 36, 55n.1, 57n.10, 62, 66–8, 75–6, 89n.1, 121, 156, 201
Rossetti, C. 7, 10–11, 92–4, 97–100, 103–7, 112, 117–23, 201
and Charles B. Cayley 103–4
'Dante: An English Classic' 105–7
as Dante critic 105, 120–1
'Dante: The Poet Explained out of the Poem' 120
as editor of Cayley's translation 104–5
as literary executor of Maria Francesca 117–18
and Maria Francesca 112, 121–2
and the Rossetti family *dantismo* 107, 118, 119–21
study of Dante 100, 104, 119
use of Dante in *Monna Innominata* 119
Rossetti, D. G. 99, 112, 121, 148
as book designer of *A Shadow of Dante* 117–19
theory of translation 106, 121
as translator of *Vita Nuova* 26, 44, 83, 102–3
Rossetti, G. 19, 35, 40, 43, 82–84, 87, 99, 101
and Maria Francesca Rossetti 101, 103–4, 108, 113
see also dantismo, Rossetti family
Rossetti, M. F. 11, 44, 92–3, 97–103, 107–13, 115–23, 171, 201
approach to translation 101–2
assistant to Charles Lyell 101
correspondance with Henry Longfellow 103, 107
early childhood 100–1
and Gabriele Rossetti 101, 103, 108, 113
A Shadow of Dante 107
in the *Academy* 114
in the *Athenaeum* 113–14
composition history of 107
'Mudie's Circulating Library' 116–17
in the *Nation* 115–16
in the *North American Review* 114–15
publication history of 111, 116
reception of 111–16
and Ruskin 112–13
in the *Saturday Review* 114
study of Dante 101
Rossetti, W. M. 44, 99, 107–8, 111–12, 115, 117–18, 175
as editor to Maria Francesca Rossetti 108

as family biographer 104, 107
as translator of Dante 102–3
Ruskin, J. 15–16, 28, 41, 101, 112, 175, 202
  opinion on Maria Francesca Rossetti 112–13
Rylands, E. A.
  as book collector 192–4
  personal Dante collection 193
  and the Rylands Dante collection 192–4
  and Valgimigli 94
  and the wholesale of the Biblioteca Spenceriana 193

Saglia, D. 4
Saly, J. 29, 56n.5
Sandhurst, E. 60, 65
Saturday Review 84–5, 114, 170, 188–9
Scartazzini, G. 40, 43, 46, 53, 165, 177
Schlegel, A. W. 69–70
Schlegel, F. 69
Scott, A. J. 73–4
Shakespeare, W. 8, 42, 70, 76–7, 149, 203
Sheehan, D. 189
Shelley, M. 16, 30–1, 56n.6, 94
Shelley, P. B. 3, 5, 16, 28–33, 104, 201
  annotations to *Inferno* 32
  history of Dante reading 29–31, 56n.6
  intertextual appropriations of Dante 30, 32–3
  poetry criticism 5, 33
  translations from Dante 32
  and Venturi's edition 31–2
Sherif, A. 7
Shore, A. 44, 92, 95, 97, 171
  see also dantismo, female
Società Dantesca Italiana 159, 193
  connection to Oxford Dante Society 175–6, 179
St Clair, W. 3
Straub, J. 82
Super, R. H. 81

Taylorian Institution 81, 96, 168, 170–1
  see also Moore, E.
Thomas, J. W. 15, 43, 105
Tomlinson, C. 12, 180–3
  as Barlow lecturer 119–20, 180
  and the linguistic *querelle* with Ricci 182–3
  and the London Dante Society 181
Toynbee, P. J. 12, 57n.10, 93, 96, 131, 151, 153, 198
  and the Oxford Dante Society 41, 173, 175–9
  reception theory 1–2, 5–6, 54
  and the Società Dantesca Italiana 175
Tozer, H. F. 15, 114, 168, 172–3, 176
  see also Athenaeum

Underdown, E. 44, 95
  see also dantismo, female
University College London 12, 96, 100, 119, 123, 132, 139, 158, 167, 169–70, 180–2, 186
  see also London Dante Society; University Extension Movement; Wicksteed, P. H.
University Extension Movement 132
  Dante courses 136
  organisation of courses and materials 135–6, 141, 145
  selection of lecturers 137
  women as students 134
  and women's organisations 133
University of Cambridge 96, 132–3, 137, 148, 185
  University Extension centre 132–3, 139–40, 142
  see also University Extension Movement
University of Oxford 75, 80, 96, 137, 139, 171, 174, 185, 188
  University Extension centre 132–3, 135, 140, 146

see also Oxford Dante Society; University Extension Movement

Valgimigli, A. 5, 12
  and *dantismo*, female 93–5
  as lecturer on Dante 190
  and the Manchester Dante Society 190–1, 194, 198, 200
Venturi, P. 17–18, 24, 28, 30–1
Vernon, G. 15, 17, 82–3, 161, 165, 195
Vernon, W. W. 17, 165, 176, 185, 195–6
Victoria University of Manchester 133, 140, 190
  see also Owen's College; University Extension Movement
Virgil 3, 64, 76, 78–9, 82, 125

Waller, R. D. 101, 112
Ward, T. H. 66
Webb, T. 30
Westminster Review 63, 84
Wicksteed, P. H. 7, 12, 15, 38, 93, 96–7, 123–32, 136–53, 155n.6, 156, 159, 171, 178, 181, 195, 197–8, 201
  as Dante scholar 151
    Dante and Aquinas 152
    From Vita Nuova *to* Paradiso 153
    periodical reviews and articles 152–3
  as editor and translator 128–9, 147–51
    collaborative work 147, 148–51
    Early Lives of Dante 148
    Essays on Dante by Dr Karl Witte 148
    of Giovanni Villani's *Cronache* 147–8
    Temple Dante 148–51
  Extension courses on Dante 139–40
    attendance to 146
    content and structure of 141–5
    examination papers 144, 146
    geography of 140
    organisation of 140–6
  as Extension lecturer 137–40
  Herford's biography of 124–6
  as Unitarian minister 126–7
    Sermons on Dante 127–8
    Six Sermons 12, 38, 124, 126, 128–32, 139, 143–4, 171
Winscheffel, R. C. 35, 55
Witte, K. 43, 46, 101, 148, 151, 169, 193
  and Barlow 158–63, 165–7
  and Moore 169, 171
  see also Deutsche Dante-Gesellschaft; Oxford Dante Society, *Oxford Dante*
Woolford, J. 9
Wordsworth, W. 24, 87, 124
Wyld, A. 95, 97
  see also *dantismo*, female

Yonge, C. M. 92, 95, 97–8
  see also *dantismo*, female

Zatta, A. 18–19, 23
Zimmerman, S. 67, 89n.1
Zweig, R. M. 65

EU authorised representative for GPSR:
Easy Access System Europe, Mustamäe tee 50,
10621 Tallinn, Estonia
gpsr.requests@easproject.com

www.ingramcontent.com/pod-product-compliance
Lightning Source LLC
Chambersburg PA
CBHW070816250426
43671CB00037B/2391